THE ENVOY

THE ENVOY

The Epic Rescue of the
Last Jews of Europe in the
Desperate Closing Months
of World War II

ALEX KERSHAW

Da Capo Press
A Member of the Perseus Books Group

Editorial production by *Marra*thon Production Services, www.marrathon.net
DESIGN BY JANE RAESE
Set in 11-point Fairfield Light

Library of Congress Cataloging-in-Publication Data is available for this book.
LCCN 2010927187
ISBN 978-0-306-81557-7

Published by Da Capo Press
A Member of the Perseus Books Group
www.dacapopress.com

Da Capo Press books are available at special discounts for bulk purchases in the U.S. by corporations, institutions, and other organizations. For more information, please contact the Special Markets Department at the Perseus Books Group, 2300 Chestnut Street, Suite 200, Philadelphia, PA 19103, or call (800) 810-4145, ext. 5000, or e-mail special.markets@perseusbooks.com.

2 4 6 8 10 9 7 5 3 1

FOR MY SISTERS

Contents

Acknowledgments

I'D FIRST LIKE TO THANK my agent, Derek Johns, for over eighteen years of great times. My editor, Bob Pigeon, was once more a true friend. Writers can't ask for more. At Perseus, David Steinberger has also given great support for almost a decade. I am deeply grateful once more for superb production work by Christine Marra and Susan Pink, and for the jacket design by Alex Camlin. Thanks also to the finest publicist, Kate Burke. George Bishop kindly read the manuscript and Paul Sidey in London and his team were wonderfully encouraging and helpful from the start. Janos Beer at MIT in Boston very kindly gave fantastic testimony, read the manuscript and provided a very useful overview. Diane Blake in New York provided great leads. In Budapest, John Snowdon was again the best companion on assignment, and his photographs are always beautiful. He also joined me in Stockholm, where Ben Olander and his wife Toni provided the best two days of fun and exploration one could hope for. Nina Lagergren was also most generous with her time—she is one of Sweden's greats. Another truly remarkable woman in Stockholm is Alice Breuer, who very kindly delved into a painful past, and I cannot thank her enough for her testimony. Alice is one of several other survivors of the Holocaust in honor of whom this book is written: Erwin Koranyi in Ottawa; Vera Goodkin in New Jersey; and Marianne Lowy in Palm Beach. These men and women, among the many thousands helped by Wallenberg, helped me to finally understand so very much and I am deeply grateful for their time and patience. This book clearly would not exist without them. Thanks finally to the Epriles, especially Tony for his company, friendship, and photos in Canada. And, last but not least, I am as ever very grateful for the support of my family on both sides of the Atlantic, especially that of my wife Robin and son Felix—my own angels of rescue.

THE ENVOY

Hungary
1944

N

0   30   60
SCALE OF MILES

POLAND

★ Auschwitz

Zilina

CZECHOSLOVAKIA

Banska Bystrica

VIENNA

Danube River

Hegyeshalom

Kistarcsa

Debrecen

BUDAPEST

Sarvar

Kormend

H U N G A R Y

AUSTRIA

Danube River

Szeged

YUGOSLAVIA

ROMANIA

RLP

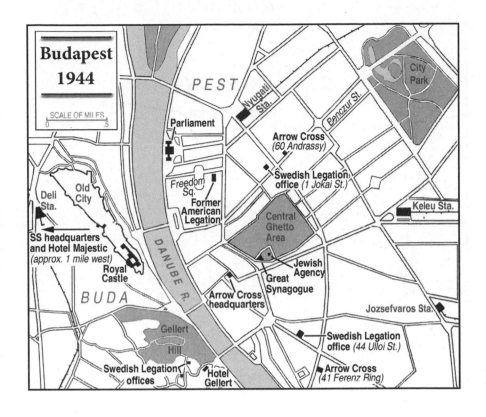

Part One

THE FINAL SOLUTION

1

Wannsee

IT WAS A SNOWY TUESDAY as the Mercedes staff cars pulled in, one after the other, wheels crunching the gravel on the driveway that led past a circular flower bed and to the entrance of a large, imposing villa at 56–58 Am Grossen Wannsee on the outskirts of Berlin.[1] Senior bureaucrats of the Third Reich, middle-aged SS officers, and Gestapo officials then stepped out of the cars and hurried inside. Around noon that day—January 20, 1942—they entered a large dining room, where they were soon seated at assigned places at a long table. Thirty-eight-year-old SS General Reinhard Heydrich was already waiting for his distinguished guests.

As a general in the SS and chief of the Reich Main Security Office (RSHA), Heydrich enjoyed enormous power in the Third Reich. He pulled all the levers of terror, being in charge of the Gestapo, the Nazi Security Service (SD) agency, and the Criminal Police (Kripo) agency. A musically gifted and well-educated former Catholic, he knew he could count on the obedience and win the cooperation of even the most recalcitrant of Hitler's senior bureaucrats. To cross him was to risk fatal repercussions, which many of his enemies had discovered in the last decade as he had risen inexorably through the ranks of loyal and dedicated Nazis in the RSHA.[2]

The meeting began as Heydrich, with his piercing blue eyes and aquiline nose, sat down in a leather chair. In all, fifteen men were at the conference, eight of whom had doctorates—not an uneducated group by any means.[3] Also present was Heydrich's fellow Austrian, the head of the Gestapo's Section IVB for Jewish Affairs, thirty-six-year-old Lieutenant-Colonel Adolf Eichmann. Among the assembled "popes" of the Third Reich, he looked like an attentive secretary, a junior clerk even. It was his job today to take the minutes—at a top secret meeting that would determine the fate of Europe's eleven-million-odd Jews.

Eichmann had worked for several months to arrange this conference and had prepared a detailed agenda for the attendees. But now he was starting to feel the accumulated fatigue of so many months of hard work. And last night had been taxing indeed. He had traveled by staff car to Berlin, along dark and slushy roads, hundreds of miles from Theresienstadt, a so-called model camp used to fool international Red Cross inspectors into believing that the Nazis were not killing undesirables in vast numbers—the mentally handicapped, Gypsies, Poles, the list went on and on, growing with each year of Hitler's tenure.

Heydrich began the meeting by saying that the Fuhrer had entrusted him with a grave responsibility. He had been ordered to bring about a complete solution of the Jewish question in the German sphere of influence in Europe.[4]

"Under proper guidance, in the course of the final solution, the Jews are to be allocated for appropriate labor in the East," continued Heydrich. "Able-bodied Jews, separated according to sex, will be taken in large work columns to these areas for work on roads, in the course of which action doubtless a large portion will be eliminated by natural causes. The possible final remnant will, since it will undoubtedly consist of the most resistant portion, have to be treated accordingly, because it is the product of natural selection and would, if released, act as the seed of a new Jewish revival."[5]

None of the men around the table was in any doubt what "treated accordingly" meant.

Heydrich spoke for about an hour before opening up the meeting to questions. Several concerns were raised. When would the final solution begin? Should it not start with mass evacuations from the crowded, diseased ghettoes in Poland? How exactly would the millions be shipped to the so-called resettlement camps? Would there be allowances made for Jews working in key war industries who had irreplaceable skills?

Some of the more zealous bureaucrats in attendance believed that half-Jews, though clearly not "real" Jews, should be killed too now that Eichmann's department of Jewish Affairs had solved the problems of how to get rid of undesirables in vast numbers and dispose of the corpses. In the East, gassings of Russian POWs had been highly effective. And at Auschwitz, an amethyst-blue crystal called Cyclon B, produced by the German industrial giant I.G. Farben, had proved even more deadly.[6] Pellets reacted instantly when released into the air, producing hydrogen cyanide. In theory, there was now no limit to how many people the Nazis could exterminate.[7]

It was after 1 p.m. Servants brought in refreshments. The attendees drank and ate and talked about finally ending the Jewish problem not just in Germany, but in all of Europe, including Britain and the Soviet Union, two enemy territories that would be finally subdued, all in good time, and from which all Jews would be deported as well. The meeting formally ended after ninety minutes, with Heydrich and the Gestapo chief Heinrich Muller being last to leave the large dining room. They asked the thorough Eichmann to share a drink with them. Soon the three men were beside a fire, warming themselves. Eichmann would never forget how honored he felt to be asked to join these two giants of the Third Reich for a celebratory tipple. "After the conference," he remembered, "Heydrich, Muller, and little me sat cozily around a fireplace. I saw for the first time Heydrich smoking a cigar or cigarette, something I never saw; and he drank cognac, which I hadn't seen for ages. Normally he didn't drink alcohol."[8]

Heydrich might have appeared relaxed, but he was not about to make an elementary mistake that might come back to haunt him. He made sure Eichmann understood that he was not to write up the minutes verbatim. He wanted the discussion sanitized, placed in appropriately euphemistic language, so there would be no explicit mention of mass murder. As Eichmann recalled: "Certain over-plain talk and jargon expressions had to be rendered into office language by me."[9]

It had been a most satisfactory day, surely worth a toast or two. And so Eichmann, Heydrich, and Muller refilled their glasses with cognac and proceeded to get drunk.[10] "After a while," recalled Eichmann, "we got up on the chairs and drank a toast, then on the table and then round and round—on the chairs and on the table again. Heydrich taught it to us. It was an old north German custom . . . We sat around peacefully after our Wannsee Conference, not just talking shop but giving ourselves a rest after so many taxing hours."[11]

Eichmann had no qualms. "I felt something of the satisfaction of Pilate, because I felt entirely innocent of any guilt. The leading figures of the Reich at the time had spoken at the Wannsee Conference, the 'Popes' had given their orders; it was up to me to obey, and that is what I bore in mind over the future years."[12]

Orders were orders. His oath of allegiance to Hitler, the Reich, and the SS brotherhood meant that he had to do what was necessary. He had been instructed, as had Heydrich, to deal once and for all with the Jewish problem. This seemingly bland and rather obtuse RSHA bureaucrat, Adolf Eichmann, would be the chief administrator of "the greatest single genocide in history."[13]

2

On the Run

THE HERMANS CAREFULLY picked off the six-inch-wide yellow stars of David on the left chest of their coats, making sure that no telltale yellow threads were visible—even the thinnest wisp of cotton might be spotted by a vigilant SS man or a collaborator. Twelve-year-old Vera Herman later remembered watching her mother remove the six-pointed stars of cadmium yellow: "Our lives literally hung on removing every one of those threads."[1]

The Hermans—father Emil, wife Margit, and their daughter, Vera—left their latest refuge, a house owned by Vera's youngest uncle, a respected pharmacist, and in complete secrecy, terrified they would be stopped, they made their way quietly at dusk through the streets of Banska Bystrica to its railway station. Were they being watched? Had someone betrayed them to the SS? They could not be sure.

Margit knew they had no choice but to leave. The Nazis were about to begin deporting the Jews who still lived in the small town in central Slovakia, some hundred miles due north of Budapest. The Hermans either stayed in Banska Bystrica "like sitting ducks" or they took a chance. Margit also knew that taking risks was not in her husband Emil's nature. He was a precise, methodical doctor who had prided himself on careful and rigorous diagnosis. "If taking a chance had been his thing," recalled Vera, "we would have been in the United States by then, because we were on the American quota. We had received our quota numbers. The only thing we couldn't get was a valid passport." Others might have tried to leave the country without one, but Vera's father, a physician as well as a proud officer in the Czechoslovakian National Guard's elite cavalry regiment, hadn't wanted to break the law.

They waited nervously on a platform and boarded a train, just another family going into the country for a short break from the war, or so they hoped it appeared.[2] It was a local milk train that seemed to stop at every telephone pole. Thankfully, they did not look stereotypically Jewish. They were fair-skinned, and Emil and Vera blue-eyed. Vera, in fact, looked more Aryan than Jewish, with her dark blonde hair, held in braids, which was the fashion for girls her age at the time. "We blended in," she recalled. "We were all thin. My father was about five six, my mother, around five foot. I was tall for my age at five foot two. My mother and I wore little babushka scarves."[3]

Some time later, they got off at a small village. On the platform, they looked to their left, as they had been instructed. There, at the far end of the platform, stood a tall young man. They began to follow him, out of the station and into the country.[4] Mercifully, they had not been stopped and asked for their papers. They approached a dilapidated farmhouse, more like a barn than a home, shared by three generations of a family and their small animals.[5] It was around 11 p.m. when the young man placed a ladder against a wall. They could see an open window above. He told them to climb up the ladder and into the attic—their new hiding place.

"Please be very careful," said the young man. "Don't move around too much because my mother-in-law is here, and she's a Nazi sympathizer. If she finds out about you, you won't be here very long."[6] The young man had not expected his mother-in-law to visit. He looked as disappointed as the Hermans as they climbed the ladder. Clearly, as with so many other collaborators in Nazi Europe, she wouldn't think twice about reporting them and her own son-in-law to the Nazis.[7]

FOR MORE THAN THREE YEARS, the Hermans had evaded capture in Nazi-occupied Europe, moving from one cramped attic to another, hiding in dark forests, hunched together in freezing crawl spaces and dank cellars, sometimes starving, never losing hope but always afraid. They had been on the run, a step ahead of the Nazis, since the fall of 1939. "My memory of that period," recalled Vera, "was of constant fear, of total uncertainty." There were times when she had wanted it all to end because it was just too much to be always so afraid.[8]

In the spring and summer of 1942, the Hermans had hidden in the forests of the Tatra Mountains, and as winter approached they had found refuge in Banska Bystrica, where they had lived in an attic from December 1942 to April 1943 and then, until recently, in a cellar.[9] Through it all, Vera had kept a diary in a small notebook. On the flyleaf of the notebook, she had jotted a refrain from a contemporary Hungarian ballad about the hardships of hiding: "Egyre konny, konny, konny; egyre menj, menj, menj; egyre fuss, fuss, fuss; pihenore sohse juss!" "Always tears, tears, tears; always flee, flee, flee; always run, run, run; but never find a respite!"[10]

The bound notebook was all she had been able to save from her old schoolbag before she had left her expansive, tastefully decorated home in a luxury apartment building, with large stone balconies and marble stairways, in a small town in Czechoslovakia in 1939. She had begun writing in it in 1942, and had tried to make an entry in it every day. Jotting in it relieved the boredom of waiting for hours, sometimes days, hidden in one place or another. "The Hungarian ballad was something that I would hear when we were hiding out in the woods," she recalled. "There was once a pub within hearing distance, and when the singing got loud and drinks got more plentiful, I heard it."[11]

In November 1943, the family's luck, it seemed, had finally run out and they learned that they, along with other Jews known by the Nazis to be living in Banska Bystrica, would soon be deported. They had been betrayed to the authorities by a local collaborator. Before the inevitable herding onto trains got under way, four men had arrived at their hiding place, part of a Jewish "property confiscation team" that included an SS officer who had made Vera's father sign papers that meant they were stripped of everything of value that they owned. Thin and fragile Vera had wondered what these cruel men could possibly want from her parents. What could they confiscate? They had nothing material of value.

The SS man with the confiscation team wore an immaculate uniform. His boots were so polished that Vera could see her reflection in them. He was handsome, the kind of young man who could easily have gone home, she thought, and taken off his black uniform and gotten down on the floor to play with his own children.[12] But still he and the others took what they could, seizing a beautifully embroidered tablecloth that Vera's mother had managed to save so that she could lay it down on the forest floor and use it for picnics, a brightly colored reminder of the lives they had lost. The team also tried to take a pair of boots, but Vera watched her mother hold onto them fiercely, and the men finally left with just the tablecloth and an old pair of shoes, all that the family possessed other than the clothes they were wearing.[13]

A few days after this visit from the confiscation team, the Hermans had learned that the SS had kidnapped local Jewish women aged eighteen to twenty-five to be used as sex slaves on the Eastern Front. The SS simply banged on doors in the middle of the night and seized terrified, screaming women, pulling them from their parents' and husbands' arms. Vera knew two sisters who were taken. One was a newlywed. The other had been born with an inverted hip and limped but was considered too beautiful to be left behind.[14]

The Hermans knew they would in all likelihood be next because they were alien Jews—Jews from another country. They had just one option: flee to Hungary, the last country in Europe from which Jews had not been deported *en masse* to the death camps, although sixty-thousand-odd had been killed in forced labor battalions. But did they still have the energy and will to make the dangerous crossing into Hungary? Vera's forty-five-year-old father, Emil, had begun to tire of the constant stress of trying to stay a step ahead of the Nazis. Their years on the run had worn down this once proud and ebullient doctor's strength and stamina.[15]

Emil always tried to put on a brave face. Vera had seen him cry only once, when he thought she was not looking, his shoulders shaking as he looked out of a window and realized how desperate their situation was.[16] "By now, he was, perhaps, just content to be a sitting duck," she recalled. "But mothers in the Holocaust were not inclined to be sitting ducks."[17]

Margit, Vera's forty-one-year-old mother, had heard about an underground railroad: peasants and partisans who could take Jews across the border into Hungary and all the way to Budapest. Margit didn't have a contact in the organization, but she was determined to get in touch with it, no matter how. At great risk, she knocked on doors, asked around, ignored cruel rebuffs, and finally discovered someone who would help her. And that was how the family now came to be in the attic above a Nazi sympathizer's farmhouse.

THE HERMANS HID IN THE ATTIC and tried to be as quiet as possible. To her horror, Vera discovered rats scurrying around the attic. Their frantic scratching interrupted the happy chatter of young children in a room below. She was worried that the rats might attack her father's balding head, so she wrapped her scarf around it for protection.[18]

The Hermans spent the night and the following day in the attic. Unrelenting rain lashed against the barn's roof. When they finally climbed down from their hiding place, they were drenched. They started walking with the man who had hidden them but didn't get far before they were bogged down. "We sank into the mud, to mid-calf, and we literally had to lift each foot out to take the next step," remembered Vera. "I was just so exhausted that I wanted to sit down in the mud and lean against one of the trees and take a nap. I said that to my mother, but she wasn't impressed."[19]

They followed the young man through the woods, but then he spotted a light in a building that was usually dark. Something was wrong. He lost his nerve, not wanting to be caught with three Jews, and scurried away, leaving the Hermans alone in the dark forest. The rain still pelted down.[20]

Margit ran after the young man and Vera watched, astonished at her mother's speed.

"You have children of your own," Margit screamed at the young man. "Are you going to let this one die?"[21]

No. He wasn't. The young man said they would try again and took the Hermans back to the farmhouse. Forty-eight hours later, he collected them and they tried to escape Czechoslovakia once more. This time, the man led them along winding paths through a dense forest until they found themselves near the border with Hungary, and he directed them toward the local Hungarian railroad station.

The Hermans took the first train to Budapest.

Vera sat looking out the window, trying to look as "normal as possible" but feeling as if she were "going to explode" at any moment.

Did we really make it? Vera asked herself. *When are we going to get caught?*

Finally, the train pulled into Budapest. Germans, green-uniformed Arrow Cross men (Hungarian Nazis), and Hungarian soldiers crowded the platforms. From the train station, the Hermans set out for the Central Jewish Agency. They passed through the streets of Pest. Domes, spires, turrets, and cupolas jostled for attention. Balconies boasted bizarre mythological figures. Many buildings had a gaudy confidence with their imitation marble, fake bronze, art deco stained glass, and peeling stucco walls in every pastel shade imaginable.

At the Central Jewish Agency, someone consulted a roster of Jews willing to take in other Jews and directed the Hermans to a family in Pest that had two girls, one of whom was about Vera's age.[22]

The Hermans had finally made it to Hungary, "a promised land for Jews on the run; the only place where you could be a Jew and stay alive."[23] Their escape had brought them a few more months of survival: "a miracle [that] we," recalled Vera, "at the time could appreciate more than the native Jewish population."[24]

Vera and her family joined three hundred thousand Jewish refugees from Nazi-controlled Europe who had already made it to Hungary. Despite the introduction of ever more punitive anti-Semitic laws under his quarter-century rule, Admiral Horthy had not agreed to liquidate these or his own country's Jews, who constituted much of the middle class. After almost four years of genocide, the Hungarian Jews, who made up 5 percent of the population, still lived in relative safety.

Most Hungarian Jews in fact felt utterly assimilated in Hungary, and many were fierce Magyar nationalists in a country that had been deeply scarred by the humiliation of defeat in the First World War and then the subsequent dismemberment under the Treaty of Trianon, in which two-thirds of the nation's territory had been lost.

Despite the resentments of a large, uneducated feudal class whose prejudices and hatreds were easily aroused, the Jews had nevertheless enjoyed an extraordinary prominence in the nation's cultural and economic affairs, being especially prevalent in such professions as law, journalism, medicine, and academia. In the 1920s, an astonishing half of all Hungary's lawyers were Jewish.[25]

Horthy's own views were common among Hungary's elites at the time: "As regards the Jewish problem, I have been an anti-Semite throughout my life. I have never had contact with Jews. I have considered it intolerable that here in Hungary everything, every factory, bank, large fortune, business, theater, press, commerce, etc. should be in Jewish hands, and that the Jew should be the image reflected of Hungary, especially abroad. Since, however, one of the most important tasks of the government is to raise the standard of living, i.e., we have to acquire wealth, it is impossible, in a year or two, to eliminate the Jews, who have everything in their hands, and to replace them with incompetent, unworthy, mostly big-mouthed elements, for we should become bankrupt. This requires a generation at least."[26]

Although they had been gradually pauperized and their civil rights stripped from them, the Hungarian Jews were for the most part confident in early 1944 that nothing apocalyptic would happen to them. As Vera recalled: "They said: 'It happened in Germany and in Czechoslovakia, but it is never going to happen in Hungary.' They said this even though they knew that Jews [in labor brigades] had already been deported from the countryside. But it was not going to happen in Budapest, where Jews had been living for a thousand years."[27]

The Hermans, by contrast, knew only too well what could happen to Budapest's Jews: Vera's grandparents had already been sent to a death camp, revealed after the war as Auschwitz.[28] They were among an estimated 90 percent of the prewar Jewish population—263,000 people—who were killed in the Final Solution in Czechoslovakia.

3

Mauthausen

THE MERCEDES STAFF CARS passed through an entrance into the vast concentration camp of Mauthausen, situated on the northern bank of the Danube in upper Austria. One after another the SS officers stepped out of the cars and headed inside an SS barracks. The most ruthless and efficient mass murderers in all Nazi-occupied Europe, they were about to be briefed on how they were going to complete the Final Solution.

As elsewhere in the vast gulag of Nazi concentration camps, it was just another day in Mauthausen. In a quarry in one section of the camp, emaciated Jews, communists, homosexuals, Gypsies, and any other so-called enemies of the Third Reich were being worked to death on the infamous Stairs of Death. Inmates carried rough blocks of stone, weighing more than a hundred pounds, up 186 uneven, often slippery and icy steps. Over and over, they climbed them, until they slipped or fell to their deaths. Today, as usual, prisoners collapsed and fell back, knocking others over, falling into each other like dominoes. So it went, from dawn until dusk.

The SS guards at Mauthausen quickly grew bored, even by this frequent spectacle, and would create their own sport, forcing inmates to race each other up the steps and then placing the survivors at the edge of a cliff, known as the Parachute Wall. At gunpoint, Jews and other inmates would then be given a quintessentially Nazi choice—be shot or push the person in front of them off the cliff.[1]

As Adolf Eichmann and his men gathered, they had every reason to be confident yet again of success. Indeed, Eichmann had already carried out orders from his superiors—SS Reich Leader Heinrich Himmler, RSHA Chief Ernst Kaltenbrunner, and the Gestapo boss Heinrich Muller—with extreme diligence, not to mention impressive results, in Poland, Romania, Germany, France, Italy, Holland, Belgium, Denmark, Slovakia, and Austria.[2]

This cold March morning in Mauthausen, Eichmann reportedly gave a pep talk to his men. Time was of the essence, he stressed. In a week, a new operation vital to the survival of the Reich would begin: the German military occupation of Hungary, code-named Operation Margarethe. Eichmann's men would follow in the footsteps of the occupying German forces and then set about removing the country's million-odd Jews, the last significant population in Europe. The cleansing of Hungary would be fast and systematic.[3] From east to west, Hungary would be rendered "Jew clean." Each province would be cleared of Jews, with the capital, Budapest, saved until last. This final operation of the Final Solution would be completed in a matter of weeks, not months.

"Now the turn of Hungary has come," said Eichmann. "It will be a deportation surpassing every preceding operation in magnitude."[4]

"SEND DOWN THE MASTER IN PERSON," Heinrich Himmler had commanded when told of the Nazi plans to occupy Hungary.[5] "Comb the country from east to west! Begin with the eastern provinces, which the Russians are approaching. See to it that nothing like the Warsaw ghetto revolt is repeated in any way."[6]

That Master was Adolf Eichmann. He had been involved with the Final Solution from its inception and was now the key functionary in the Gestapo department assigned to ridding Europe of the Jews. In the words of his deputy, Dieter Wisliceny, he was "very cynical in his attitude to the Jewish question. He gave no indication of any human feeling toward these people. He was not immoral: he was amoral and completely ice-cold in his attitude."[7]

It seemed that nothing could stop Eichmann from killing Jews. According to Rudolf Hoss, commandant of Auschwitz, who knew Eichmann well and worked closely with him, "Eichmann was sharply opposed to every suggestion to sift out the Jews capable of work from those deported. He regarded this as a constant danger to his plans for the Final Solution, in view of the possibility of mass escapes or some other event that might permit the Jews to remain alive . . . He showed himself to be completely obsessed with the idea of destroying every single Jew he could lay his hands on."[8]

In 1942, Eichmann had argued against the mobilization of his men to deal with the partial deportation of alien Jews, such as the Hermans, from Hungary. But now, with Horthy under intense pressure from Hitler to cooperate fully with Nazi demands, there was the opportunity to carry out a total deportation, no piecemeal affair. Then he had advised: "Experience has proved [that] a partial action requires no less effort in preparation and execution than a total measure against all the Jews of a country . . . We had better wait till Hungary is ready to include all its Jews in the necessary measures."[9]

That time had come.

DRESSED IN A SILVER-GRAY UNIFORM, Adolf Eichmann stood at the front of the column of 140 vehicles. It was now midday on March 19, 1944, a red letter day for the hard-drinking, increasingly dissolute colonel—his thirty-eighth birthday.[10] Dragging on a cigarette, he surveyed his two-hundred-odd men as they readied to leave for Hungary. A corner of his thin-lipped mouth twitched. He had a nervous tic. From a distance, he was an unimposing figure with his thin frame, light brown hair, and impassive gray-blue eyes. He walked with a slight stoop, his legs bowed like a cowboy.

Engines cranked up, clouds of exhaust fumes formed, and Adolf Eichmann stepped into his Mercedes staff car. He gave the command to move out, hot on the heels of no less than eleven Wehrmacht divisions that had stormed into Hungary and occupied it in the early hours of that morning. The ensuing journey to Budapest was almost a festive affair. En route, Eichmann and his closest advisers stopped in his hometown of Linz and gathered around to celebrate his birthday with a bottle of rum.

Among the well-wishers were Herman Krumey, Dieter Wisliceny, and Theodor Dannecker. Krumey, a bespectacled toady who had earned the nickname "Bloodhound of Vienna," had cleansed Amsterdam, Warsaw, and Paris of "dirty" Jews. Like many of Eichmann's men, he had a weakness for prostitutes, and in Budapest he would soon find himself a new mistress, Eva Kosytorz—a notorious courtesan who would become as loathed and feared as her porcine lover.

Perhaps the most fanatical anti-Semite among Eichmann's aides was Dannecker, dubbed the "Exterminating Angel." He had earned his reputation for diligence in the French countryside, hunting down Jewish children who had somehow escaped the Nazis' massive Europe-wide dragnet. According to Xavier Vallat, the first French commissioner for Jewish Questions in Vichy, France, Dannecker was "a fanatical Nazi who went into a trance every time the word *Jew* was mentioned."[11] He was also something of a fusspot, according to his colleagues, and a superb pimp, Eichmann's ever-ready provider of sexual distraction. In Paris, he had organized several clubs, along the lines of Salon Kitty, the famous brothel in Berlin. The most beautiful girls were easy to procure: Most often, they were pulled from the terrified lines of deportees at Drancy by Dannecker's men and told they could "spare themselves the journey East" by becoming high-class whores. According to one source, Dannecker himself liked to select them from a distance. Later, at his office, they were told to strip and were then marched back and forth so he could inspect their suitability. They could either serve the SS or die. It was that simple. Few refused.[12]

The Austrian Dieter Wisliceny, Eichmann's obese, sometimes jocular deputy, had cleared out Slovakia and Greece. Rumor had it that all a smart, wealthy Jew had to do was slip a diamond into an expensive white chocolate truffle and Wisliceny would arrange for his death list to be one name shorter. He would soon become so fat, gorging on Hungarian cuisine, that he would find it difficult to sit comfortably in a chair.

It was Wisliceny whom Eichmann had first informed in 1942 of plans for the Final Solution to the Jewish problem. "I was sent to Berlin in July or August 1942 in connection with the status of Jews from Slovakia," Wisliceny recalled. "I was talking to Eichmann in his office in Berlin when he said that on a [written] order of Himmler all Jews were to be exterminated. I requested to be shown the order. He took a file from the safe and showed me a top secret document with a red border, indicating immediate action. It was addressed jointly to the chief of the Security Police and SD [Security Service] and to the inspector of concentration camps. The letter read substantially as follows:

> The Fuehrer has decided that the final solution of the Jewish question is to start immediately. I designate the Chief of the Security Police and SD and the Inspector of Concentration Camps as responsible for the execution of this order. The particulars of the program are to be agreed upon by the Chief of the Security Police and SD and the Inspector of Concentration Camps. I am to be informed currently as to the execution of this order.

"The order was signed by Himmler and was dated sometime in April 1942. Eichmann told me that the words *final solution* meant the biological extermination of the Jewish race, but that for the time being able-bodied Jews were to be spared and employed in industry to meet current requirements. I was so much impressed with this document which gave Eichmann authority to kill millions of people that I said at the time: "May God forbid that our enemies should ever do anything similar to the German people." He replied: "Don't be sentimental—this is a Fuhrer order."

An order, Wisliceny realized, that was in fact the "death warrant for millions of people."[13]

THE GERMAN OCCUPATION of Budapest on March 19 came as an enormous shock to the Jews living there. One Jewish refugee from Czechoslovakia, who would soon become active in the Hungarian Zionist Youth

Resistance movement in Budapest, vividly recalled "the endless columns of gray tanks, the motorbikes, the vehicles in military camouflage, everything moving forward wordlessly with clockwork precision, spreading fear and terror across the snow-covered city. What we had so feared and had warned of so often was now happening."[14]

Eighteen-year old Marianne Lowy, an attractive, dark-haired aspiring actress and dancer, was due to meet with her fiancée, Pista Reiss, at 11 a.m. on the Corso, Budapest's famous riverside promenade, where families and young lovers would sit on beautiful spring Sunday mornings. Marianne and Pista, ten years her elder, had just furnished an apartment in the hills of Buda with Swedish modern furniture and Oriental rugs. They couldn't wait to move in after their marriage in three weeks' time. Marianne had already picked out a dress and a veil of finest Brussels lace.

Around 10 a.m., just as Marianne was about to put on a new spring dress, the telephone rang. It was Pista, calling from the new apartment, which had a superb view of the Danube. "Don't go out of your house," he said. "The Germans . . . I'm looking out the window and I can see the German army marching across the bridges."[15]

And so it was, Marianne recalled, that the "world of my girlhood suddenly ended."[16]

4

The Last Refuge

ICHMANN ARRIVED IN BUDAPEST on March 19, 1944, with the swagger and ambition of a man who knew he was close to ridding all of Nazi-occupied Europe of its Jews. Hungary was the last place where they could be found in large numbers, more than 725,000 of them, and if he had his way, they would be dispatched in record time to the gas chambers in Auschwitz.[1] Almost half had already escaped his grasp and were refugees, like Vera Herman and her family, from other countries.[2].

Eichmann and his aides quickly set up their operation in the leafy, haute bourgeois neighborhood of Svagheny Hill in Buda. And so, just like Mafiosi with unlimited appetites, financial resources, and power, Eichmann and his most trusted associates settled in for what promised to be a long, hot summer of sending Hungary's Jews, "spiced with paprika," to the "Auschwitz mill," as Eichmann was wont to say.[3]

Eichmann chose the elegant Hotel Majestic as his headquarters. Eichmann's aide, Herman Krumey, took an office next to Eichmann's. A large and detailed map of Hungary, indicating the regions where the Jews were to be deported, was quickly pinned to one wall. Eichmann also secured for his personal retreat a spacious villa on Apostol Street, atop the beautiful Rose Hill. The home had been seized from a Jewish businessman called Aschner. The gardens sloped gently toward the Danube and would soon be full of fragrant spring flowers. The nearby streets were

lined with chestnuts that were starting to leaf, bright green buds spring-
ing to life.

Eichmann now answered to only two men: his immediate boss,
Gestapo Chief Muller, and Reichsfuhrer Himmler, head of the SS. Heydrich, his mentor, was no more; he had died of blood poisoning, caused
by the dirty shards of a grenade that had exploded beneath his car and
splintered into his spleen, back in May of 1942 in Prague—the victim of
Allied-trained assassins.

The morning after his arrival in Budapest, Eichmann dispatched his
key henchmen—Wisliceny and Krumey—to begin a dialogue with the
leaders of Hungary's Jewish community. On March 20, 1944, Krumey
duly stood before a group of nervous Jewish leaders. A pharmacist before
joining the SS, Krumey was known to be a stickler for detail, "meticu-
lous, always punctual, excellent at following instructions."[4] He had
known Eichmann since 1938, when they had been in Austria together.

Krumey began by informing the Jews that, from now on, "all the affairs of Hungarian Jewry are transferred to the competence of the SS."[5]
Then Krumey told the assembled leaders that Jews were not to leave the
city. There was to be no panic. The Jewish press as well as rabbis were
to call for calm. Disaster was not imminent. Indeed, the Gestapo was
not in Budapest to kill the Jews, stressed Krumey, but to protect them
from lawbreakers. In the following days, a senior group of Jewish leaders, the Jewish Council, was to be formed to liaise with the Gestapo.
Eichmann would address the first formal meeting of the Jewish Council
on March 31.

CRUCIAL TO EICHMANN'S PLANS were Laszlo Baky and Laszlo Endre,
two Jew-hating, fiercely nationalistic state secretaries in the Hungarian
government. Thanks to their enthusiastic assistance, Eichmann would
later recall that the deportation process in Hungary succeeded like a
"dream."[6] A week after arriving in Budapest, Eichmann met with the
pair; for several hours, they sat and munched on pretzels and drank Hungarian wine in the Majestic's carefully tended gardens, gazing down on
the Danube curling lazily through the city below. From time to time, they

examined a large map of Hungary, which Eichmann had brought with him, so they could be sure of the utmost efficiency in cleansing the provinces before emptying Budapest.

The two Hungarians were eager to begin the very next day by deporting one hundred thousand alien Jews (including Vera Herman and her parents). But Eichmann did not want the operation to go off half-cocked and insisted on moving at a more measured pace, not wanting to overload the railway system, nor the gas chambers and crematoria at Auschwitz, which was then ramping up to handle the hundreds of thousands of Hungarian Jews targeted for liquidation.

Eichmann was delighted by the Hungarians' enthusiasm. He left the meeting assured of their full backing. The Horthy regime had finally agreed to the Nazis' requests for the delivery of "Jewish workers for German war production purposes."[7]

"On that evening," Eichmann later recalled proudly, "the fate of the Jews of Hungary was sealed."[8]

Eichmann was a master at deferring responsibility to others, and so he made sure Baky and Endre agreed to provide him with a formal request from the Hungarian government for the deportation. That way, the Gestapo and SS could claim that they had been invited to carry out the deportations. Baky immediately went to meet with Lieutenant Colonel Laszlo Ferenczy, who headed the largely corrupt, anti-Semitic, and uneducated Hungarian gendarmerie, around five thousand men in all. "[Ferenczy] had a strongly chiseled, attractive face, a thick, muscular neck," recalled a Jewish contemporary. "I hoped the hangman's rope would look good on it." Ferenczy was just as eager as Baky and Endre to get started. He would later tell his men to go ahead and torture Jewish children if they thought it necessary—it was the best way of forcing their parents to say where they had hidden their valuables.

Rudolf Hoss, the commandant at Auschwitz, later recalled—while under interrogation for war crimes—that he visited Budapest three times that spring of 1944 to "obtain an estimate of the numbers of able-bodied Jews that might be expected." During these visits, added Hoss, he was able to witness Eichmann's winning ways with both the Hungarian government and its army. "[Eichmann's manner of approach] was extremely firm and matter-of-fact, but nevertheless amiable and courteous" re-called Hoss, "and he was liked and made welcome wherever he went. This was confirmed by the innumerable private invitations he received from the chiefs of these departments."[9]

Hoss also remembered how fiercely determined Eichmann was to complete his mission to destroy European Jewry. "Eichmann was ab-solutely convinced that if he could succeed in destroying the biological basis of Jewry in the east by complete extermination, then Jewry as a whole would never recover from the blow. The assimilated Jews of the West, including America, would be in his opinion in no position (and would have no desire) to make up this enormous loss of blood, and there would therefore be no future generation worth mentioning."[10]

WHY WAS EICHMANN SO DETERMINED on this course of action? Was he just another zealot, his mind poisoned by decades of anti-Semitism and the virulent hatreds of National Socialism? Or was there something in his past—some scarring encounter or episode perhaps—that had cat-alyzed his loathing of Judaism? Or was he so inadequate, so brutalized, that sheer envy and the lust for a scapegoat explained his utterly profes-sional dedication to the murder of eleven million people?

Simon Wiesenthal, the celebrated Holocaust survivor and Nazi hunter, later investigated whether anything in Eichmann's childhood in-dicated that he might become a mass murderer. "I didn't find anything," Wiesenthal recalled. "Eichmann came from a religious, quiet family. His father, a member of the Presbyterian church, once spoke as the guest of honor at the synagogue in Linz, when the head of the Jewish community there, Benedikt Schwager, was awarded a high Austrian decoration."[11]

Wiesenthal elaborated further, telling the journalist Alan Levy in 1985: "Look, I've studied the life stories of too many Nazi murderers. Nobody was born a murderer. They'd mostly been farmers, workers, clerks, or bu-reaucrats—the kind of people you meet every day. Some had good early childhoods; some didn't. Almost all had religious instruction of some kind; none had a prior criminal record. Yet they became murderers—expert murderers—out of conviction. It was like they put on their SS uniforms and replaced them in the closet by hanging up their consciences with their civilian clothes. In the moment Eichmann put on the swastika, the first casualty he deported was not a Jew, but his own conscience."[12]

THE PATTERN OF DECEPTION was by now well established. First, con the Jewish community, through its frightened yet ever hopeful leaders, into believing that nothing fatal was about to happen. Second, quickly and decisively place Jews into holding prisons, camps, and ghettoes. Last, but not least, keep to a strict timetable of deportation, ensuring that as many Jews as could be taken by train were deposited as close to the gas chambers as possible.

Eichmann began his operation by calling Budapest's Central Jewish Council to a meeting at his office at the Majestic Hotel. The men of the council gathered nervously on March 31, 1944, some of them having packed suitcases in the expectation that they were going to be imprisoned immediately. Eichmann entered his office, dressed in his immaculate gray uniform, wearing a cap, a gun holstered at his waist. One of the Jewish leaders present was bespectacled thirty-eight-year-old Hungarian lawyer and journalist Rudolf Kasztner, a committed Zionist, canny negotiator, and leader of the Aid and Rescue Committee, which had helped Jews escape Nazi Europe.

According to Kasztner, who would deal with Eichmann and his lackeys a great deal in the coming months, Eichmann was abusive from the start.[13]

"Do you know what I am?" he shouted. "I am a bloodhound! All opposition will be broken. If you think of joining the partisans, I will have you slaughtered. I know you Jews. I know all about you. I have been dealing with Jewish affairs since 1934."

In Kasztner's memoirs, Eichmann then lied brazenly. "If you behave quietly and work," promised Eichmann, "you'll be able to keep your community and your institutions. But—and I am being frank with you here—where Jews opposed us, there were executions." Once the war was won, the Jews could return to their former lives. "We Germans will again become good-natured," vowed Eichmann, "as we were in the past."

Then Eichmann made an announcement. Starting April 5, all Jews would have to wear the yellow Star of David badge. "Not just your membership," stressed Eichmann. "I will make no distinction between religious Jews and converts. As far as I'm concerned, a Jew is a Jew, whatever he calls himself."

Making the badges would be good for Jewish businesses, sneered Eichmann. "[But] to be fair, you can't keep it an exclusive business for Jews," he added. "Of course, we have to open up the bidding to gentiles." Eichmann chuckled. He told Kasztner and the others before him that no one was going to be killed. The Hungarian Jews would be put to work to help the German war effort. Then came the same lie Eichmann had used so successfully to deport communities throughout Europe: families would be sent away together, "out of consideration for the close family life of the Jews."

Eichmann knew that the leaders before him desperately wanted to believe him. And according to one of them, Samuel Stern, he was a convincing operator, a skilled charmer. "I will visit your museum soon," Eichmann promised, "because I am interested in Jewish cultural affairs. You can trust me and talk freely to me—as you see, I am quite frank with you. If the Jews behave quietly and work, you will be able to keep all of your community institutions."[14]

Eichmann was finished. He stood up and marched out.[15]

ANTI-JEWISH DECREES FOLLOWED FAST. All Jews now had to wear six-inch-wide cadmium-yellow stars. They could not travel freely; Eichmann alone would decide who would receive a travel permit.[16] All synagogues were closed and turned over to the Gestapo.

On April 5, as these and other decrees took effect, Marianne Lowy was married in a civil ceremony. The following day, she had a religious service in secret. "There were not synagogues available," she recalled. "The one I belonged to became a stable for the Germans. We had an upstairs neighbor who had an open-roofed terrace. We used my grandfather's tallis for the canopy. There were four men, two cousins and two neighbors, who held it up. It was not a wedding that an eighteen-year-old girl visualizes, but we did it."

An hour after the ceremony, Marianne removed the yellow star she had sewn onto her coat and threw it away. "If they get me," Marianne told herself, "they get me. I'll take a chance."[17]

THE FIRST DEPORTATIONS to Auschwitz would begin in just a matter of weeks, on May 15, 1944, and then proceed at such a startling pace that by July all but those living in Budapest would have been removed, the vast majority ending up in the ovens of Auschwitz. As many as three hundred thousand would be shot or gassed, their bodies thrown into hastily dug pits and burned, in just forty-six days.[18]

First the Jews in the provinces were to be taken from their homes to special encampments, ghettoes, and containment areas such as brick-yards and disused factories. Helping Eichmann's deportation would be thousands of Hungarian gendarmes, arguably the most enthusiastic of all foreign collaborators with the Final Solution. In their black, cock-plumed hats, they looked like faintly ridiculous throwbacks to the days of the Austro-Hungarian Empire, but there would be nothing picaresque about their treatment of their fellow Hungarians.

With intentional cruelty, if not irony, the first day of the round up was scheduled for the first day of Passover, the Jewish holiday that celebrates the Jews' escape from Egyptian oppression.[19]

That morning, around 7 a.m., Marianne Lowy was spending Passover with her parents in Pest. She heard the doorbell ring. Her parents were still asleep, so she went to open the door. Three Gestapo men stood out side. They said they wanted to talk to her father.

"What for?"

"He was listening to the BBC."[20]

This was a common justification. By this stage of the war, everyone had access to a radio, and most listened if they dared to the BBC, its broadcasts signaled by the famous opening notes of Beethoven's Fifth Symphony.[21]

Marianne's mother emerged from her bedroom in a negligee, followed by Marianne's father. The men began to ask him questions. Then they told him to pack—they were taking him away for questioning.

Marianne began to pack a bag for her father.

"Oh, he'll be back," said one of the men. "It's just for questioning."

Marianne watched aghast as her mother dropped to her knees and began to beg the men not to take her father. "She held onto the coat of one of the men," Marianne recalled, "trying to hold him back, but it didn't help. The men said that if my father hadn't done anything, he'd be released after the interrogation."[22]

They were lying. That morning, Marianne's father was taken to a prison in Budapest to await deportation to Auschwitz.[23]

PERHAPS THE MOST MOVING testimony from this period comes from Eva Heyman, a thirteen-year-old girl not unlike Vera Herman. Eva scribbled her last entry in a secret diary on May 30, 1944: "Yet, my little Diary, I don't want to die, I still want to live . . . I would wait for the end of the war in a cellar, or in the attic, or any hole, I would, my little Diary, I would even allow that cross-eyed gendarme who took the flour from us to kiss me, only not to be killed, only to be left alive!"

Eva Heyman and her grandparents were arrested and deported to Auschwitz on June 2, 1944. Her mother, Agnes Zsolt, would be liberated from Bergen-Belsen in 1945 and return to Hungary to search in vain for her daughter. Eventually, she learned that Josef Mengele had sent her to be gassed at Auschwitz: "A good-hearted female doctor was trying to hide my child, but Mengele found her without effort. Eva's feet were full of sore wounds. 'Now look at you,' Mengele shouted, 'you frog, your feet are foul, reeking with pus! Up with you on the truck!' He transported his human material to the crematorium in yellow-colored trucks. Eyewitnesses told me that he himself had pushed her onto the truck."

Eva Heyman was gassed on October 17, 1944, according to her mother, who would later commit suicide after securing publication of her daughter's diary.[24]

Among others who were deported was Elie Wiesel, who famously re-counted his experiences in *Night* and other works, and the writer Imre Kertesz, whose book, *Fateless,* paints an equally haunting picture of Hungary's darkest summer. When sixteen-year-old Wiesel arrived with his family in Auschwitz that May, he was separated on the ramp from his mother and sister. He and his father were marched toward a crossroads in the camp. "Standing in the middle of it was, though I didn't know it then, Dr. Mengele, the notorious Dr. Mengele," recalled Wiesel. "He looked like the typical SS officer: a cruel, though not unintelligent, face, complete with monocle. He was holding a conductor's baton and was surrounded by officers. The baton was moving constantly, sometimes to the right, sometimes to the left."[25]

Wiesel and his father were waved to the left.

Mengele had deemed them fit enough to work.

Nearby, someone among the weeping men and boys began to recite the Jewish prayer for the dead, Kaddish.

"*Yisgadal, veyiskadash, shmey raba* . . . May His name be celebrated and sanctified," whispered Wiesel's father.[26]

Wiesel would be the only one of his family to survive the camps.

GAINING ENTRY TO the heavily guarded SS and Gestapo compounds in the leafy streets and hills of Buda, where the rich had built impressive villas and mansions, was dangerous that spring for any Hungarian civilian without the correct papers and a valid reason to be on the streets. But it was madness for Alice Breuer, an eighteen-year-old Jewish medical student with bright eyes and raven-black hair.

Alice looked through the windows of a rattling streetcar, passing across the fast-flowing Danube and heading toward the hills of Buda. She wore a yellow star on her coat. At any moment, she knew she could be arrested. Thousands of other Jews had already been dragged from their beds, from offices, from bars, and randomly off the streets, then sent to a Gestapo prison to be tortured or to a holding camp such as Kistarcsa—the last stop for many before the ramps at Auschwitz. But

Alice, nicknamed Lici, was undeterred as she got off the street car and took the cogwheel railway up toward the Majestic Hotel, Adolf Eichmann's headquarters. At all costs, she had to get back to the town of Kormend in the provinces to see her family. If that meant asking Eichmann himself for a travel pass, that was clearly what she had to do. He had decreed that only he could authorize such a pass.[27]

Alice had left the home of her husband's parents early that morning, knowing it would take several hours to get to the Majestic and back. She hadn't told her husband, Erwin, of her plan to get authorization to travel from Eichmann himself. Had Erwin known, he would probably have barred her from even leaving the house. It was a crazy idea, sheer madness.

ALICE AND ERWIN had known each other less than a year, first meeting as medical students in the pathology department at the Jewish General Hospital in Budapest in the fall of 1943.[28] "The first thing she did was try to kick me out of the laboratory," recalled Erwin. "But then I explained to her that I was studying the same subject. We talked. She was brilliant, very fast thinking, well informed. She loved classical music and lived and breathed medicine."[29]

It was not long before Erwin, with his dark, swept-back hair and fine Slavic features, had fallen in love with Alice. Then came the German occupation of March 19, 1944, and everything the future promised was stolen. The Nazi war machine held Hungary firmly in its vice, and Alice had begun to worry about her family, who lived in a small town near the Czech border. All she had wanted was to be with them, even if that meant she might not see Erwin again. "I tried to console her [Alice]," remembered Erwin, "but the repeated screams from a nearby police station, heard clearly from [Alice's] apartment, meant that somebody was being beaten, which did not mitigate her worries [about her family]."[30]

Alice had decided to return to her family. With heavy heart, Erwin had kissed her goodbye at a train station in Budapest.[31] "I was very worried what would happen to her," he remembered. "I realized that the Jews in Budapest were in a better situation because of the sheer number of them, over one hundred thousand, plus a lot of illegal people who had come from various countries. But in Kormend, a small little town with just three hundred Jews, it would be so easy to round them all up and put them on a train to Auschwitz."

Erwin's worst fears were soon confirmed: A few weeks after Alice returned to Kormend, she and her family were taken to a ghetto.

Erwin had acted fast. With a friend of his, he had stolen a letterhead and rubber stamps from his university—these had been crucial because with the officious yet uneducated Hungarian gendarmes, Erwin recalled, "any piece of paper, even toilet paper with a stamp on it, became unbelievably important. We wrote a letter that was so stupid that we laughed at it. It ordered Alice to immediately report in Budapest in the national interest because of the need for medical staff. We placed all kinds of stamps all over it."[32]

It worked. Alice was allowed to return to Budapest at the end of April. She joined Erwin and his family in their new home: an apartment building, marked by a large yellow star, in a run-down part of Pest that had been designated for the Jews. Gone forever was the stylish, elegantly furnished home that Erwin had grown up in, its huge garden filled with more than three thousand sweetly-scented rose bushes.[33] Reunited, Erwin and Alice discussed marriage. "My mother and Erwin's parents also talked about me and Erwin getting married," recalled Alice. "Everybody thought it was better, safer to be married. We had ten days to marry— then I could legally stay in Budapest. At this time, boyfriends were not just boyfriends."[34] They were potential saviors for young women from the provinces.[35]

Erwin's mother had told Alice that she would care for her as if she were her own daughter. "I will love you my girl," she had said. "You will be my daughter. I will be your mother."

"I don't need a mother," Alice had replied. "I have one."

But in the end, Alice agreed to become Erwin's wife. And so she and Erwin were married in a rushed civil ceremony at City Hall. To celebrate, they had gone to one of the few restaurants in Budapest where Jews were still permitted. For a honeymoon, recalled Erwin, they had sipped an "espresso coffee."[36] Not long after, Alice had somehow learned that her family was going to be deported from Kormend. "My whole family—all my friends, everybody I knew," she recalled. "I was desperate. So I decided to go to Eichmann's place."[37]

ALICE GOT OFF THE COGWHEEL RAILWAY at a stop a few hundred yards from the Majestic Hotel. Gray-uniformed German soldiers patrolled the winding, steep streets lined with elegant mansions. Not far from the heavily guarded entrance to the Majestic, a German soldier approached Alice. To her amazement, he did not want to spit on her or kick her. He smiled at her and appeared friendly, even though she was wearing a yellow star on her coat.

It was soon clear to Alice from the German soldier's polite questions that he had taken a fancy to her. "It's such nice weather," the German said. Alice was too afraid to turn her back on him. So they talked. The German soldier explained that he had been a teacher before the war, and for a few minutes they had a "nice conversation." As they approached the entrance to the Majestic, Alice told the German soldier it would be embarrassing for him to be seen with her. Guards were watching. She was a Jew, after all.

The German held out his hand.

"Thank you for the nice company."

They parted and Alice then walked fearlessly right up to the SS guards outside the Majestic.

"I would like to talk to Colonel Eichmann."[38]

Alice was ushered inside the entrance, across a small bridge, and into Eichmann's luxurious headquarters. To her surprise, the guards did not search her. Clearly, she must have been summoned by Eichmann himself; all sorts of Jewish and Hungarian riffraff turned up at his office these days. Why else would a young Jewish woman be asking to go inside the Majestic?

"Go in," a guard said.

One of Eichmann's men opened a door. Eichmann was in his office. Alice stepped inside. The thin-lipped, chain-smoking Eichmann was sitting at a table with several of his aides. A window behind his desk allowed a magnificent view of Budapest.

Eichmann looked up.

"What's this about?"

Alice nervously tried to explain that she needed a travel pass to Kormend.

"What's she saying?" said Eichmann. "What's she saying?"

Eichmann clearly couldn't understand what she was doing there. "He could have just shot me, but he was so astonished," she later recalled. "He was very ordinary looking. He had a gun and he was wearing a gray uniform."

"Out! Out!" snapped Eichmann. "Out! Out!"

Alice left quickly. Amazingly, she was seen out of the Majestic by Eichmann's own guards. She was not harmed. Then she began to walk down toward Pest, back to the small, cramped apartment where there was no privacy, no place even to sit alone with one's fears.

Soon, the episode with Eichmann seemed like a dream. She had so desperately wanted to go home to Kormend and be with her friends and family. But now she knew there was no way she could get to them. Her visit to Eichmann had failed. "It was a terrible time," she recalled. "Every day I woke up and decided 'this is the day I am going to die. I don't want to live.'"[39]

Part Two

DARKNESS AT NOON

5

Escape from Auschwitz

HE TWO MEN, wearing suits taken from murdered Dutchmen, scrambled out from their hiding place beneath a pile of wood and into the cold Polish night. For a second or so, the two men sat on the pile of wood and looked back at the most notorious death camp in history—Auschwitz. "The brilliant lights painted a soft yellow patch in the darkness," recalled one of the men, twenty-year-old Rudolf Vrba, "giving the whole place a mysterious aura that was almost beautiful. We, however, knew that it was a terrible beauty, that in those barracks, people were dying, people were starving, people were intriguing, and murder lurked around every corner."

The two Slovak Jews finally turned their backs to the camp. They dropped to the ground, lay flat, and began to crawl slowly on their stomachs, away from the watchtowers and toward the first cover they could find, a copse of birch trees. "We reached it, rose, and ran, stooping through it until we came to open ground again and began to crawl once more," recalled Vrba. "It was dark and, if we did not keep going, the dawn would catch us in the open. We moved on; and then, when we least expected it, we came to an entirely unexpected obstacle. At first I thought it was a river. It was about eight yards wide, with a whitish ribbon stretching as far as I could see on either side."[1]

Vrba bent down to investigate. It was sand. If they stepped in it, their footprints would tell the Germans where they were headed. But they had no choice but to continue, so they sprinted through the miniature desert, then across a field of ferns.

They slowed down to read a sign:

Attention! This is Auschwitz concentration camp.
Anyone found on these moors will be shot without warning![2]

BEFORE TRYING TO ESCAPE, Vrba had worked on the Canada ramp as part of the cleaning up detachment. It had been his job to sort new arrivals' possessions and search them for precious objects and money. He had himself been part of the selection process, going to the right rather than the left on his arrival in 1942. He knew now that he had been saved only so he could help Germany profit from the industrial slaughter of his fellow Jews, by scavenging among their cast-off possessions and the piles of rags and clothes for objects and materials that could be put to use. He would forever bear the evidence of his slave labor for the Third Reich—a tattoo with his number, 44070.

Cursed, or perhaps blessed, with a photographic memory, Rudolf Vrba had kept a tally of how many other Jews had arrived at Auschwitz since he had been there. He was able to make reasonable estimates because his job meant he was on the ramp when transports unloaded and when they left. He could tell by looking at the belongings of new arrivals that they did not know they were about to be exterminated. These Jews had believed the Nazis' lies about being resettled to the East, the same lies Eichmann repeated that April to the gullible in Budapest.

Someone had to warn people about Auschwitz, and Vrba was determined to try. There had come a point that winter of 1943–44, he recalled, when "it was no longer a question of reporting a crime, but of preventing one; of warning the Hungarians, of rousing them, of raising an army one million strong, an army that would fight rather than die."[3] In January 1944, Vrba saw that a new railway line was being built. This would mean that transports could be taken from sidings in faraway communities, such as Kormend, right to the gas chambers, a significant improvement in the machinery of death.

Vrba had thought about escape since the moment he arrived. But he had soon become aware of just how difficult it would be and therefore had planned his attempt meticulously. "Auschwitz was the most heavily guarded camp in Europe," he recalled. The camp was a "secret which the Nazis were determined would never be revealed, for once even a whisper about it escaped, the sheep would no longer walk quietly into the slaughterhouse."[4]

Since arriving in Auschwitz, Vrba had befriended a twenty-two-year-old called Alfred Wetzler, who came from his hometown in Slovakia. Wetzler had a job in the Birkenau mortuary, where among other tasks he counted the amount of gold taken from dead Jews' teeth. That winter of 1943–44, the two men had agreed to try to escape together. The date they had set for their escape was April 7, 1944, on the eve of Passover.

Unknown to both men, just four days before, on April 3, U.S. aircraft had photographed Auschwitz and its crematoria. There would soon be strident calls for the camp to be bombed, not simply photographed, but Allied strategists decided that history's greatest death factory was a "secondary war target" and did not do so, a failure that continues to ignite fierce debate to this day.[5]

WETZLER AND VRBA PASSED BY the warning sign. They knew they had to reach the cover of the nearest forest before it got light. By dawn, they were crossing a cornfield. Suddenly, they saw a group of women guarded by SS men. They threw themselves to the ground, hearts racing, then crawled on their stomachs through the field. Two hours later, they reached the forest. They stopped to rest for a few minutes before continuing onward, through the tightly bunched firs. But then they heard children's voices. Peeking through bushes, they saw a large group of Hitler Youth, chattering away innocently, as they wound through the forest. The children sat down only thirty yards from the men. "We were trapped," recalled Vrba, "not by the SS this time, but by their children!"

For around an hour, the men lay in the bushes. It began to rain. The children quickly left to escape the downpour and the men hurried onward, boots sinking into the now soggy ground. Several miles from

Auschwitz, exhaustion caught up with them. "It's time we slept," Vrba said. "Let's find somewhere to hide, somewhere that not even the SS would bring women." They looked around and found some bushes. "A watery sun filtered through the branches," recalled Vrba. "The more enthusiastic birds twittered over our heads; and Fred lectured me amiably on the finer points of chess until we fell asleep."

They awoke a few hours later and headed toward the Slovak border, several miles away. On a mountainside near the border, as they again lay resting, there was a rifle shot. They had been spotted by a German patrol with dogs. "We ran, scrambling, stumbling up our hill through the snow," recalled Vrba. "If we could reach the top and disappear into the valley on the other side, we had a chance, but we had to cover that ground under fire and the Germans were blazing away."

Fred was ahead of Vrba and dived behind a large rock. Vrba followed him but then fell. Bullets ricocheted off stones nearby. Vrba pressed his face to the dirt and tried to remain still.

"We've got him!" shouted a German. "Cease fire!"

As the Germans moved toward Vrba, he made a dash for it. The Germans opened fire again, but he reached the rock and took cover.

"C'mon!" said Fred. "Head for the trees."

They made it to a tree line, across a cold stream and into a forest. It seemed as though they had thrown the Germans off their scent by crossing the stream because the baying of dogs became more and more distant. On they trudged. The next day, Vrba and Fred Wetzler crossed into Slovakia. It was April 21, 1944. A local farmer helped the two men reach a Jewish doctor in a town called Cadca who guided them to Zilina. By April 25, 1944, Vrba and Wetzler were drinking sherry in the headquarters of the Jewish community in Zilina, celebrating their escape.

Then they began to tell the Jewish leaders in Zilina about their time in Auschwitz. "For hours I dictated my testimony," recalled Wetzler. "I gave them detailed statistics of the deaths. I described every step of the awful confidence trick by which 1,760,000 in my time in the camp alone had been lured to the gas chambers. I explained the machinery of the extermination factory and its commercial side, the vast profits that were reaped from the robbery of gold, jewelry, money, clothes, artificial limbs, spectacles, prams, and human hair, which was used to caulk torpedo heads. I told them how even the ashes were used as fertilizer."[6]

Vrba stressed that there was no time to lose.

"One million Hungarians are going to die," he said. "Auschwitz is ready for them. But if you tell them now, they will rebel. They will never go to the ovens. Your turn is coming. Now it is the Hungarians' hour. You must tell them immediately."

"Don't worry," one of the Jewish leaders assured Vrba. "We are daily in contact with the Hungarian leaders. Your report will be in their hands first thing tomorrow."

Every day that spring, Vrba asked for news from Hungary, hoping to hear about an uprising. But the Jewish leaders there, including Rudolf Kasztner, did not warn the Hungarian Jews about Auschwitz. In their defense, they later claimed with some justification that they wanted to avoid an uprising, which they believed would be savagely repressed, as one had been in the Warsaw ghetto. With the Soviets advancing fast toward them in the East, the Jewish leaders in Budapest decided to try instead to buy time by negotiating with Eichmann. It was a terrible gamble, for in doing so they played right into Eichmann's hands. By now, he had finalized transport schedules for the swift and massive deportation of Hungary's Jews.

Kasztner would later be shot dead on a street in Israel after a trial in which he was accused of collaborating with the Nazis and roundly criticized for failing to warn Hungary's Jews about Auschwitz, even though he had read the Vrba report.* Indeed, it emerged that he had even discussed it with Eichmann while trying to negotiate for the safe passage of a train of Jews, which included his own relatives, to Switzerland. In a meeting in Eichmann's office at the Majestic, recalled Kasztner, he showed Eichmann a German translation of the so-called Auschwitz Protocols. He hoped it would increase pressure on Eichmann to slow down deportations.

"How long?" asked Kasztner, "will it take for the Jewish Agency, for American Jewry, for the world, to find out about this?"

---

*The verdict was appealed and Kasztner was fully exonerated.

Eichmann smiled as he flicked through the report. Then he threw it across his desk at Kasztner.

"Herr Doktor, do you really believe this nonsense?"

Kasztner did not reply.

"I had thought better of you," continued Eichmann. "Surely you recognize this as another fairy tale. I warned you people to stay clear of horror stories. This is the kind of bullshit that will get your slandering body in front of a military judge. It's treason to spread this kind of nonsense, Kasztner—the kind of treason that would see you and your stupid little bunch hanged!"[7]

6

The Cruelest Summer

T HAT MAY OF 1944, newlywed eighteen-year-old Alice and her husband, Erwin, tried to continue their studies, still determined to become doctors. But it was practically impossible. New laws restricting the movement of Jews meant they could leave the "crowded, seedy hole" they shared with Erwin's parents in an apartment block only between 11 a.m. and 2 p.m.[1]

Like all other Jewish men of arms-bearing age, twenty-year-old Erwin now worked in a forced labor battalion. By an order of the Jewish Council, shortly after Eichmann's arrival, he had been transferred to a group that was building an air-raid shelter in Budapest's leafy suburb of Schwabenberg, where Eichmann had set up his headquarters at the Majestic Hotel.

One day, Erwin received a letter that had been smuggled out of the Kormend ghetto.[2] It was from Cecil, Alice's mother. Cecil admitted in the letter that Alice had always been her favorite child. She also begged Erwin to take care of Alice. "From now on," Cecil stated, "Lici [Alice] is your responsibility."[3]

"Her words remained etched in my soul," Erwin later recalled. "I made a solemn pledge to myself to fulfill Cecil's last wish."[4]

Alice's mother had sent a little package with the letter. It contained wedding cake that she had prepared in the ghetto from the last of her food supplies.

Not long after, Alice's mother, father, and sister were among the first people to be deported from Hungary.[5]

SANDY-HAIRED JOEL BRAND, a squarely-built and broad-nosed thirty-eight-year-old Jew, was ushered into Adolf Eichmann's office. It was May 8, 1944. The sharp-witted adventurer with extensive underground connections worked that spring, as his colleague Rudolf Kasztner did, for the Aid and Rescue Committee, a Zionist organization. The Committee had already helped thousands of Jewish refugees in Nazi-occupied Europe escape to Hungary and beyond.[6]

Brand would never forget his first impression of Eichmann. He "had narrow shoulders slouched forward in his gray, tight-fitting SS officer's jacket, epaulets displaying a lieutenant colonel's four stars, a thick leather belt, light-brown hair cut short, large ears, a wide forehead, narrow lips, and flat blue eyes, small for his long, pale face."

"I believe you know who I am," Eichmann told Brand. "I was in charge of the actions in Germany, Poland, and Czechoslovakia. Now it is Hungary's turn."

Brand could barely believe what he heard Eichmann say next.

"I am prepared to sell you one million Jews," said Eichmann, "blood for money, money for blood. You can take them from any country you like, wherever you can find them—from Hungary, Poland, the eastern provinces, Theresienstadt, Auschwitz, wherever you wish. Whom do you want to save? Men who beget children? Women who can bear them? Old people? Children? Sit down and tell me."

Brand tried to keep his wits about him.

"We want to ransom our people and save them from extermination," Brand replied carefully, "but all our Jewish factories and businesses in Hungary are closed, and all our property has been seized."

"I know, of course," said Eichmann, "what you say is true. I am not interested in Hungarian goods. I had you brought here to make a proposition [to me] that I believe will achieve our mutual objective. I want you to go abroad and get in direct touch with your people and with representatives of the Allied powers. Then come back to me with a concrete proposal. When we reach an agreement, you can rely on us to perform our part with our usual German thoroughness. I will get you the necessary documents for your journey."[7]

Brand would later recall the meeting with Eichmann in extraordinary detail, perhaps because he was quick to make notes after the meeting, knowing that it was crucial that he remember as clearly as possible what Eichmann was proposing.

Brand met as soon as possible with other leaders of the Jewish Agency. They agreed that Brand should go along with Eichmann's plan.

On May 10, Eichmann called Brand back to his office at the Majestic.

"I have obtained assent to our negotiations," said Eichmann. "Are you ready to go?"

"I am ready to leave at once," Brand replied, "and I think I can offer you a large amount of foreign currency."

Eichmann was not interested in money. "Give me ten thousand trucks," he said, "and I will give you one million Jews. You can give the Allies definite assurance on my word of honor that these trucks will never be used in the West. They are required for exclusive use on the Eastern Front."

"What kind of guarantee can you give that a million Jews will really be set free?" Brand asked.

"If you return from Istanbul," said Eichmann, "and tell me that the offer has been accepted, I will close Auschwitz and bring back ten percent of the promised million to the frontier. You can take one hundred thousand Jews away and afterward bring me one thousand trucks. We will go on like that, a thousand trucks for every hundred thousand Jews. You cannot ask for anything more reasonable than that."

Brand stood up. He made to leave.

As he reached the door, Eichmann called to him.

"Hurry, Herr Brand, and come back quickly. I am not joking."[8]

MEANWHILE, TIME WAS RUNNING OUT for Vera Herman and her mother and father, just one of the tens of thousands of families now trapped in Budapest. There was nowhere left to run. "Somebody had convinced Adolf Eichmann," recalled Vera, "that his headquarters would be safe from bombing if he left the Jews in Budapest, judiciously scattered throughout the city. He did that, but after two months, he realized that not knowing where the Jews lived would make it more difficult for him when the time came. So he rounded up the native Jews—the Jews of Budapest—into ghettos, and he put the alien Jews, like my family, into holding prisons."[9]

The Hermans were taken to a prison called Tolonc, a fieldstone medieval fortress on the outskirts of Budapest. "The first night," recalled Vera, "it was filled to capacity, so we stood in the courtyard all night, packed so tightly that we could not even sit down. As we kept dozing off in a standing position, we resembled a field of wheat swaying in the breeze. Next morning, when they made room for us by deporting two thousand so-called inmates to Auschwitz, it was hardly an improvement."[10]

Also that morning, Emil Herman was separated from his wife and daughter. Vera believed she had seen the last of her father. Then she and her mother were herded into the fortress's concrete dungeons. There was no furniture, not even bunks to lie on, just a cold floor and countless bedbugs and lice crawling the walls. But her mother, Margit, stayed strong, telling Vera that at least their rusting cups, which held a watery soup made from potato peels, provided much needed traces of iron; they had to spoon the soup into their mouths with stale crusts of bread.[11]

Several days later, Vera and her mother were surprised by the visit of a missionary. He gave Vera and Margit some blankets.[12] They did not know that he had hidden a thermos, full of hot tea, inside one of the blankets. As they walked back to their dungeon, one of them tripped and the thermos smashed to the ground, shattering into hundreds of pieces. "We could almost taste the incredible treat slowly soaking into the ground," recalled Vera.[13]

Not long after the missionary's visit, Vera and her mother were taken to another prison—Kistarcsa, a holding camp for those bound for Auschwitz, run by the SS and administered by the Hungarian gendarmerie. Prominent Jews had been sent there as soon as the Nazis had arrived in Hungary that March. The first Jews from Hungary to be killed in Auschwitz—some eighteen hundred men and women—had, in fact, been dispatched from Kistarcsa on April 29, 1944. Another eighteen trains, with the same number of victims, had followed that summer.[14]

JOEL BRAND ALSO KNEW that time was fast running out as he arrived in the Syrian city of Aleppo on June 10, 1944. It had been almost a fortnight since he had left Budapest, aiming to make contact with Allied officials through Jewish intermediaries. At all costs, he needed to discuss Eichmann's offer—"blood for goods"—with the British and Americans so that he could return to Budapest and begin negotiations with Eichmann. The Gestapo were meanwhile holding his wife, Hansi, hostage during his absence.

Brand's train pulled into the station at Aleppo. Brand gave his luggage to a porter and was about to follow him onto the platform when an Englishman, wearing civilian clothes, entered his compartment.

"Mr. Brand?"

"Yes."

"This way please."[15]

At the compartment door, a jeep was waiting, its engine purring. Men in the jeep forced Brand into it, and he was driven away at high speed and taken to an army barracks. Brand realized that he had been seized by British intelligence. After breakfast the next morning, he was taken to a luxurious Arab villa and shown into a room full of British officers. He explained in great detail the proposals made by Eichmann, then begged them to let him go.[16]

Despite his protests, Brand was taken to Cairo, where the British again questioned him, this time for ten or twelve hours, day after day. In a report to the State Department, the British stated: "Assuming suggestion was put forward by Gestapo in form conveyed to us, then it seems to be sheer case of blackmail or political warfare . . . Implied suggestion that we should accept responsibility for maintenance of additional million person[s] is equivalent to asking the Allies to suspend essential military operations."[17]

On the tenth day of his imprisonment, Brand went on a hunger strike, writing in a letter that: "It is apparent to me now that an enemy of our people is holding me and does not intend to release me in the near future. I will do my utmost to break through the bayonets guarding me."[18]

Brand was eventually persuaded to give up his hunger strike. He later testified that Lord Moyne, the British minister resident in the Middle East and a close friend of Winston Churchill, was present during one of his interrogations and said: "What can I do with this million Jews? Where can I put them?"[19]

AT THE SAME TIME, back in Hungary, twelve hundred people were indeed being sent to their deaths in Auschwitz each day.

Brand's colleague, Kasztner, went to see Eichmann at the Majestic and begged him to stop the deportations.

"It's up to you and your people to have everything settled quickly," said Eichmann. "If I stop the deportations, you'll all take me for a weakling, and you'll make no effort at all to have the negotiations started."

After the meeting, Kasztner sent a telegram to Istanbul, hoping it would reach Brand and speed his return: "Deportations have been resumed."[20]

But Brand did not return. And the deportations would not stop until the provinces had been emptied of Jews.

On July 6, after more than four hundred thousand Hungarian Jews had been sent to their deaths in Auschwitz, British Foreign Secretary Anthony Eden explained why the British had to block the "blood for goods" negotiation with Eichmann. There could not be "anything that looked like negotiating with the enemy."[21]

Brand was finally released by the British in October 1944 but did not return to Budapest, fearing correctly that the Gestapo would kill him. After the war, he joined the Stern gang, which fought to expel the British from Palestine, permanently embittered at his treatment by British intelligence. At no point, he maintained, had he believed that the Allies would make a deal with Eichmann. But he felt that, at the very least, they should have tried to negotiate to stall deportations and buy time for Hungary's doomed Jews. This, in fact, had been the recommendation of the War Refugee Board's representative, Ira Hirschmann, who had urged in early July 1944 that Brand be sent back to Budapest as soon as was possible, armed with careful instructions "indicating that consideration is being given to the proposals in connection with money and possible immunity."[22]

A tragic figure, Brand would die in the 1960s of a heart attack in Germany, of all places, after testifying at a trial of Auschwitz officials.

When later questioned about his "blood for goods" discussions with Brand, Eichmann did not deny making the astonishing offer, which had originated, he stated, with Heinrich Himmler. Whether he or Himmler would have made good on it is another question.[23]

ONE MORNING IN ZILINA in June 1944, an old and sad-faced woman brought Rudolf Vrba his breakfast.

He noticed that she was in tears and asked what was the matter.

"They're deporting the Hungarians," she cried. "Thousands of them. They're passing through Zilina in cattle trucks!"[24]

Vrba was stunned. His escape from Auschwitz had seemingly been for nothing.

7

The Swedish Pimpernel

I N WASHINGTON, the fate of Europe's Jews had not passed unno-
ticed, though there had been scandalously little done about it.[1] In
the words of historian Arthur Morse, whose 1967 book, *While Six
Million Died,* revealed the extent of inaction and obstruction among the
Allies: "As [Hitler] moved systematically toward the total destruction of
the Jews, the government of the United States remained bystanders . . .
Those who tried to awaken the nation were dismissed as alarmists,
cranks, or Zionists. Many Jews were as disinterested as their Christian
countrymen. The bystanders to cruelty became bystanders to genocide."[2]

There were a few notable exceptions. In 1943, the Secretary of the
Treasury, Henry Morgenthau, himself a Jew, had asked aides to prepare a
report titled "The Acquiescence of This Government in the Murder of
the Jews." The eighteen-page report concluded that State Department
officials "have not only failed to use the governmental machinery at their
disposal to rescue Jews from Hitler, but have even gone so far as to use
this governmental machinery to prevent the rescue of these Jews . . . In
their official capacity [they] have gone so far as to surreptitiously attempt
to stop the obtaining of information concerning the murder of the Jewish
population of Europe."[3]

In late 1943, Morgenthau passed the report on to President Roosevelt.
"The matter of rescuing the Jews from extermination is a trust too great to
remain in the hands of men who are indifferent, callous, and perhaps
even hostile," Morgenthau stressed in an accompanying letter. "The task

is filled with difficulties. Only a fervent will to accomplish, backed by persistent and untiring effort, can succeed where time is so precious." Roosevelt set up the War Refugee Board just a week later, on January 22, 1944. Its mission was to deal with the "the rescue, transportation, maintenance, and relief of the victims of enemy opposition and . . . the establishment of havens of temporary refuge for such victims."[4]

By early summer 1944, it was clear that the War Refugee Board would need to establish a rescue operation in Hungary itself, on the ground, if any Jews were going to be saved. But it could not send an American because the United States was at war with Hungary, an Axis power. It needed to find someone from a neutral country to head the rescue mission. The Swedes had a sizeable diplomatic presence in Budapest, and so the War Refugee Board's representative in Sweden, Iver Olsen, was instructed to look for a Swedish citizen who would be willing to organize the rescue in Budapest. American funds would support the operation.

Olsen had worked in the Treasury Department before being sent to Sweden with the War Refugee Board. He already had a formidable record of success, having managed to arrange and finance the rescue of more than a thousand political and intellectual refugees from the Baltic States. He had even gone so far as to hire high-speed boats, which could outrun German U-boats and patrol craft. But his greatest single achievement had come through working closely with American and Norwegian trade unions to organize the transport from Norway to Sweden of over ten thousand endangered Norwegians.[5]

Olsen's search for someone to head a rescue effort in Hungary began with a June 12, 1944, cable from Washington. The well-connected Olsen had only to walk down a corridor in his building that day to the headquarters of the Middle European Trading Corporation to get started. He knew its director, Kalman Lauer, a small, rotund, middle-aged Hungarian Jew, whose wife's parents were now trapped in Budapest. The two men are said to have first talked about someone to head up the rescue as they shared the elevator in the eight-story office building in Stranvagen, where both Olsen and Lauer worked. "I'm looking for a Swede," Olsen apparently said. "Someone with good nerves, good language ability. He'll have to speak both German and some Hungarian.

Someone who would be willing to go to Budapest and spend the next two months trying to save Jews from the Nazis. An independent spirit who does not need much direction. It's a big order."[6]

Lauer told Olsen about his thirty-two-year-old colleague, Raoul Wallenberg, a dynamic, quick-thinking young businessman, fluent in German and Russian, and already familiar with Budapest. As it happened, Wallenberg had been planning for several weeks to visit Budapest, hoping to be able to rescue Lauer's relatives, but the Germans had not yet granted him a visa allowing him to travel via Germany to Hungary.[7]

Wallenberg had been born into the most powerful family in Sweden. Its motto "Esse, non Videri"—"To be, not to be seen"—was fitting for a dynasty of highly influential Lutheran bankers, archcapitalists, and diplomats who had long been accustomed to dominating Swedish society and industry, particularly through the immensely powerful Enskilda bank, whose tentacles reached into every profitable business sector in Scandinavia and beyond.

Raoul Wallenberg had some Jewish blood: his great-great grandfather was Jewish before converting to Lutheranism.[8] His grandfather, Gustaf Wallenberg, had encouraged his education abroad and extensive travels in America and the Middle East. A diplomat and envoy, Gustaf had been a dominant influence on Raoul, whose father, a Swedish naval officer, had died of cancer at age twenty-three, three months before Raoul was born. "It was a great loss for Raoul and for everyone in the family," recalls Wallenberg's half-sister, eighty-nine-year-old Nina Lagergren. "His mother—my mother—was left alone. Raoul was a great comfort. Of course, they were very close. He was a loving, empathetic child, very clever and artistic, with a beautiful voice."[9]

Raoul Wallenberg was no ordinary young aristocrat with an outsized sense of entitlement. From an early age, he had shown an extraordinary determination to learn all he could about the world beyond Sweden. He read the encyclopedia, *Nordisk Familjebok*—all thirty-five volumes—from cover to cover. According to one schoolmate: "Even his appearance was remarkable, with his large, brown eyes and his wavy, dark hair. His way of expressing himself and his interest in everything between heaven and earth were new to us. To begin with, we were cautious—we couldn't understand how anyone could be so totally uninterested in football and getting up to mischief, but the dreamer, as we called him, won our respect with time."[10]

Determined to become a naval officer like his father, Wallenberg must have been bitterly disappointed when he learned that because he was color blind—he had drawn green horses on red grass as a child—he would not be able to follow in his dead father's footsteps. Eager to spend time abroad, Wallenberg left Sweden in 1931 to study architecture in America at the University of Michigan in Ann Arbor. When he returned to Sweden, he tried but failed to find a job as an architect even though he had won the only medal to be awarded by the American Institute of Architects to his class in Ann Arbor of more than a thousand students.

In 1936, Wallenberg worked at a branch office of the Holland Bank in Palestine's port city of Haifa, where he met and befriended Jews who had escaped persecution in Nazi Germany. "Their stories of suffering had a great influence on him," biographer Jeno Levai noted. "His sense of justice was outraged by what he heard."[11] Wallenberg's character traits, added Levai, were by now "well defined. He was generous and enjoyed having lots of people around him. He was a moderate man, drank very little, and was content to chat all evening over one bottle of beer. He loved beautiful women [but] could not find a partner who suited his demanding standards of beauty and intellect. He joked with his favorite aunt that women might only want to marry him for his wealth."[12]

After returning from Haifa, Wallenberg wrote his grandfather: "I am not made to be a banker. There is something about the profession that is too calm, cynical, and cold for me. I think that my talents lie elsewhere. I want to do something more positive than sit behind a desk all day saying no to people." He wanted to do more with his life than work in banking—"a glorified pawnshop."[13] Yet it was with the help of his wealthy and influential cousin and godfather—the banker Jacob Wallenberg—that Raoul had then found a job at the Central European Trading Company, owned by Lauer. In 1938, Hungary, under the fascist sway of Miklas Horthy, had passed anti-Jewish laws, which meant Lauer had faced serious problems traveling to Hungary. So he had sent Wallenberg in his place, once in 1942 and most recently in autumn 1943.

To Iver Olsen, Wallenberg seemed an ideal candidate. Crucially, he knew Budapest and how to make deals, perhaps even with the Nazis.

ON JUNE 9, 1944, the intense young Wallenberg, the demure and tall Olsen, and the stocky Lauer met at the summer resort of Saltsjobaden at the Grand Hotel. It was 7 p.m. as they sat down in its luxurious, oak-paneled dining room. They talked late into the Scandinavian white night, Wallenberg agreeing to go to Budapest for two to three months, and finally left the hotel as the sun rose the next morning at around 5 a.m.[14]

Before parting, Olsen told Wallenberg he would arrange for him to meet with the American ambassador in Stockholm, Herschel Johnson. The savvy, highly experienced Johnson was just as impressed as Olsen and cabled Washington: "There is no doubt in my mind as to the sincerity of Wallenberg's purpose because I've talked to him myself. I was told by Wallenberg he wants to be able to help effectively save lives and he was not interested in going to Budapest merely to write reports to be sent to the Foreign Office."[15]

In Washington, War Refugee Board officials arranged for more than $200,000 in financing and other support for Wallenberg's rescue mission.[16] Meanwhile, Wallenberg visited the Swedish Foreign Office, where he read reports about the deportation of Jews from Hungary's provinces. Clearly, not a moment more could be wasted, for it meant another life lost. Each day that June, an estimated twelve thousand Hungarian Jews were being killed in Auschwitz, five hundred each hour, an average of thirty a minute, one every two seconds.

Wallenberg brought forward his planned time of departure.[17]

"I can't stay in Sweden until the end of July [as planned]," he told Lauer. "Every day costs human lives. I'm going to get ready to leave immediately."[18]

Before leaving Sweden, Wallenberg spent several days in intense negotiations with officials at the Swedish Foreign Ministry. He was afraid his rescue work would become "dragged into the processes of state bureaucracy and into the quagmire of diplomacy." The long tradition of Swedish neutrality, especially the Foreign Ministry's aversion to "conflict with the Nazis," might undermine his mission, and he wanted written guarantees that he could "get a free hand in the field of rescue."[19]

Wallenberg's demands were extraordinary. Nevertheless, after much wrangling, the Foreign Ministry agreed to them. He would even be able to use bribery to save lives, they agreed, and would act in Budapest in the official capacity of secretary to the Royal Swedish Embassy. Much to the further chagrin of Swedish officials, no doubt, he even insisted on devising his own basic code, to use in telephone conversations with Lauer, so convinced was he that the Gestapo had broken the Swedish diplomatic codes. Iver Olsen would, for example, be referred to as Larsson.[20]

On July 5, 1944, on the eve of his departure, Wallenberg met with the leading members of the Jewish community in Stockholm. The Chief Rabbi of Stockholm, Professor Marcus Ehrenpreis, was present. Following a previous meeting, he had had misgivings about Wallenberg, especially about his youth and his eagerness to spend large sums to bribe the Germans, but now he gave the slightly balding young man his full support.

"Those who set off on a mission of humanity can be assured of God's special protection," Ehrenpreis told Wallenberg.[21]

It was clear to the men at the meeting that Wallenberg was moved by the rabbi's words. Wallenberg then stood and thanked them for their support.

"It's late and I have yet to pack my clothes," he said. "I'm sorry, but I must leave now. Thank you, my friends . . ."

Ehrenpreis accompanied Wallenberg to the door.

"You are in the hands of God" were Ehrenpreis's words of parting.[22]

By EARLY JULY 1944, only the Jews of Budapest had been spared the roundup in Hungary. "Technical details will only take a few more days in Budapest," Eichmann reported to Berlin.[23]

If all went according to plan, Eichmann might win promotion and what he apparently craved most: Hitler's appreciation. But then Eichmann ran out of luck. On July 7, as Wallenberg was preparing to leave

Sweden, the Hungarian regent, Admiral Horthy, finally bowed to intense international pressure—notably from the King of Sweden—and ordered the suspension of "the transfer of Jews to Germany."[24]

Horthy's decision incensed Eichmann: "In all my long experience, such a thing has never happened to me. It cannot be tolerated."[25] He complained bitterly to Berlin but was informed that until the political situation in Hungary changed, Horthy's decision would have to be respected. "Eichmann was terribly angry," recalled Wilhelm Hottl, a Gestapo colleague. "He called Horthy an old *depp,* an Austrian word for nitwit. 'Horthy's got no say in this. *We* decide what happens in Hungary.'"[26]

The Jews of Budapest had gained a temporary reprieve.

RAOUL WALLENBERG LEFT STOCKHOLM at 1:50 p.m. on July 7, 1944, traveling to Budapest via Berlin, where he met his twenty-five-year-old half-sister, Nina, at Tempelhof Airport, on the afternoon of July 8, 1944. Tall and slim, with high cheekbones and intense blue eyes, Nina was married to a Swedish diplomat, Gunnar Lagergren, head of the Foreign Interests Section of the Swedish legation in Berlin. She was delighted to see her brother, whom she idolized. Today, more than sixty years later, she remembers him as a quick-witted, dynamic, gifted actor and a brilliant impersonator, able to bring jollity to even the most somber situations.[27] She stresses that she and Raoul had grown up together in a "loving, close family" after Raoul's mother had remarried.

Brother and sister made their way to a waiting car. Nina's husband sat behind the wheel. Luftwaffe fighters soared above as Gunnar pulled away from the airport, past antiaircraft guns and giant webs of camouflage netting concealing gray planes and bombers. Wallenberg was carrying his belongings in two knapsacks and was dressed in a long leather coat and a black felt hat. "He had sent a message to the Swedish Embassy, in Berlin, saying that he was coming, and that he would like to stay overnight with [me]," recalls Nina. "Then the ambassador thought it would be nice for me to have him two nights, so he ordered train tickets for a day later to Budapest. We spoke in the car from the airport to my home, and he talked about his mission for the first time. Then he asked if they had booked tickets for him. I said: 'Yes, but you are going to stay for two nights.' He got very upset. He said he was in a great hurry to get to Budapest."[28] There was no time to waste. He would leave the next day, on the first available train.

Wallenberg told his sister that he had a list of prominent Jews and others in one of his knapsacks. "I had no idea at the time that his mission would be as dangerous as it turned out to be," she later recalled. "I assumed he would carry it out according to the usual diplomatic methods, although knowing him as I did I should have known better. But I was seven months' pregnant with my first child at the time, so I suppose I wasn't concentrating much on anything else."[29]

It was dusk on July 8 as Nina and Wallenberg arrived at her home, the gatehouse of a large house in Wannsee beside the lake, not far from where Eichmann and others had planned the Final Solution. Wallenberg and Nina talked late into the night but were forced to a nearby bomb shelter when RAF bombers paid yet another visit to the city. The raids were now a nightly occurrence over central Berlin and outlying industrial areas, but they were rare in Wannsee itself.[30] "We saw these Christmas trees, as we called them, lighted [squares] they would send down before a raid to illuminate the area before they were going to bomb. It looked like it was going to be a big raid, so we decided to take shelter."[31]

It was Wallenberg's first experience of war. Perhaps only now did he begin to consider the enormity of what he had taken on: trying to rescue enemies of the Reich from under the noses of some of the most ruthless and amoral men in Europe.

The following day, Wallenberg kissed his sister goodbye. He was about to be driven across rubble-strewn Berlin to the railway station. "We'll get together soon and catch up on old times," he reportedly told Nina. "The war can't last much longer. It'll soon be over and we'll all be together again at home with mother." He paused. "I'm going to be an uncle!" Wallenberg then cried. "Great news! Let me know as soon as the baby is born."[32]

ALMOST SEVENTY YEARS AFTER their parting, eighty-nine-year-old Nina Lagergren says her brother was, on reflection, ideally suited to the task ahead of him. "It was his nature to act swiftly and be very inventive. In the Swedish Home Guard, he had excelled as a leader under pressure. He was quick to make decisions. He could perform."

Wallenberg's idols had been altruistic, intrepid Swedes. According to Nina, he had two main heroes as a young man: Elsa Brandström and Fridtjof Nansen, whose acts of courage during World War I had left a lasting impression. Brandström had been a courageous, self-taught nurse who had helped save thousands of lives in Siberia in 1915. Nansen was a polar explorer, but he also worked for the League of Nations, returning half a million refugees from Germany and Austria-Hungary to their countries after the conflict.

Wallenberg had recently found another inspiration, this time cinematic, in the 1941 film *Pimpernel Smith,* which Nina had seen with him the last time they had been together in Sweden, in December 1942. The film's main character, Horatio Smith, played by actor Leslie Howard (the son of a Hungarian Jew), saves persecuted Germans from the Nazis. "We were not allowed to see it in cinemas in Sweden because of [our] proximity to Germany," recalls Nina. "So we were invited by the British embassy to see it in a closed session. When it ended, and we were leaving the cinema, Raoul said to me: 'This is something I would like to do.' It was quite amazing. He immediately felt it."

Like Horatio Smith, Raoul Wallenberg could not "just stand by."[33]

WALLENBERG ARRIVED THE NEXT AFTERNOON at the Anhalter rail station to take the 17:21 train to Budapest. The station was as usual crammed with anxious German troops leaving for the Eastern Front and for France, where the Allies had landed months earlier on June 6 and were now battling ferociously to break out of Normandy. Wallenberg had not reserved a seat and was forced to sit in the crowded corridor on one of his knapsacks, a pistol hidden in his pocket; he'd bought it second-hand, telling Lauer he didn't want to waste funds on a new one.[34]

Through the train's windows that evening, Wallenberg could soon see shattered Germany slip past as the train headed south. He reportedly spent most of the journey trying to memorize the names on his list of key resistance figures, socialist politicians, and Jewish businessmen. It was important to remember their names, just in case he had to destroy the list in a hurry.

Wallenberg's train finally pulled into a station on the Austro-Hungarian border at Hegyeshalom. Border officials boarded the train and began to check people's identities. Wallenberg handed over his passport. Its personal description stated that he was "aged 33, born 4.8.1912 in Stockholm, Protestant, 170 cm tall, brown hair, brown eyes."[35]

As his papers and passport were being examined, a transport comprised of twenty-nine boxcars was heading that day—Sunday, July 9, 1944—from Hungary, through Hegyeshalom, toward Poland. As Wallenberg sat on his knapsack and perhaps tried to snatch some sleep, his train could in fact have passed this transport of two thousand Hungarian Jews bound for the ovens in Auschwitz. They had been seized from the Budapest suburbs of Ujpest, Kispest, and Pesterzsebet, and on the evening of July 8, Eichmann had given orders for them to be deported as soon as possible. Admiral Horthy had suspended deportations, but Eichmann had just beaten the deadline.[36] The transport marked the end of the liquidation of Hungary's provincial Jews, what Eichmann called a "deportation surpassing every previous deportation in magnitude."[37]

The Reich plenipotentiary in Budapest, SS Brigadefuhrer Edmund Veesenmayer, would soon report to Berlin that in fact 437,402 Jewish men, women, and children had been deported to Auschwitz from Hungary's provinces on 148 trains in just seven weeks, from May 14 to July 8. There were now around 230,000 Jews left in Hungary, stranded in its capital, Budapest, waiting in trepidation for the day when deportations would be resumed.[38]

8

The Majestic Hotel

THE BERLIN-BUDAPEST TRAIN arrived in Nyugati Palyaudvar, the main railway station in the west of the city, on July 9, 1944. The art deco–styled station was the same as Wallenberg remembered it from his last visit, the previous fall of 1943. But the city beyond was much different, a more somber, darker place, now full of fear and uncertainty, where the Nazis and Hungarian fascists were clearly in control. Walls were covered with swastikas, daubed with anti-Semitic slogans and scarred with German propaganda posters. Along the elegant Corso, in the numerous world-famous Turkish spas, and in the embankment cafes and restaurants, there was none of the bustle and gaiety that had so charmed prewar visitors.

Wallenberg's taxi wound through the narrow streets of Pest and then crossed the Danube, heading for the Hotel Gellert, not far from the Swedish Embassy. To Wallenberg's right, looming above central Europe's great artery, stood the Royal Palace, residence of Admiral Horthy. Wallenberg checked into the hotel, and the following morning, Monday, July 10, he went straight to work, making his way up Gellert Hill toward the Swedish Embassy a few hundred yards away, at 8 Gyopar Street.[1] Most days that summer, one could find a long line of people, many of them shabbily clothed, some hysterical and in tears, most wearing the yellow Star of David. The desperate, sad line sometimes stretched all the way down the steep Gellert Hill. The Jews in line were trying to obtain

Swedish passports, which would exempt them from wearing the yellow star and being deported.

Wallenberg knew at least one person on the staff at the embassy: thirty-one-year-old Per Anger, a blond-haired career diplomat. Anger had socialized with Wallenberg before the war and they had also met during Wallenberg's visits to Hungary while working for the Central European Trading Company; Wallenberg had already assigned him the codename Elena. "I was convinced that no one was better qualified for the assignment than Wallenberg," recalled Anger. "He was a clever negotiator and organizer, unconventional, extraordinarily inventive and cool-headed, and something of a go-getter. Besides this, he was very good at languages [fluent in Russian] and well grounded in Hungarian affairs. At heart, he was a great idealist and a warm human being."

Anger also remembered that Wallenberg was oddly equipped for a diplomat. He was carrying "two knapsacks, a sleeping bag, a windbreaker," and a black revolver, which he had been able to bring into the country because his diplomatic passport meant customs officials were not able to search his belongings.

"The revolver is just to give me courage," Wallenberg told Anger. "I hope I'll never have to use it."

Wallenberg was clearly anxious to get to work.

"I've read your reports," he told Anger. "But could you bring me up to date?"

Anger briefed Wallenberg on what had happened that summer. The deportations from the provinces to Auschwitz had been suspended only the day before. As many as 230,000 Jews were still alive in Budapest, some of them under protection from neutral legations such as the Swiss and Portuguese. The Swedish ambassador, Danielson, had already begun the Embassy's rescue operation, having issued six hundred provisional passports to Jews who could prove that they had "personal or commercial ties to Sweden."[2]

"Everything depends on what the Germans have in mind," explained Anger. "It's hardly believable that they will go along with sparing the Jews of the capital for good."

"What documents have you issued the Jews?" asked Wallenberg.

Anger pulled out Red Cross protection letters, examples of the temporary Swedish passports that Danielson had issued, and other documents. Wallenberg looked at them and then, according to Anger, said: "I think I've got an idea for a new and maybe more effective document." Wallenberg explained how a newly designed safe-passage document—a Schutzpass—might be printed in the thousands so that more people could come under Swedish protection. "In this way," recalled Anger, "the idea of the so-called protective passports was born at our first meeting. These were the identification papers in blue and yellow with the three crowns emblem on them that would come to be the saving of tens of thousands of Jews."[3]

The Schutzpass that Wallenberg had in mind would signify that the bearer was under the official protection of the Swedish Embassy and therefore could not be deported to death camps such as Auschwitz. The Nazis and Hungarian authorities were often impressed by official documents, especially ones printed in color with royal insignia stamped on them. And so he stressed to Anger that the protective passes be as convincing as possible—they should be printed in yellow and blue colors and embossed with Sweden's national coat of arms.

Wallenberg soon found the resources to print fifteen hundred passes. Later, when he discovered how effective they were, he would print many thousands more.[4] And to help distribute them, Wallenberg quickly hired dozens of Jewish coworkers for a Section C department at the embassy, which he would run with Per Anger and other diplomats' assistance. Because these Jews worked in an official capacity for the Swedish embassy, they and their families did not have to wear the yellow Star of David. Wallenberg discovered, within days of arriving in Budapest, that he had his choice of the most effective Jewish managers and administrators still alive in Hungary; several had worked in senior positions for a Hungarian subsidiary of the Phillips Corporation.

On the evening of July 14, Wallenberg made his first telephone call to Lauer in Stockholm, using their agreed code. The call lasted less than thirty minutes and was interrupted several times by German censors. Wallenberg was able to confirm to Lauer that the Jews from the provinces had been deported. He could not mention Auschwitz directly by name but hinted at it, and stressed that he needed "money, money, and more money" to begin his rescue work. Lauer contacted Iver Olsen, and 110,000 Swiss crowns ($100,000) were paid into an account in Wallenberg's name at Enskilda Bank in Stockholm. Finally, Wallenberg had the funds he needed to begin saving lives.[5]

ANOTHER GENTILE IN BUDAPEST already knew how to deal with the Nazis and Eichmann, and had managed to protect thousands of the city's Jews—the vice consul at the Swiss Embassy, Carl Lutz, a dark-haired, bespectacled forty-nine-year-old who had also devised his own system of protective passes. A career diplomat, the formidable Lutz had spent twenty years in the United States before being posted to Palestine, where, like Wallenberg, he had befriended Jews who had suffered Nazi persecution. He had been working in Budapest since 1942 and was therefore intimately aware of the political situation.

Lutz came from a far more modest background and was more than a decade older than Wallenberg, but they would soon become close colleagues, equally determined to save Jewish lives.[6] Their first meeting took place at Lutz's office on July 15, 1944, in the former U.S. Embassy overlooking Freedom Square. Most days that summer, this large square in front of the building was crowded, as were the streets around the Swedish Embassy, with long lines of desperate people trying to obtain Schutzpasses.[7]

According to Lutz's biographer, Theo Tschuy, Wallenberg explained that several officials and diplomats he had consulted in recent days had mentioned Lutz. He was, apparently, the man to talk to if Wallenberg wanted advice on how best to help protect Hungary's last Jews. Could he share his expertise? Lutz was only too happy to oblige, and quickly explained his methods, mentioning how he had acquired buildings where those with Swiss protective passes could live. Being creative and breaking the rules were essential. The Nazis could be beaten at their own game—by exploiting their weakness for bureaucracy and slavish obedience to well-spoken superiors. Crucially, as long as Horthy was able to control Ferenczy's gendarmerie and key officials in the government, there was time and space in which neutral diplomats could outmaneuver Eichmann and the Gestapo. But Eichmann was not to be underestimated. Lutz had met with him in recent weeks and had been left with the impression of a "forceful, intrepid officer, a daredevil who knew what he was about."

Eichmann had told Lutz: "We German soldiers aren't afraid. Where would we be if we were scared to death? My comrades are fighting in Russia, and I'm fighting in this job."[8] Anyone who tried to obstruct him would, sooner or later, be regarded just like the Russians—as his sworn enemy.

Wallenberg apparently made an extraordinary confession to Lutz—his mission was in part a public relations exercise. In the United States, there had been allegations that Jacob and Marcus Wallenberg—Raoul's opportunist cousins—had undermined the Allied war effort through extensive business dealings with the Nazis. To deflect criticism, the Wallenberg family lawyer, Allen Dulles, had suggested that it might look good for Jacob and Marcus if their cousin, Raoul, tried to help the Jews. Indeed, Wallenberg's presence in Budapest might perhaps restore the family's good name in Washington.

Wallenberg was now determined, however, to do far more than save his cousins' reputation in the eyes of the Allies. He told Lutz he had wanted for some time to throw himself into important work that "went beyond" mere moneymaking. This was his chance.

Lutz quickly warmed to Wallenberg and was impressed by his honesty. He told Wallenberg that he hoped that Switzerland, which had its own share of nefarious dealings with the Nazis, would also step up its efforts to save Jews, just as Sweden had now that the Nazis looked certain to be on the losing side.

Wallenberg then handed over his list of prominent Jewish businessmen: famous industrialists, tycoons, and exporters, some of whom had connections with the Wallenberg family. According to Tschuy, Wallenberg explained that he was no longer content to save solely those on the list. Only since his arrival had he come to realize the extent of the tragedy that had occurred that summer. Lutz warned Wallenberg that he would encounter opposition from his own embassy, and perhaps his cousins, if he stepped too far beyond diplomatic protocol. But Wallenberg didn't appear to care. He said it didn't matter what Stockholm wanted. What were a few hundred rich men compared to a quarter-million lives?[9]

A FEW DAYS AFTER HIS MEETING with Lutz, with some of the money deposited into his account at Enskilda, Wallenberg set about buying buildings in Pest. They were close to the seventy-two buildings that Lutz had already secured for Jews officially protected by the Swiss. To acquire the protective houses, Wallenberg had to get permission from Lieutenant Colonel Laszlo Ferenczy, the head of the Hungarian gendarmerie who had been so ruthlessly effective in carrying out Eichmann's deportations of Jews from the provinces.[10]

Wallenberg did not speak Hungarian, so he asked if a Mrs. Elizabeth Kasser, who worked for the Hungarian Red Cross, could interpret for him during his meeting with Ferenczy.[11] Her husband, Alexander Kasser, general secretary of the Swedish Red Cross, accompanied his wife and Wallenberg, hoping to win concessions from Ferenczy, too.[12]

Many years later, Elizabeth Kasser recalled that Wallenberg was kept waiting in Ferenczy's office, much to Wallenberg's obvious irritation.[13] He was literally a man on a mission, eager to get down to business, with no time for formality unless it suited his interests—he had just angrily rebuked seventy-six-year-old Admiral Horthy in person over the deportations. ("Horthy is an imposing figure, but I felt morally taller," Wallenberg had told an aide.[14]) When Ferenczy finally turned up, he made a long speech about how Wallenberg and the Kassers should be ashamed of themselves for helping filthy Jews, what Eichmann and his men called Untermenschen—subhuman beings. Ferenczy then launched into a further diatribe, much of which Kasser did not translate because she did not want Wallenberg to explode.

When Ferenczy had finished, Wallenberg apparently handed over his list of 630 prominent and wealthy Jews, for whom the Swedes had already arranged visas. Perhaps impressed by Wallenberg's calm and collected response, Ferenczy agreed to deal with the matter. Before the meeting was over, Wallenberg had also persuaded Ferenczy to allow him to acquire buildings to house the Jews on his list until they could leave for Sweden. It was Wallenberg's first victory. "As soon as we were out of sight of that building," recalled Elizabeth Kasser, "we put our arms around each other and did a sort of Indian dance in the street."[15]

Others would not be so easily charmed.

It was around this time that Marianne Lowy and her family heard from other Jews about a "miraculous person who had arrived with the sole purpose of saving Hungarian Jews." It was said that he came from a prominent Swedish family, who were like the Rockefellers in America. Marianne's husband, Pista, decided to act on the rumor. He visited the Swedish embassy, where he met Wallenberg and was issued Schutz-passes for his family. "They stated that we were under the protection of the Swedish king," remembered Marianne. "My father had been in an internment camp for six weeks by now. So when we got the Schutzpasses, we sent a messenger to where my father was, and lo and behold, the Gestapo let him go. The next morning, there he was, standing on the doorsteps of my parents' home. He had been beaten but he was alive . . . That was the first miracle that Wallenberg performed for us."[16] Marianne and her family would later discover that just hours after her father was released, those who had been imprisoned with him were taken to Auschwitz.

Thanks to their Schutzpasses, Marianne's parents were able to move to one of Wallenberg's newly acquired protected houses in Pest, where properties were selling at knockdown prices. Marianne decided to stay in Buda with her husband Pista, who had been released from a forced labor battalion because of the Schutzpass from Wallenberg. Eventually, he would find refuge in one of several satellite embassies, which Wallenberg soon set up to house his workers and other protected Jews. Marianne, strong-minded and stubborn, had already acquired false papers and had opted to stay with a relative outside the city. When she wasn't pretending to be a good Catholic housemaid, she tried to find food for her family, scavenging and bartering whatever she could. Thankfully, she was not stopped and searched on her many visits to her family and the false papers she carried with her were not discovered.[17]

But soon her daily wanderings became even more dangerous as the Allies started to bomb Budapest. "The air raids didn't make us unhappy," recalled Marianne. "We told ourselves that if we got hit by a bomb, we'd never know it, so what was the difference. On the other hand, if the bomb missed us, it meant we'd get one day closer to the time when we'd be liberated. That was our one pleasure from the bombings. The other pleasure was that the gentiles were getting a kind of poetic justice. They didn't allow us to go to the public swimming pools, or on picnics or excursions. Well, now they couldn't go either; they had to spend their Sundays running to the air-raid shelters and waiting for the all-clear."[18]

DIPLOMATS NORMALLY REQUIRED several months to become acquainted with a new posting. Remarkably, Wallenberg hit the ground running, taking only a few weeks to understand how best he might be effective. He had spent a total of almost eight weeks on previous visits to Budapest and knew his way around the city. He had also been superbly briefed by Danielson, Anger, Lutz, and other diplomats already involved in rescue activities. But he proved remarkably adaptable and well organized from the start, and was soon working long hours to expand the Swedes' humanitarian efforts. He joined forces with other neutral diplomats; bombarded the Hungarian authorities, the War Refugee Board, and Stockholm with official reports on the plight of the Jews; and exerted greater and greater pressure on officials he believed he could influence.

Nevertheless, it was quickly clear that Wallenberg would need to organize a "man-made miracle" if he was to succeed against the Gestapo and its Hungarian accomplices.[19] Indeed, the sheer scale of the challenge he faced in Budapest was made painfully obvious when he learned that the relatives of his business partner, Kalman Lauer, had already been sent to the gas chambers. From the day he had arrived in Budapest, Wallenberg had known how worried Lauer was about them and how urgently he had wanted news of their fate.[20] "Please be so good as to inform Dr. Lauer and his wife," Wallenberg wrote his mother, Maj, only a week after entering Hungary, "that I have unfortunately found out that his parents-in-law and also a small child belonging to his family are already dead. That is to say, that they have been transported abroad, where they will not live for very long."[21]

Wallenberg had indeed found a formidable adversary in the Gestapo. Clearly, as he had anticipated, he would need to be unconventional in his methods. He was soon prepared, according to Per Anger, to try almost any tactic to succeed. He was also willing to form relationships with anyone who could provide inside information about what the SS and the Hungarian fascists were planning next.[22] Under the circumstances, Wallenberg was determined to ignore legal niceties, a fact that fast annoyed some of his diplomatic colleagues, who would later describe his actions as *dumdristig*—dumb-daring. They reportedly resented this rather distant, aristocratic workaholic putting all their lives at risk by stepping beyond diplomatic protocols.[23]

Word quickly got back to the Swedish Foreign Office in Stockholm about the energetic young Wallenberg. In a report to the War Refugee Board in Washington, Iver Olsen noted that "the Swedish Foreign Office is somewhat uneasy with Wallenberg's actions in Budapest and perhaps feels that he has jumped in with too big a splash. They would prefer, of course, to approach the Jewish problem in the finest traditions of European diplomacy, which wouldn't help much."[24]

Before agreeing to the mission in Budapest, Wallenberg had pointedly demanded assurances that he could use the funds provided him for any means, including bribery. That July, in Budapest, he told Alexander Kasser, the Swedish Red Cross official: "The times are such that nobody has the opportunity, the patience, or the time to analyze what is illegal because everything that is done by the Nazis in the name of law is inhuman, unjust. Therefore, whatever is illegal becomes legal. The main thing is to help."[25]

IT HAS BEEN CLAIMED that Wallenberg had his first meeting with Eichmann that July. According to Per Anger, it may have occurred on July 19,
at Eichmann's office at the luxurious Hotel Majestic.[26] Going by the experiences of visitors such as Joel Brand and Kasztner, who had already
visited Eichmann at his headquarters, Wallenberg would have been carefully searched at the entrance to the hotel—Eichmann was increasingly
paranoid about assassins.[27] Wallenberg would have been pointed upstairs by two gun-wielding SS men.[28]

Eichmann's large office on the second floor had a magnificent view,
but he was often to be found seated behind his large walnut desk, his
back to the windows. On his desk were a framed photograph of a dull-
haired woman and two children—Eichmann's family back in Austria—
and usually his revolver and holster, near his right hand. Thick smoke
from his cigarettes often clouded the view through the large windows behind him.[29] He looked like a harried bureaucrat, albeit in a Gestapo uniform. "It was only his eyes that were unusual," recalled Joel Brand.
"Steel-blue, hard, and menacing, they seemed to be boring into the person facing him . . . He wore an elegant uniform and his movements were
brisk and somewhat jerky. His way of speaking was unusual, too. He
would fire off a few words and then pause. When he was talking, it always reminded me of the chatter of a machine gun."[30]

It was possibly at this meeting that Eichmann made a key revelation,
according to some sources: The Gestapo had already investigated the
young Swedish diplomat with the famous name and had not liked what
they had found.[31]

"Why did you go to Palestine in 1937?" asked Eichmann.

"Because it interested me," Wallenberg is said to have replied. "I believe the Jews should have a state of their own, don't you?"[32]

"I know all about you," snapped Eichmann. "You're a Jew-lover who re-
ceives all his dirty dollars from Roosevelt. We know that the Americans
have put you in Budapest and we know that your cousin Jacob is another
Jew-lover and an enemy of the Reich."[33]

The Gestapo knew that the Wallenberg brothers were sophisticated
operators, with connections to both Allied and Axis leaders. Marcus Wal-

lenberg had represented Swedish trade interests with Britain. Jacob, "cool and cynical," had dealt with Germany, milking contacts and making healthy profits from the Nazi war machine. But then, because of his association with groups plotting to replace Hitler, Jacob had been warned to stay away from Germany, given his connections to Hitler's enemies.[34]

"We know about your so-called passes," blustered Eichmann. "They're all frauds! The Jews who've escaped to Sweden with them are all enemies of the Reich."[35]

Wallenberg apparently did not reply to Eichmann's boorish outburst. Instead, he is said to have calmly given him a carton of cigarettes and a bottle of whisky. The gesture was appreciated. Eichmann's mood improved. He then offered to allow a trainload of "protected Jews" to go to Sweden if Wallenberg could come up with a ransom. The same kind of deal had been arranged with Rudolf Kasztner of the Jewish Council; there was in theory no reason why Wallenberg shouldn't also get in on the action: Jews' lives were for sale, and Eichmann was willing to offer a fair price.

The story goes that Wallenberg did not take up the offer—he was not interested in Eichmann's "token generosity," and the meeting was soon over.[36]

What can be confirmed is that Wallenberg's issuing of thousands of Schutzpasses did indeed irk Eichmann. He was eventually so angered by it that he snapped at a Red Cross official: "I am going to kill that Jew dog Wallenberg."[37] Word of Eichmann's threat made its way back to the Swedish Embassy in Berlin, and a formal complaint was lodged with Veesenmayer, who retorted unapologetically that Wallenberg "operated in an unacceptable manner for the benefit of Hungarian Jews."[38]

Eichmann also complained to Rudolph Kasztner about Lutz and Wallenberg's actions, and the rapid increase in forged Schutzpasses. "Lutz and Wallenberg will pay for this damned mess," Eichmann threatened.[39]

At some point during his stay in Budapest, according to several credible sources, a German armored car rammed Wallenberg's official limousine at high speed. Fortunately, Wallenberg was not in the car and his driver was not hurt.[40] Some have claimed that Eichmann was behind the so-called accident and that his aide Dannecker was also involved. The collision may have been intended as a warning rather than an attempt to murder the Swede.[41]

FIFTEEN MILES NORTH of Budapest, the conditions in Kistarcsa deteriorated quickly that July. Vera Herman was one of many children there who now suffered from malnutrition. Disease in the prison was rampant. Then one morning, all children and their mothers were told to assemble in the prison's courtyard. The prison commander explained that three men, who represented the Swedish Red Cross, had come to collect children under fourteen and take them to a Red Cross children's home. Margit and the other mothers were told that they could hand over their children if they wanted to.

Margit Herman faced the most difficult decision of her life. But nothing mattered more now than the survival of her only child. So Margit pushed twelve-year-old Vera into the arms of one of the Swedish Red Cross officials. If her daughter could eat a real meal and sleep in a bed that night, it would be worth it, even if she never saw her again. But suddenly, realizing the enormity of what she had done, Margit fainted.

Vera rushed toward her mother, who was lying unconscious in the courtyard. In the commotion, two strange men in suits grabbed her, lifting her off her feet, and took her out of the courtyard to a car waiting outside the prison.[42] Kistarcsa's gates closed behind them. The car pulled away. One of the men in the car, Dr. Alexander Kasser, told Vera that he was working with a Swedish diplomat called Raoul Wallenberg, who was trying to save as many children as he could.[43]

They reached the outskirts of Budapest and headed into the city, where they stopped outside the Swedish Red Cross Children's Home. Then Dr. Kasser took Vera inside, where she joined twenty-six other children whose mothers had done as Margit Herman had done.

Vera was bereft: "I can't even find words to describe it—my whole world was gone, everything I knew," she later explained. "I tried to stay strong because I knew that was what my mother would want."[44] Vera began to care for the other children, some as young as five. But one of the smaller children had scarlet fever, and soon Vera had contracted such a severe case that she was taken to a hospital.

"What hurts?" asked a nurse.

"Life."[45]

Vera was quarantined in the hospital for six weeks. One Sunday afternoon during her stay there, a mob of drunken Hungarian Arrow Cross men attacked the Swedish Children's Home and then, in a stunning act of barbarity, murdered all twenty-six of the children who had earlier been saved and whose mothers had so agonizingly given them up to Wallenberg's protection. Vera was not told of her friends' fate; when she left the hospital, she was placed in an orphanage also run by the Swedish Red Cross. She now believed that she was an orphan, that she would never see her parents again.[46]

Meanwhile, back in Kistarcsa, Vera's mother was selected for deportation to Auschwitz and placed in a cattle truck on a train. It left one morning, bound for the death camp. Earlier, she had hidden poison, and now, as the train headed toward Auschwitz, she was tempted to take it. The only reason she didn't was the thought that someone in her wagon might survive and tell her daughter, Vera, that she had taken her life.[47]

Some of the women in the cattle truck who still had the strength to stand were gathered near a small grill and looking outside. To their surprise, they saw that the train was heading down a sidetrack. They passed through gates and entered what was clearly another prison.[48] It was Sarvar, a holding camp similar to Kistarcsa, on the Austro-Hungarian border. Guards ordered the women off the train.[49]

Vera's mother managed to get out of the boxcar. Then she saw a man who looked familiar. She stared at him. The man had a face just like her husband, Emil. Was she hallucinating?

It was Emil. Incredibly, he too had been sent to Sarvar and now worked there as a doctor. Emil spotted Margit and walked toward her. But he suddenly turned away and was gone. A few minutes later, he was back. He brushed lightly against Margit. "Take this!" he whispered as he slipped her a vial.

Margit took the vial, swallowed its contents, and collapsed. Emil rushed over and placed her on a stretcher. As he began to carry her toward the sick bay in the prison, an angry SS guard decided Margit would have to be put back on the train bound for Auschwitz. He ran after Emil, shouting, "I have to deliver two thousand bodies. I don't care whether they're dead or alive."

Before he could reach Emil, however, the guard was called to the telephone. Someone was on the line from SS headquarters.

"Don't bother bringing them anymore," the guard was ordered. "Just take them outside the prison and machine-gun them."[50]

The SS guard did as he was told.

According to Vera: "There were only [three] survivors from that transport of two thousand: my mother and two resourceful souls who must have hidden somewhere. They remained in this facility, in this last holding prison on Hungarian soil."[51]

Margit had avoided Auschwitz. For the time being, she learned, she would stay in Sarvar and join other women making uniforms for the SS.[52] As she sewed the black jackets of her would-be murderers, she must have wondered if she would see her husband again, let alone her only child, Vera, the daughter she had pushed into the arms of strangers.

ALICE BREUER LOOKED AT HER WATCH, a beautiful Swiss-made Longines that Erwin had bought for her.[53] It was past 11 a.m., just after the curfew for Jews, as she walked along a street in Pest on a shopping errand. Two Arrow Cross men saw her yellow star and approached her.

"It's not eleven o'clock and you are not allowed to be in the street," one of them said.

Alice checked her watch again. It was after 11 a.m., she protested. But the Arrow Cross men took her away and placed her in a Budapest detention center.

Somehow, Erwin managed to track her down and smuggled her some food. His father tried, without luck, to bribe officials into releasing Alice.

In the detention center, Alice soon befriended an old woman, who was later transferred to the sick ward in the prison, where she tried to commit suicide by jumping out a window. She had told Alice that she simply could not live with the shame of being in prison. Alice also shared a cell with talkative, "fascinating" street prostitutes, who cared for her and tried to lift her spirits.[54]

But the attempted bribe by her father-in-law was discovered, and a guard took Alice to a cell to be punished. She stared back defiantly at the guard, who told her he would "push out" her eyes. Instead, he beat her until she blacked out. "I was unconscious, lying on the floor," she later recalled. "The next thing I remember is that I looked up, and the guard was standing with a gun. I didn't know what happened but I was conscious. 'Everything is alright,' I thought. 'I see stars.'"[55]

At some point that July, Alice was transferred to Kistarcsa, the holding camp for Auschwitz. "It was not a nice place, but it wasn't Auschwitz," she recalled. "I was so confused. But I was very lucky because there were people who helped me, who gave me a little bread and some soup. I could not manage on my own. There always seemed to be someone who helped me, took care of me, maybe because I looked like I didn't want to live."[56]

Meanwhile, Erwin tried once more to find Alice. He succeeded in tracking her down at Kistarcsa, where he again tried to bribe officials into releasing her.[57] He had no luck. "Some officials could be bribed," he remembered, "but in Jewish matters it was very difficult because the officials knew they could be caught easily and would be in big trouble."[58] Then Erwin heard about a young Swedish diplomat who had just arrived in Budapest and was trying his best to help Jews. "This sounded quite unlikely," recalled Erwin, "but I understood that the help consisted of putting them under the protection of the Swedish embassy 'until their immigration to Sweden.' Thus, they were no longer Hungarian citizens and, as such, they became exempt from all the anti-Jewish laws, including wearing the yellow star and being subjected to forced labor."[59]

Erwin thought the young Swede and his passes sounded too good to be true. Perhaps it was another SS myth, propagated to give Jews a grain of hope. Nevertheless, he set out as soon as he could for the Swedish Embassy on Gellert Hill and was amazed to discover that the rumors about Wallenberg had substance.[60] All he had to do to get Schutzpasses for himself, his family, and Alice was prove some kind of connection to Sweden. That was easily accomplished. For many years, Erwin's father had conducted business with a Swedish firm; Erwin found the papers establishing this among his family's few belongings and rushed back to the Swedish Embassy.

It was just after 4 p.m. on Saturday, August 5, 1944, when Erwin met with Wallenberg—a "young, intense, and energetic man, clearly driven by some deep inner force."[61] He gave Erwin a Schutzpass, which he signed in the lower-left corner.[62] It bore the serial number 0176. "The number was very low," recalled Erwin. "Wallenberg had just begun his work because only a week later there was a tremendous number of people with Schutzpasses. I remember that he was very busy, tense, organized, very fast thinking. His phone was ringing and he was making notes and giving instructions in fluent German. He seemed to have all kinds of tricks up his sleeve."[63]

Wallenberg also promised to do what he could to find Alice, although there was no guaranteeing that she was still alive. She could have been sent to Auschwitz, in which case he could do nothing. But he would try to find her. Wallenberg was true to his word. On Monday, August 7, at 10 a.m., he kept an appointment, according to his diary, to discuss the fate of Alice and four other prisoners—5 *Fanger*.[64]

Later that same day, a guard approached Alice in Kistarcsa.

"You are a Swedish citizen," the guard said, to her utter surprise. "The consul is here for you." This man must be mad, she thought. She didn't believe him. But then, when she got to the camp exit, she saw a car and Hungarian police waiting. "I was taken," she recalled, "together with others, to the Swedish Embassy in Budapest. There I met Raoul Wallenberg for the first time."[65]

Wallenberg offered her chocolate, handed her a Schutzpass, and explained that she was now a Swedish citizen with nothing to fear from the Germans and the Hungarian Nazis.

"Remember that your connection with Sweden is [the business] AB Kanthal Hallstahammar," Wallenberg stressed. "This is important. Don't forget it. Now hurry home to your husband and his parents. They are waiting for you."[66]

It was an intensely emotional reunion later that day with Erwin, who had also been able to obtain safe passes for his parents and sister, as well as for Alice's brother, George, who was in a forced labor camp. That night, a dazed Alice celebrated her release with Erwin. Thanks to the Schutzpasses from Wallenberg, they did not have to wear yellow stars and went for dinner at Gundel, a famous restaurant in the wooded City Park area. There, surrounded by gold leaf-framed mirrors, below elegant crystal chandeliers, they toasted what felt like a miracle. Alice had been saved from deportation. Erwin no longer had to work in the forced labor battalion, digging the bunker near Eichmann's headquarters. The evening was "out of this world," he remembered.[67] Alice also would never forget it: "Erwin wanted to do something for me, and invited me to a very good restaurant. So I went from one extreme to another. I remember thinking: 'This can't be true. I must be in a dream.'"[68]

BY AUGUST 1944, it was increasingly clear that the Germans were losing the war. The Soviets had crossed the Hungarian border, and the Red Army was massing for a final push across the Hungarian plain toward Budapest. Emboldened by the Soviet advance, Alice and Erwin joined an underground group, whose members were given a typed document, signed by three Auschwitz escapees, including Alfred Wetzler, who had escaped with Vrba on April 10. The document included their eyewitness accounts of the killings in Auschwitz. The underground organization, based in the Jewish General Hospital, was committed to trying to rescue or gain the release of imprisoned Jews.

One day, Alice and Erwin took a train to the countryside near the Austrian border, intent on trying to locate Alice's brother George, who was still working in a forced labor camp. They managed to get a Schutzpass to George, but on their return to Budapest, while waiting for a train, there was an air raid. They lost sight of each other. Gendarmes patrolled the station. Agonizing minutes passed as they tried to find each other again. Erwin realized just how dangerous leaving Budapest had been. Then he saw Alice. "I thought the embrace would never end," he recalled. "We took a crazy chance by undertaking such a dangerous trip . . . but in the end, the document saved George's life."

Back in Budapest, Erwin and Alice rented a room in leafy Buda and began to help out at the Jewish General Hospital, where they assisted in several operations. Like the rest of Budapest, they waited for the Soviets to arrive or the Germans to leave. In the evenings, they read aloud from Roger Martin du Gard's *Family Thibault,* an epic saga about the collapse of French society on the eve of the First World War.[69] "I cannot die before I finish reading this hefty book," Erwin told himself.

The book must have made for particularly fitting reading late that summer as the Americans and British began to bomb Budapest in earnest. Hungary, like France in 1914, now confronted imminent ruin and defeat. The Allied bombing was particularly ominous, setting all of Budapest on edge as people fled to cellars and shelters, where many would remain, night after night, until liberation by the Soviets. "Sometimes, houses came apart like sand castles in the waves of an angry sea," remembered Erwin, "emitting a peculiar smell of cooking gas, dust, death, and incinerated, acrid wood."[70]

It would be only a matter of weeks, Alice and Erwin thought, before the lightning Soviet advance reached Budapest and the war for all Hungarians would finally be over. Then on August 23, the Romanians made peace with the Soviets, thereby speeding the Red Army's advance. Realizing full well that the Axis was doomed, Horthy resolved to do the same as Romania before Stalin crushed Hungary in a prolonged and bloody occupation. As a precursor to ending Hungary's involvement in the war, he reasserted his power, calling the Nazis' most senior diplomat in Budapest, Veensenmayer, to Buda Castle. Among other demands, Horthy insisted that Eichmann and his special commando—Sonderkommando—be withdrawn from Budapest.[71]

During a tense meeting, Laszlo Ferenczy, the head of the Hungarian gendarmerie, made it clear to Eichmann that nineteen thousand men were loyal to the Horthy regime and would resist any attempt by the SS to resume the deportations. It was the greatest setback in Eichmann's career and he was enraged. According to Ferenczy, Eichmann shouted: "In all my long experience, such a thing has never happened to me before . . . That won't do . . . This is contrary to our agreement . . . It cannot be tolerated . . ."[72]

Eichmann contacted Berlin and asked for instructions. Himmler sent orders on August 24, confirming that Eichmann's mission in Hungary was suspended until the political situation changed.[73] Eichmann, according to several accounts, was inconsolable. He had been so close to completing his mission—the liquidation of the last Jews of Europe. Now recognition by the Fuhrer was unlikely. "The greatest thing he wanted," recalled Eichmann's SS colleague Wilhelm Hottl, "was to be received just once by Hitler, for Hitler to thank him for the extermination. That was his dream."[74]

A twenty-nine-year-old Austrian doctor of history, the pudgy-faced Hottl had enjoyed a rapid rise through the ranks of RSHA agents. As acting head of intelligence and counterespionage in central and southeast Europe, he was now in charge of a spy network that ran from inside Russia to Hungary and Romania. Before the German occupation on March 19, it had been his job to draw up lists of Jews and opposition figures to be arrested and sent to Auschwitz.[75] This "minor aide in the most evil intelligence service in the world" was not particularly close to Eichmann—only perhaps Wisliceny enjoyed that privilege—but he had known him for some time, having first met him in Vienna in 1939 when Eichmann had run a so-called Central Office for Jewish Emigration from the appropriated palace of the Jewish banker Louis von Rothschild.

Late that August, Eichmann visited Hottl at his apartment. "He was wearing battledress, not his dress uniform, which he had worn on his other visits to me," recalled Hottl. "He gave the impression of being very nervous, and this became even more marked when I told him about the disastrous situation on the German front. Doubtless I, too, was very dejected at the time, because I was afraid that there was nothing that could stop the Russian advance through Hungary to my native Austria."

For the next hour, Eichmann drank at least four glasses of brandy, so much that Hottl suggested he not drive.

Eichmann got up to leave.

"We shall probably never see each other again."

Eichmann then told Hottl that he knew his days were numbered if the Germans were defeated, which now looked inevitable. "When I asked him why he thought this," recalled Hottl, "Eichmann said that, in view of his role in the program to exterminate the Jews, he was considered by the Allies to be a top war criminal. When he made this comment, I immediately grasped the opportunity to say that I had always wanted to hear reliable information about the extermination program, and particularly about the number of Jews exterminated."[76]

According to Hottl, Eichmann "said that the number of murdered Jews was a very great Reich secret, but with the situation in which he, Eichmann, found himself today, he still could tell me something about it, particularly since I was an historian. Eichmann then told me that, according to his information, some six million Jews had perished . . . , four million in extermination camps and the remaining two million through shooting by the Operations Units and other causes, such as disease."[77]

"What will happen after the war," asked Hottl, "when the world asks about these millions?"

"A hundred dead are a catastrophe," said Eichmann. "A million are a statistic."[78]

IT SEEMED AS IF Hungary's last surviving Jews would be saved. Wallenberg expected the invading Soviet troops to quickly defeat the Nazis and soon occupy Budapest. Within a few weeks, by October at the latest, he believed his mission would be over and he would be able to return to Sweden, having proved himself and added luster to the Wallenberg family name. He would be able to get on with his life, expanding his business partnership with Lauer or perhaps even finding work at his cousins' behemoth, Enskilda Bank.[79] He was still only thirty-two years old and was eager to make his mark back in Sweden. "I am doing everything in my powers to return home quickly," Wallenberg wrote his mother, Maj von Dardel. "But you understand that one cannot disband a large operation such as this on a moment's notice. When the invasion comes, the disbanding will take place more swiftly and I will try to return home in eight days."[80]

The Red Army was just fifty miles from Budapest when Wallenberg sent a dispatch to Stockholm on October 12. "The Russian advance has increased the hope of the Jews that their unfortunate plight will soon end," he wrote. "Many have voluntarily stopped wearing the Star of David. Fears that the Germans might, at the last moment, carry out a pogrom remain, despite no positive signs of such an occurrence."[81]

Wallenberg was right to be cautiously optimistic. The Jews' "unfortunate plight" was about to get even worse.

9

Operation Panzerfaust

H E HAD A LARGE SCAR across his left cheek, a gruesome memento from a duel he had won as a student, one of no less than fifteen ritual saber fights during his youth. The scar only added to the glamour and mystique of the burly, chain-smoking Austrian, thirty-six-year-old SS Major Otto Skorzeny. By September 1944, Skorzeny was a legendary figure—the Third Reich's most effective and feared commando, soon to be dubbed the "Most Wanted Man in Europe" by the Allied press.

Skorzeny had led several spectacularly successful missions during the war, most notably the freeing of Il Duce—Benito Mussolini—from a mountainside prison in Italy in September 1943. Now he had been selected for yet another high stakes hit-and-run operation, this time to kidnap Admiral Horthy's son, Miklas, Jr. With Horthy's son as their hostage, the SS and Gestapo could pressure Horthy into stepping down as leader of Hungary and installing a fascist regime, under the Arrow Cross, to run the country in his place.

Skorzeny recalled how he arrived late—it was past midnight—at Hitler's command headquarters, the Wolf's Lair, a complex of concrete bunkers near Gierloz in northern Poland. He listened as Hitler and his inner circle discussed the state of the war, particularly the grave developments in the southeast sector.

At the end of this situation report, Hitler gestured for Skorzeny to remain behind, along with Field Marshal Wilhelm Keitel, General Alfred

Jodl, Foreign Minister Joachim von Ribbentrop, and Reich Leader Heinrich Himmler.

The men sat down in armchairs around a small table.

Hitler concisely explained what had been happening in Hungary and elsewhere in the southern sector of the Eastern Front. He stressed that the Soviets had to be held at the border of Hungary. More than a million German troops would be taken prisoner if Hungary collapsed.[1]

"Now," Hitler added, "we have received confidential reports that the regent of Hungary, Admiral Horthy, is trying to establish contact with the enemy to negotiate a separate peace. The success of his discussions would spell the loss of our army. Horthy wishes to [make a peace treaty] not only with the Western Powers but also with Russia, to which he has offered unconditional surrender."

Hitler turned toward Skorzeny.

"You, Major Skorzeny, are going to prepare the military occupation of Castle Hill, in Budapest. You will start this operation as soon as we learn that the regent is about to betray the duties incumbent upon him according to his treaty of alliance with Germany. You will begin your preparations today. To permit you to surmount any difficulty you face, I shall give you a written order that gives you the most extensive powers."[2]

Jodl read from a piece of paper, which listed units available for the operation. They included a battalion of Waffen-SS paratroopers.

"For the duration of the operation," said Jodl, "a plane from the squadron detailed to the Fuhrer's general headquarters will be given you for your personal movements."

Hitler then discussed with Ribbentrop recent reports from Veensenmeyer, the German consul in Budapest.

The atmosphere in the capital was "very tense," he said.

Hitler signed Skorzeny's orders.

"I rely on you and your men."

Skorzeny left Hitler's situation room around 2 a.m. After a few hours' sleep, he boarded a Heinkel plane bound for Vienna, where he would gather his troops and make final preparations for his Budapest operation, code-named Panzerfaust.

Skorzeny was soon gazing down on the rolling hills and wide valleys of southern Germany as the Heinkel flew toward his native Austria. "The stakes of the game I was about to play were enormous," he later recalled. "If the Hungarian divisions in the Carpathians were to cease fire or, worse, go over to the enemy, a whole German army of a million men would find itself in a precarious or even desperate situation. And if, later, we were to lose Budapest, the turntable of our communications, we would face an unimaginable catastrophe. If only I could act in time."[3]

ON OCTOBER 15, Miklas Horthy, Jr., was scheduled to meet with Yugoslav agents in a large building beside the Danube to discuss Hungary's withdrawal from the Axis. The meeting duly began at 10 that morning. Skorzeny arrived on the scene a few minutes later. As he drove up to the building, he saw stationed in front of it a Honved truck and a civilian car, probably Miklas Horthy, Jr.'s. Without hesitation, he parked in front of the Hungarian vehicles to prevent them from making a quick getaway.

Skorzeny's account of what happened next reads like the stuff of SS pulp fiction: the tale of a swashbuckling SS knight's caper in the Carpathians. Hitler's favorite commando recounted how he got out of his car and was pretending to look at its engine when two German policemen arrived. There was a burst of machine-gun fire from the Honved truck. One of the policemen fell, severely wounded in the belly, close to Skorzeny, who had just enough time to take cover behind his car; a second later a fresh burst of fire from the Honved truck made a sieve of its open door.

Skorzeny blew a whistle: the signal for his men to swing into action. He tried to hold off several Hungarians with his revolver. The car took many more rounds. Bullets ricocheted against the pavement. Two long minutes passed and then, to Skorzeny's relief, he heard his men approaching. They opened fire and the Hungarians fell back and disappeared. Skorzeny rushed into the entrance of the building. Gestapo officers appeared, dragging four prisoners. Skorzeny and his men helped pile Miklas Horthy, Jr., and three others into a military truck. To avoid notice, the Gestapo had rolled up their hostages in large carpets. "From what I saw, this astute stratagem was proving none too successful," recalled Skorzeny. "The conspirators were struggling violently; our policemen were forced to bind them in their carpets and to hoist them none too gently into the truck, which sped off at once."[4]

When Skorzeny reached a local airport later that morning, he was pleased to find Horthy's son already aboard a plane. Skorzeny watched it leave with Hitler's latest hostage, bound for the Third Reich. Operation Panzerfaust had succeeded beautifully.

IT WAS A GLORIOUS DAY. The leaves were turning red and copper and gold on St. Margaret Island in the middle of the Danube. Alice and Erwin planned to have lunch with Erwin's parents that morning of October 15 in Buda, where they were now living in relative safety, thanks to their status as "foreign citizens of a neutral country."

Alice and Erwin were with a six-year-old orphan as they made their way across Budapest. They often took Pipez, Alice's nickname for the boy, away from his orphanage on weekends, and they did so that Sunday. When they got to Erwin's parents' place in Buda, they listened to the radio, enjoying each other's company, confident that the war was drawing to a close and their suffering would soon be over. "My in-laws had a family dinner at the very nice summer house they were renting in Buda," recalled Alice. "They invited the whole family: my husband and me, my sister-in-law. It was a big get-together."[5]

It was around 1 p.m.

"Today it is obvious to any sober-minded person that the German Reich has lost the war," announced Admiral Horthy over the radio. "Conscious of my historic responsibility, I have the obligation to avoid further unnecessary bloodshed . . . I informed a representative of the German Reich that we were about to conclude a military armistice with our previous enemies and to cease all hostilities against them . . . I appeal to every honest Hungarian to follow me on the path beset by sacrifices that will lead to Hungary's salvation."[6]

Across Budapest, people flooded into the streets. Jews ripped off their yellow stars.[7]

In Buda, beside their radio, Erwin and Alice celebrated with their relatives and Pipez.

"We were saved," remembered Erwin. "We had survived. The war was over."[8]

LATER THAT AFTERNOON, Admiral Horthy was arrested by the Gestapo and taken to SS headquarters, where he was placed in a bare room and guarded by an SS private in case he tried to commit suicide. Horthy later recalled in his memoirs how he was about to take an aspirin when the guard snatched it and the glass of water from his hand.

A German officer entered Horthy's room.

"The premier would like to speak with you," he said.

Horthy walked to the room next door. There stood the psychopathic Ferenc Szalasi, head of the Hungarian Nazi party—the Arrow Cross. Szalasi gave Horthy the Nazi salute and asked him to make him prime minister. Disgusted, Horthy told Szalasi to ask the Germans to appoint him. "As I am a prisoner here," said Horthy, "I cannot perform my official duties, and in any case you are the last person I should choose to appoint to that function."

Szalasi left but returned later that day to make the same request. He got the same answer. Not long after, Horthy was startled by a gunshot. One of his most trusted aides, Lieutenant Colonel Tost, had shot himself in a nearby room. "By his death, I lost one of my most faithful officers," recalled Horthy, "no doubt he preferred to escape by suicide from prolonged imprisonment and Gestapo interrogations that he knew might force him to betray others."

At 6 p.m., Horthy was allowed to return to the Royal Palace on Castle Hill so he could gather some of his personal belongings. He was shocked by the chaos and mess left by Skorzeny's men, who'd made themselves comfortable on the damask-upholstered furniture. Cupboards and drawers had been broken open. Horthy's rooms had been pillaged, and anything of value stolen.[9]

General Geza Lakatos, Hungary's premier, suddenly appeared. He was with forty-year-old Reich plenipotentiary Edmund Veesenmayer,

Hitler's personal representative in Hungary. Lakatos handed Horthy a sheet of paper. In German, it announced his abdication and the appointment of Szalasi as premier. Horthy examined the typewritten page. At the bottom of the German text he read the words: *Signed, Horthy.*

"What's this?" said Horthy. "Am I supposed to sign this?"

Lakatos said that he was.

Horthy said Szalasi had twice asked him that day to appoint him. He had twice refused. He turned away and continued to pack his belongings. Lakatos hesitated, and then told Horthy that his son's life was at stake. Horthy was stunned. Veesenmayer soon confirmed that the life of Horthy's son did indeed depend on the signature.

"I see that you seek to give your coup d'état an air of legality," said Horthy. "Will you give me your word of honor that my son will be liberated and will join us if I sign?"

"Yes, Your Highness," Veesenmayer replied. "I give you my word of honor."

Horthy said that he neither resigned nor appointed Szálasi premier. He was merely exchanging his signature for his son's life.

For too long Horthy had tied his fortunes to the swastika. He had allowed Eichmann and his Hungarian accomplices to kill more than half a million of his people in just a few months that summer. Yet only now, apparently, did he see through the Nazis' veneer of respectability—now that they were threatening to take the life of his own son.

BACK AT THE VILLA IN BUDA, where Alice, Erwin, and his family were gathered later that day, the radio announced that Horthy had abdicated and that the Hungarian Nazi party, the Arrow Cross, was taking power. The war was not over. Hungary would fight on.

Everyone was stunned. Only a few minutes ago, they had been free, the yoke of Nazi terror and murder finally lifted. But now the most virulently anti-Semitic fascists in Europe were in charge of their fate.[10]

The pogroms began that very evening. Hundreds were pulled from their homes or off the streets and slaughtered in plain sight in the first hours of the Arrow Cross regime. Forced laborers were marched to bridges across the Danube, shot, and their bodies dumped into the river.[11] The first Jewish suicide was recorded at 7:32 p.m. that day. Before the year was out, there would be more suicides on any one day than in all of Hungary in 1943. Mothers would soon knock daughters unconscious with rolling pins and then lie down with them beside open gas pipes.

Erwin and Alice were only too aware of the true nature of the Arrow Cross. "They were scum," recalled Erwin. "The garbage of the nation." Its many factions could agree on little other than that the Jews should be done away with. "Posters were quickly plastered everywhere in the city. One said that the government did not recognize any protected Jews. They must all go to the ghetto. Anybody who was not there, who was hiding, and those hiding them, would be butchered. That was the precise word used by our new government—butchered."[12] Arrow Cross official Pal Hodosy was typical of the new masters of Budapest. "The problem is not that Jews are being murdered," he would declare publicly. "The only trouble is the method. The bodies must be made to disappear, not put in the streets."[13]

No one was safe. At any minute, the Arrow Cross might appear, on the hunt for Jews and their valuables. So Erwin and Alice left that night, October 15, and hid in the nearby garage of a Hungarian politician, Tivadar Homonai, who had known Erwin and his family since Erwin was four years old.[14] It was just as well. "We learned that on the very same night, just a few hours after we left my parents' house," recalled Erwin, "the Arrow Cross killers were indeed looking for us there. We had just left in the nick of time. But the next morning, we had to be on the move once again, like sheep in a lion's cage."[15]

The morning of October 16, 1944, Alice and Erwin took Pipez and crossed the city to try to find some Christian friends, the Arpadfys, who had bravely agreed to hide them. It was a harrowing journey through a city where Jews were now to be killed at random, often on the drunken whims of brutal, illiterate teenagers—young fascists pumped full of a lethal cocktail of testosterone and hate. Jewish corpses lay pooled in blood on the streets.

Alice, Erwin, and Pipez were not wearing yellow stars, but they felt extremely vulnerable all the same. And Pipez looked very Jewish, especially with his cap. Surely, thought Erwin, everyone was looking at them, thinking the same thing—they were a Jewish family. [16]

"Pipez, take off your cap."

Without the cap, Pipez looked even more like a Jewish orphan, with his short cropped hair.

"Pipez, put your cap back on."

Alice told Pipez not to say a word. They crossed the Danube, heading toward Pest.

"Lici—why don't the fascists do anything against us?" Pipez asked. "Is it because we don't have a yellow star?"

There was a deathly silence in the streetcar. No one moved. No one said a word.

"Pipez—shut up!" said Alice.[17]

They left the streetcar as soon as they got to the other side of the Danube. Thankfully, they were not followed. That night, they hid at the home of the Arpadfys. They had survived their first day on the run.

The following morning, Erwin tried to obtain false papers from an unnamed criminal he knew, fearing that Wallenberg's Schutzpasses would no longer be valid under the Arrow Cross regime. Alice and Pipez were with Erwin. The criminal glanced at Pipez, who looked more than ever like a Jewish orphan. "If this boy is found with you," the criminal told Erwin, "all of you will be killed. He's under Red Cross protection. Why don't you send him back to their orphanage? He will be safe there and won't expose you to this danger."[18]

It was a difficult decision, but Erwin and Alice agreed that this would be safer for all concerned. The criminal's wife took Pipez back to his orphanage. She returned in tears. Six-year-old Pipez had begged her not to leave him at the orphanage. "I have one dollar," he had pleaded with her. "I'll give it to you. I want to live."[19]

The criminal told Erwin that he knew a place where Erwin's parents, his sister Marta, and her fiancée could hide: a rented apartment in Pest. He warned Erwin that they were to stay as quiet as they could in case neighbors reported them to the Arrow Cross.

Erwin and Alice hopped on a rattling yellow streetcar that took them into the working class outskirts of the city, where Erwin hoped to pick up forged papers. They finally got off the streetcar near the address Erwin had been given. Erwin told Alice to stay and wait for him.

"I'll go alone and get the papers," said Erwin.

As Erwin walked along the street, he sensed that something was not right. Then he saw several men. They spotted him, and he turned and started to walk back toward Alice, trying to look calm. The men began to run after him, and Erwin sprinted toward Alice. He saw a streetcar headed their way.

"Jump on it," shouted Erwin.

Alice did so. Erwin was close behind. At the next stop, they got off and took another streetcar, having managed to shake off their pursuers. That night, they hid with a laborer and his family, in a one-room apartment. "He was a communist," recalled Erwin. "He didn't ask any questions. I wanted to give him money, but he would not accept it." They left the next morning and were soon drenched because of the pouring rain. "Wherever we went, we saw groups of fifty, a hundred, two hundred Jews—all in line, hands above heads. Boys of sixteen with tommy guns were rounding them up, kicking, using whips, taking them toward the ghetto."[20]

They kept on moving, trying to get across Budapest without being stopped by the Arrow Cross and asked for their papers. One of Alice's shoes fell off because it was so old and worn. Erwin found a drugstore and bought some bandages and, hidden in a doorway, he tied Alice's broken shoe to her foot with gauze. To buy them a little extra time, Erwin took Alice into a hairdresser, anywhere off the street would do. Finally, they managed to get to the apartment in Pest where Erwin's parents were hiding. Erwin knew immediately that it was unsafe because it was in an area of Pest where the Arrow Cross thugs were particularly thorough in their searches. He told them to leave immediately and they did so. Not long after, the Arrow Cross raided the apartment. One of the neighbors had reported hearing strange noises.

Erwin and Alice decided to take their chances and return to a small room they had found in Buda that summer. Erwin's parents and sister Marta found refuge elsewhere. Later that day, Erwin and Alice arrived in Buda in time to beat a curfew. "Finally, we could clean up and get into dry clothes," recalled Erwin. "We were aware of the continuous mortal danger but at this point we no longer cared. If this was the end, so be it."[21]

THAT SAME DAY, October 17, 1944, Horthy left Hungary as a prisoner. At 4:30 that afternoon, he was escorted to a special train, in which his wife and daughter-in-law with her small son were already seated. Air-raid sirens sounded at all the stations along the route toward Austria, to make sure that any who wanted to see the regent leave Hungary would be in shelters instead. "We arrived in Vienna at midnight in the deepest depression," recalled Horthy. "Here, Veesenmayer had told me, my son would join us. I strained my eyes in the hope of seeing my son, Miklas, but neither in Vienna nor at Linz nor in Bavaria did we find him. We did not even know where he was or whether he was still alive. Our request to be allowed to receive word from him for Christmas was not granted. Ribbentrop merely advised my daughter-in-law in a letter that he was 'suitably housed,' a cynical description of his residence in the Mauthausen concentration camp."[22]

Horthy remained under house arrest in Bavaria until the war in Europe ended. On April 29, 1945, his SS guards fled in the face of the Allied advance. On May 1, Horthy was first liberated and then arrested by elements of the U.S. 7th Army, and eventually taken to the prison facility at Nuremberg in late September 1945, where he was reunited with his son, Miklas, Jr. After intense behind-the-scenes lobbying by a former American ambassador to Budapest, it was decided not to prosecute Horthy for war crimes. Stalin reportedly said that it "should not be forgotten that [Horthy] offered armistice in the fall of 1944."

Horthy was released from Nuremberg and allowed to rejoin his family in Bavaria. In 1948, he testified against Veensenmayer, who received a twenty-year sentence.[23] The following year, Horthy was given sanctuary in Portugal, which was under the sway of another prototypical fascist, Antonio de Oliviera Salazar, who ruled Portugal from 1932 to 1974. In his memoirs, Horthy naturally denied any knowledge of the death camps in the spring and early summer of 1944, when his own countrymen were dying at a rate of twelve thousand a day in Auschwitz. Horthy died in 1957, having escaped justice for his involvement in what Winston Churchill described as "probably the greatest and most horrible crime ever committed in the history of the world."[24]

As Horthy was leaving Hungary, the "Master" reasserted his power in Budapest. It was a smug Eichmann who stood before representatives of the Jewish Council once more on October 17, 1944.

"You see, I am back again," he told them.

Eichmann paused.

"The Hungarians thought that the events in Romania would be repeated here," Eichmann continued. "They were wrong. They forgot that Hungary still lies in the shadow of the Reich. *This* government will work according to *our* orders. I have already been in touch with Minister Kovarcz and he has agreed that the Jews of Budapest shall be deported, this time on foot. We need our trains for other purposes."

Eichmann smiled.

"Now we are going to work efficiently and quickly. Right?"

The Jewish leaders were dumbfounded.

Preparations were quickly being made to march Hungary's last Jews—as many as a quarter-million—to the border. Finally, the country would be cleansed. Reich plenipotentiary Edmund Veesenmayer cabled Ribbentrop in Berlin: "A final settlement of the Jewish question can now be expected."[25]

In the first days after the Arrow Cross came to power, thousands of Jews were corralled into synagogues and held without food or water. In the chaos, Wallenberg's car was stolen and his Jewish driver, Vilmos Langfelder, arrested. For much of October 17, Wallenberg frantically cycled around Budapest, finally tracking down his driver and car at the headquarters of the Arrow Cross. Outraged by Langfelder's arrest, he is said to have faced down several heavily armed Arrow Cross thugs before negotiating the return of both car and driver. Wallenberg then hurried to the Dohany Street synagogue—one of the largest in Europe—to try to free several hundred Jews who had been imprisoned there. He had telephoned Charles Lutz, the Swiss charge d'affaires, and Lutz had agreed to accompany him to the synagogue. Wallenberg and Lutz gained entry and walked through throngs of desperate Jews to the main altar.

"Does anyone here hold a Swedish Schutzpass?" shouted Wallenberg. Hands were raised.

"Yes, I do," someone called.

"Everyone with a pass form an orderly queue by the entrance," Wallenberg shouted. "Orderly. It must be orderly."

Wallenberg turned to several SS men inside the synagogue.

"These are Swedish citizens," said Wallenberg. "You have no right to keep them here. I order you to release them at once."[26]

Wallenberg and Lutz both gathered groups who had Schutzpasses. Then they led them out of the synagogue and to Swedish- and Swiss-protected houses, where most would hunker down in crowded, cold rooms and await the Soviets—now their best hope, other than the neutral diplomats, of surviving the Arrow Cross. Within a few days, thanks to the fierce protests of Wallenberg, Lutz, and other neutral diplomats, all the Jews held in synagogues were reportedly freed.[27]

ON THE AFTERNOON OF October 18, one of Budapest's Jewish leaders, Rudolf Kasztner, arrived for a meeting at the Hotel Majestic with Eichmann. Eichmann was in a foul mood.

"I am back, as you see," said Eichmann, who was dressed in full uniform. "My arm is long enough to reach you and your useless dung people," he shouted. "They will all be deported now, you hear me? Not one of them will be spared. This time, there are no trains, no lorries—they will march all the way. I don't want to hear any of your damned excuses. I don't care how old they are or how sick they are. It's all lies. I've heard it all before. We need workers for the defense of Vienna."

Eichmann said that two hundred thousand Jews were left in Budapest—"Jew City." They were all disguising themselves as gentiles or foreign nationals. He would get them all, one way or another.

"I am a bloodhound. Don't you forget that! You think I can't do it? You think my teeth have been pulled by Himmler?"

Eichmann dismissed Kasztner and laughed at him as he left the office. Kasztner met a grinning Wisliceny in the corridor outside Eichmann's office.

"Didn't think we'd be back so soon, did you?" smirked Wisliceny.

Wisliceny then explained to the stunned Kasztner that Eichmann's mistress had left him.

"The Obersturmbannfuhrer is in a foul mood—I wouldn't even try to argue with him," added Wisliceny. "Perhaps after the next fifty thousand have gone, you might have a chance at bargaining again."

"Fifty thousand?"

"Yes, fifty thousand Jews to work protecting the Reich."

Kasztner did not respond. Later, back at his apartment, he broke down in tears.

Part Three

RED DANUBE

10

The Arrow Cross

S O BEGAN A REIGN OF TERROR that at times allegedly unnerved even hardened SS veterans.[1] Lars Berg, one of Wallenberg's colleagues at the Swedish Embassy, vividly remembered how "all the lowest scum of the city, all crooks and street boys, came running. They were given a white party badge and an automatic weapon with plenty of ammunition . . . Nobody was safe any longer."[2]

Even though the Arrow Cross now had political power, it seemed that the status of neutral diplomats such as Wallenberg would still be respected. But none knew for how long. Meanwhile, as Wallenberg scrambled frantically for the release of Swedish-protected Jews all across the city, the Gestapo were a step ahead. They had apparently managed to persuade the Arrow Cross minister of the interior, Gabor Vajna, to once and for all put an end to Wallenberg and the neutral diplomats' interventions. On October 18, a formal announcement revoked the validity of any "letter of safe conduct of any kind [or] any foreign passport which a Jew of Hungarian nationality may have received from whatever source or person."

The tens of thousands of Jews whom Wallenberg and others had saved were now stripped of protection. Wallenberg and his fellow diplomats knew they would have to act fast or all their rescue efforts would have been for nothing. So they exerted intense pressure on Vajna and other officials.

Wallenberg was particularly effective in his dealings with the young and pregnant aristocrat, Baroness Elizabeth Kemeny—the wife of Hungary's new foreign minister Gabor Kemeny. "You [must] persuade your husband to honor the protective passes and soften his government's policy toward the Jews," Wallenberg told her, according to her recollection. "I would vouch for him. Your child would have a father, and you would know that you had helped to rebuild a world in which justice and morality are important, the kind of world you would want your child to inherit."[3]

According to several accounts, Kemeny soon buckled under pressure from his wife as well as from the neutral diplomats in Budapest, and announced on the radio that protective passes as well as the safe houses were to be once again respected. On October 22, during a power outage, a harried but no doubt relieved Wallenberg sat in his office, surrounded by dozens of his aides, and by candlelight dashed off a letter to his mother. "I can reassure you that I am fine," he told her. "The times are extraordinarily exciting and nerve-racking. We keep working and struggling on, and that is the main thing."[4]

MARIANNE LOWY WAS still living as anonymously as she could in a Buda suburb, where she pretended to be the Catholic sister of a woman whose husband had been taken to a forced labor camp. But the Arrow Cross had informers everywhere, it seemed, and there was no shortage of people who reported suspicious comings and goings.

One morning, Marianne heard the front doorbell ring. She opened the door and was shocked to find five grim-faced Hungarian gendarmes, wearing hats with cock feathers, standing before her. She was terrified but managed to appear quite calm. They demanded entry. She showed them into a large dining room. They asked to see her papers and told her to sit down at the dining room table.

She pulled out her "gentile papers."

The men examined them carefully.

"We're here to question you," one of them said.

"This is the end," she thought.

Marianne was asked to explain all about the catechism. Thankfully, she had spent many hours studying it, and was able to do so. After an hour of intensive questioning, the men stood up and made to leave. Marianne thought she had convinced the men that she really was just a good Catholic girl, not a married Jewess with false papers. One of the men addressed her. "Well, we didn't get you this time," he said. "But we'll be back."

As soon as the gendarmes left, Marianne packed her few belongings—a toothbrush and some clean underwear—and made her way across Buda, then the Danube to a protected house where her parents and several Jewish families were living. She later moved to 44 Ulloi Street, Wallenberg's main office, joining her husband Pista, who had escaped a labor battalion, and some three hundred other Jews who had found refuge there.[5]

Given Wallenberg's daily presence, it seemed to be the safest place in Budapest.

But no one knew for how long.

ALICE AND ERWIN KORANYI had also been hiding in Buda, determined to hold out until the Soviets arrived. "No Jews were supposed to be there," recalled Alice. "I worked in a library for a short time, but then German officials came to the library. One of the Germans liked me. It was a difficult situation. He said he would help me get to see my family."[6] Alice did not take up the offer and left the library in case the German became vengeful. "Every encounter with an authority," recalled her husband Erwin, "sometimes on numerous occasions during a single day, was *rouge et noir* at the roulette table."[7]

It became terrifyingly clear one day late that October that even Erwin and Alice's small hideaway in Buda would no longer be safe. Erwin was looking out a window when he saw a Hungarian soldier escorting a young Jewish man with a yellow armband. When the man reached the street corner, he made a break for it and ran for his life. The soldier took his rifle, aimed carefully, and killed the boy.

Erwin and Alice knew they had to move again. But where were they to go now? Thankfully, Erwin's sister, Marta, who had recently become a typist in Section C for Wallenberg, discovered that there was space for them at a Swedish satellite embassy, at 1 Jokai Street in Pest. With enormous relief, they quickly found sanctuary there. They had to share a room with several others, but at least Erwin and Alice could sleep on a small, straw mattress rather than a cold, hard floor. And for the time being, they hoped, the Arrow Cross would be too busy hunting for Jews on the streets to look for them in the Swedish-protected building, with its large yellow and blue flag fluttering reassuringly outside.[8]

THE SUPREME COMMANDER was on the line. It was 10 p.m. on October 28, 1944. In his headquarters in Debrecen, which he had captured a week earlier, burly forty-six-year-old General Rodion Malinovsky, commander of the 2nd Ukrainian Front, talked on a telephone.

A brilliant strategist, Malinovsky had distinguished himself during the battle of Stalingrad and was one of Stalin's most trusted generals. With a reputation for being stubborn and outspoken, Malinovksy, the hardened son of an impoverished Ukrainian peasant, did not like what Stalin, that cunning yellow-eyed Georgian, was now telling him—in essence that his exhausted men would have to return to combat before they had recovered from the fierce fighting to take Debrecen.

"Budapest must be taken as soon as possible," Stalin said. "To be precise, in the next few days. This is absolutely essential. Can you do it?"

"The job can be done within five days," replied Malinovsky, "when the 4th Mechanized Guard Corps arrives to join the 46th Army."

"The supreme command can't give you five days," Stalin stressed. "You must understand that for political reasons, we have to take Budapest as quickly as possible."

Malinovsky tried to stand his ground. "If you give me five days I will take Budapest in another five days," he argued. "If we start the offensive right now, the 46th Army—lacking sufficient forces—won't be able to bring it to a speedy conclusion and will inevitably be bogged down in lengthy battles on the access roads to the Hungarian capital. In other words, it won't be able to take Budapest."

"There's no point in being so stubborn," replied Stalin. "You obviously don't understand the political necessity of an immediate strike against Budapest."

"I am fully aware of the political importance of the capture of Budapest, and that is why I am asking for five days."

Stalin finally lost his patience: "I expressly order you to begin the offensive against Budapest tomorrow."[9]

Malinovsky knew Stalin's order was premature. The objectives he had been given were not likely to be met. Yet he had no choice. Like so many of Hitler's best generals, he could only try his best to comply with the order.

11

The Road to Hegyeshalom

S COLONEL ADOLF EICHMANN had been given a second chance. Key officials in the newly installed Arrow Cross regime—Vajna, Baky, and Endre—were eager to remove Budapest's last Jews. But he would have to act quickly and with great ingenuity if he was going to deport all of Budapest's Jews before the Soviets arrived. It was time for the "Master" to prove that his talents had not diminished.

Unable to requisition trains because of the pressing military situation in the East, Eichmann came up with a simple yet barbarously effective solution to the lack of rolling stock. He would make the last of the two-hundred-thousand-odd Jews of Budapest march to their deaths. They would be sent on foot, under armed guard, all 120 miles to the Austrian border.

The death marches began on November 8, 1944, when two thousand Jews were rounded up and sent out of Budapest. As winter set in and temperatures plunged, Arrow Cross gangs gathered thousands more terrified Jews each day and set them marching. Eventually, more than thirty thousand people would be herded into groups of a thousand and forced to walk to the border. They had no food, medical care, or shelter. Women in high heel shoes, old men without jackets, and young schoolgirls were marched out of Budapest, across the Danube toward Austria. "It was horrible for us to be standing as passive spectators," recalled Wallenberg's fellow diplomat, Lars Berg, "when young girls were driven together, arranged in files, and marched off as they were in silk stockings, high-heeled shoes, and thin office clothes."[1]

The cruelty and suffering was soon on a scale that even some of Eichmann's colleagues had not experienced. "The foot march [Eichmann] organized was pure murder," SS Colonel Kurt Becher recalled.[2] Hungarian guards whipped the Jews as they staggered toward the border, some dying on their feet, most as they lay on the ground having collapsed from exposure and hypothermia. If they slowed, they were killed. The Hungarian police and Arrow Cross youths were trigger happy, hungry it appeared to kill Jews on any pretext. One seventy-four-year-old woman, Bertha Schwartz, reached out to a guard for support and was shot dead before her hand touched him.

"This is cruel," one Hungarian guard complained. "Why don't they shoot them and toss them into the Danube instead of making them drag themselves miserably like this?"[3]

According to a young schoolgirl, Susan Tabor, when her column of forced marchers reached the outskirts of Budapest one day early that November, it was herded into a brick factory in Obuda. "Some people fell and were trampled over because the guards hurried us mercilessly into the building," she recalled. "Once we were all in, there was hardly room on the floor for everyone to sit. There was no light, no water, no food, no doctors, no first aid, and no sanitary facilities. No one was allowed outside. Armed [guards] walked around stepping on people, abusing them, cursing, and shooting . . . Our spirit was broken. We didn't talk to each other. We were treated like animals and we felt like animals. One Nazi couldn't stand the screams of a woman who had a broken foot and couldn't move, so he stamped on her head. Her brains came out. We still didn't talk to each other."

The next morning, Tabor heard SS guards barking orders. Then she saw a man silhouetted in the entrance to the building. He was a "frail-looking man with a sensitive face." Tabor stared at Wallenberg. She did not realize at first that he was talking to her and the others. "He was telling us he had negotiated with the Nazis for the release of those with Schutzpasses. When the Germans weren't looking, he slipped extra passes to some women. He also gave us food and medical supplies." But above all, he brought hope. "He gave us back our dignity, our humanity," recalled Tabor. "Here was someone who thought we were human beings worth saving."[4]

A few hours later, as the forced march began again, Susan and her mother gave their coats, marked with yellow stars, to friends who were freezing to death. As guards tried to organize columns, Tabor and her mother slipped away from the death march. "We didn't know if we were going to be shot in the back or not. Nazi soldiers were all around. No one stopped us and we just kept walking back to Budapest."[5] There, they managed to find some Christian friends who would hide them until the war was over.

It is thought that Wallenberg was able to save two hundred Jews that morning.[6] Thousands of others had to keep walking toward a town on the border called Hegyeshalom, where Eichmann's deputy, Dieter Wisliceny, and sometimes Eichmann himself would oversee their transfer to Reich authorities across the border. According to a Red Cross official: "Endless columns of deported persons were marched along—ragged and starving people, mortally tired, among them old and wizened creatures who could barely crawl. Hungarian police were driving them with the butt end of their rifles, with sticks and with whips."

Seventeen-year-old Miriam Herzog traipsed no less than twenty-five miles a day in sleet and freezing rain. She saw police beating those who could not keep up and leaving others to die slowly of exposure and ex-haustion in ditches. The older women suffered most. Sometimes at night, they lay without blankets out in the open, shivering, without any-thing to eat or drink.

One night, Miriam and the other women in her group stopped in a square in the middle of a village. They lay down on the ground to rest—there was no shelter. In the morning, many of the older women were dead, their corpses frozen to the ground.

Miriam's thirst was even worse than her hunger. Weak from dysentery, wretched from the dirt and the lice that infested her, all she could do the next night was find a space on the floor of a barn and lie down. She didn't know how much later it was—maybe days—but suddenly she heard a great commotion among the women near her.

"It's Wallenberg."

Miriam didn't know this name, but someone told her he was a Swedish diplomat who had saved many Jews already. She didn't think he would really help her, and anyway she was now too weak to move, so she lay there on the dirt floor as dozens of women clustered around him.

"Please, you must forgive me," Wallenberg told them. "I cannot help all of you. I can only provide certificates for a hundred of you."

Wallenberg looked around the room and began putting names down on a list. He saw Miriam lying on the floor and moved over to her. He asked her name and added it to the list. After a day or two, the women whose names he had taken were placed in a cattle truck on a train bound for Budapest. Because the railway lines had been bombed, the journey took three days, instead of three or four hours. Miriam and the others Wallenberg had rescued were close to death when they arrived. "There were a lot more dangers and hardships ahead of us, but we were alive," she recalled in a 1980 interview with the BBC, "and it was thanks entirely to Wallenberg."[7]

THE MAIN HIGHWAY FROM BUDAPEST to the border was soon littered with so many bodies that even hardened SS veterans were revolted. On November 16, 1944, silver-haired and bespectacled fifty-year-old SS General Hans Juettner and Rudolf Hess, the commandant of Auschwitz, drove from Vienna to Budapest and encountered scenes along the road that, in Juettner's words, left a "truly terrifying impression."[8]

When Juettner and Hess arrived in Budapest, they were told that Eichmann was not in the city. "I spoke to an SS Sturmbannfuhrer whose name I have forgotten [Theo Dannecker] and gave him a piece of my mind," recalled Juettner.

At Hegyeshalom, Juettner met Dieter Wisliceny, Eichmann's porcine aid, who told him that Eichmann had "instructed him to pay no attention to illness, age, or protective passes."[9]

Juettner later claimed that he ordered a halt to the marches, and several thousand Jews were returned to the city.[10] But a few days after Juettner returned to Berlin, the death marches resumed. "On November 21,

Eichmann immediately gave orders to continue the foot march," recalled Rudolf Kasztner of the Jewish Council. "He believed that the order to stop the foot marches had been issued on the strength of the mistaken impression of a 'few' gentlemen, who had no way of judging whether people who had been on the march for seven or eight days could or could not be regarded as fit for labor."

Eichmann also told Kasztner that he had had enough of Wallenberg and other diplomats' interference. "He went on about the abuse of the safe conducts," recalled Kasztner. "He said he would hold the Swiss consul, Lutz, and Raoul Wallenberg responsible for this outrage. But he had one suggestion: He would close his eyes to the holders of these safe conducts if we voluntarily provided him with twenty thousand pick and shovel Jews."[11]

Kasztner declined the offer.

THE LIGHT WAS FADING. Cold rain lashed across the empty avenues of central Pest. It was November 22, 1944. Raoul Wallenberg sat in the back of his Studebaker as his Hungarian Jewish driver, quiet and dependable Vilmos Langfelder, pulled away from the sidewalk and headed north, toward the border town of Hegyeshalom. In the long weeks since the Arrow Cross had taken power, Wallenberg and the twenty-two-year-old engineer, with red-blond hair and a round, amiable face, had become inseparable.[12]

Seated beside Wallenberg were his diplomatic colleague, thirty-year-old fellow Swede Per Anger, and twenty-one-year-old Johnny Moser. Moser was a blond-haired Jewish assistant chosen to work with Wallenberg because he could pass himself off as an Aryan.

Behind the Studebaker followed three wagons, loaded to capacity with medicine and food.[13] Tailing these trucks was another car carrying doctors and nurses who worked for Wallenberg's fast-growing relief organization, which now employed more than 550 Jews to administer dozens of Swedish safe houses, an orphanage, a hospital, forty doctors, and numerous soup kitchens, all funded and supervised by Wallenberg.

Wallenberg and his relief party were to be joined on their way to the Austrian border by volunteers from the International Red Cross and

Swiss Legation.[14] It was a pitiful journey, one that would never be forgotten by those who accompanied Wallenberg. As the headlights of the Studebaker stabbed the darkness that night, they witnessed soul-destroying suffering. There were gray-faced children with bare, bleeding feet, dressed in thin rags. There were old men trying to hold up their wives, hysterical or numbed, shivering with the cold and the horror of it all, clearly close to dying.

Langfelder often put his foot to the brake to avoid hitting the marchers. Some of them recognized Wallenberg and cried out. But Wallenberg could not stop now to help them. There were far more people to save further on, at the head of the endless columns of people crying out for help.

Wallenberg and his aides knew they had to reach the border town of Hegyeshalom by daylight. It would mean driving through the night to get there, but they had no choice. At 9 a.m., another two thousand Jews would be lost to Eichmann's men and deported across the border to Austria.[15]

En route to Hegyeshalom, Red Cross representatives stopped in Gonyu, where marchers were being kept on barges in the Danube. According to their subsequent report, "deportees were driven on board the ships anchored in the Danube. Many—in their great distress—committed suicide. In the still of the night, one scream followed another. The doomed people were jumping into the Danube, which was covered with drifting ice. They could not stand the tortures any longer . . . With our own eyes we saw the police driving the Jews, who arrived in pitch darkness, over the narrow gangways covered with ice, so that scores of them slipped and fell into the icy river."[16]

Per Anger arrived that night with Wallenberg and the other aides in Gonyu. As they began to hand out food, they too heard the screams of Jews who could take no more and were leaping to their deaths in the icy river. When they resumed their journey along the road heading to the border, they passed "masses of unfortunates, more dead than alive. Ashen-faced, they staggered forward under proddings and blows from the soldiers' rifle butts. The road was edged with bodies."[17]

Langfelder again put his foot to the pedal, the Studebaker passing through the central European darkness, past silent, frosted vineyards and abandoned farms. Wallenberg arrived at Hegyeshalom at 7 a.m., just after dawn. Arrow Cross guards were busy lining up marchers at the town's station. The Swiss Red Cross later reported that some of them were "in the worst imaginable condition. The endless labor of the foot march, the almost total lack of food, made worse by the torturing, steady fear that they were being taken to the extermination chambers in Germany, brought these pitiful deportees to such a state that all human appearances and all human dignity completely left them."[18]

A train stood waiting to take these Jews to Austria, where they would be worked to death building fortifications around Vienna—Stalin's next objective after Budapest. One of the Jews who stood waiting on the platform at Hegyeshalom later recalled: "For me that train meant one thing—death. I was positive that if I climbed onto that train I would die. Just as I was about to get on board and everyone was crying, I saw a handsome man, as if in a dream, who was trying to take people away. And I asked, 'Who is this gentleman?' because I thought that everyone, the whole world, was against us."

Wallenberg worked fast.

"Why, I just gave *you* a pass several days ago," Wallenberg told one Jew. "Off you go, now."

Hands rose in the air.

"I want to save you all, but they will let me take only a few. So please forgive me, but I must save the young ones."

According to Per Anger, Eichmann was also at the station that morning. Eichmann apparently stood, dressed in his customary silver gray uniform, counting off the Jews as if they were cattle. "Four hundred eighty-nine—check!"[19]

Many of the boxcars standing in the sidings at Hegyeshalom were already crammed with Jews. In a few minutes, the train was due to leave. According to one account, Wallenberg reportedly pleaded with Eichmann, who turned his back on the Swede and walked away, leaving his deputy, Wisliceny, to deal with the infuriating diplomat.[20]

Per Anger also recalled seeing Wallenberg approach hundreds of Jews gathered on a platform. He shouted that those with Swedish passes should join him. But several heavily armed Arrow Cross guards stepped into his path, placing bayonets to his chest. Wallenberg walked away. A few minutes later, he returned with a group of Hungarian soldiers and a gendarme officer whom he'd earlier bribed with cigarettes and several bottles of rum.

Wallenberg set up a table, opened his briefcase, and then took out what he called his "black book of life"—a register of protected Jews.[21] He called out the most common Jewish names and handed out replacement passes as quickly as he could. His young assistant Johnny Moser, meanwhile, moved among the Jews, whispering under his breath: "Raise your hands."[22]

It has been claimed that Wallenberg saved three hundred of the three thousand Jews assembled at Hegyeshalom that day, November 23, 1944. Most had never been issued a Schutzpass. But they had the strength and wits to respond when Wallenberg called out or walked among them. Wallenberg's helpers then unloaded the food and medicine from their three trucks, helped the Jews aboard, and drove them away. Wallenberg had bribed the Hungarian officer in control of Hegyeshalom into distributing the food to those he could not rescue.[23]

Wallenberg did not want to hand out the food to the condemned himself. He could not bear to see the looks on the faces of the people he could not save, their tears and pathetic sobs of gratitude. Instead, he walked away and watched from a distance as the food was given to marchers whose "death pale" faces "swam with tears."[24]

It was broad daylight by the time Wallenberg left Hegyeshalom. The scenes he encountered on the return journey along the road to Budapest were perhaps the most harrowing during all his time in Hungary. As Langfelder drove along the main highway, every twenty miles Wallenberg saw a column of Jews: "sick, unfortunate people, from twelve-year-old children to seventy-four-year-old matrons . . . ragged and dirty." The car continued, soon passing a group of men from the Bor copper mines. They were starving to death and were "half-naked and insane with hunger."

On they drove, through villages where some peasants had earlier laughed and mocked the marchers, especially the young, pretty Jewish women, walking in heels, their coats stolen, as they had staggered past the snarling faces of their fellow Hungarians.

"Kill those Jewish whores now!"[25]

Wallenberg stopped time and time again. It was always the children who had to be saved first. According to one particularly moving account, he pulled toddlers and babies from the thin, pale arms of their dying mothers, and then placed some of these children on the floor of his car.

Soon, Wallenberg's convoy could carry no more.

"The trucks are full," a tearful Wallenberg reportedly told one of his helpers, "and these people don't have the strength to walk back to Budapest even if the guards permitted it. They're all going to die."[26]

THE MAN WHO HAD ORDERED the death marches, Adolf Eichmann, also travelled back to Budapest on "the road of death" on November 23, 1944. As far as Eichmann was concerned, the marches had been a great success. That night, when Eichmann reached his headquarters in Buda, General Winkelmann, Himmler's representative in Hungary, and the Hungarian fascist Laszlo Endre, the Arrow Cross undersecretary of state in the Ministry of the Interior, held a soiree in honor of Eichmann. In three weeks, Eichmann had sent 50,000 Jews out of the country. That left just 175,000 in Budapest. They could be quickly liquidated by December.[27] There was plenty to celebrate.

Eichmann enjoyed the party. "I was so happy to be in the company of prominent Hungarian government members," he said later. "Winkelmann congratulated me on the 'elegant performance' [of the march]. So did Veesenmayer. So did Endre. We even toasted it, and for the first time in my life I drank mare's milk alcohol [brandy and milk]."[28]

But the performance was about to end. Just days later, the Arrow Cross premier, Szalasi, under intensifying pressure from Wallenberg and his fellow diplomats, halted his government's participation in the marches. The forty-year-old Edmund Veesenmayer, the most senior Nazi official in Hungary, cabled RSHA offices in Berlin: "Szalasi's edict is practically equivalent to canceling deportation."[29]

There was another reason why the death marches could not continue: The SS in Austria were reportedly unable to cope with the large numbers of Jews arriving every day. And they could not put the starved human wrecks that reached them to work because many were too weak even to lift a shovel.[30]

THERE WAS CHAOS AND CONFUSION. The partisans now operating in the forests near Sarvar had become more and more daring, perhaps buoyed by the rapid Soviet advance across the central plains of Hungary. This time, they managed to damage the camp's gates, and some prisoners, including the Hermans, seized their chance and escaped. Most were recaptured, but the Hermans were by now expert at fleeing the Nazis, and somehow had the strength to get clear of the camp.[31]

So began a painstaking journey across the mostly flat, deforested countryside, toward Budapest. Finally, after three weeks, they got to the city and found friends who would harbor them.[32] They discovered that the name 'Raoul Wallenberg' was on everyone's lips. His actions after October 15 had become widely known, and his success, according to one of his workers, Janos Beer, had created a "positive feedback." His example became a powerful tonic and spur to others—Jews, his aides, and fellow diplomats alike.

Late that fall, Emil Herman told his wife, Margit: "I'll try to get to the Swedish embassy and see if I can meet Raoul Wallenberg."

Wallenberg was at the embassy on Gellert Hill when Vera's father reached him. Within five minutes, he had issued Emil a Schutzpass for himself and his wife Margit, and assigned them to a protected house.

Then Wallenberg apparently smiled.

"Do you know we still have your little girl?"[33]

It is not known how Emil reacted to this stunning statement. But without doubt, Emil Herman would never forget the date—November 30, 1944, the day his daughter was brought back from the dead.

With their new passes, and not wearing the yellow star, Emil and Margit walked to a Swedish-protected house in Pest. Meanwhile, their daughter, Vera, was taken from an orphanage and brought to the same safe house, where she was miraculously, it would forever seem, reunited with her parents.

They hugged, stroked, and kissed.[34] Vera then grabbed her parents and wouldn't let go, wanting never to be separated from them again. She had to hold them tight to make sure they were real. If she just kept clinging to them, she was convinced that she would not be orphaned again. And from then on, she vowed, she would not let them out of her sight and would be the perfect daughter, utterly obedient, all that they could possibly ever want her to be.[35]

Soon after they were reunited, Vera's mother, Margit, explained why she had pushed Vera into the arms of Wallenberg's rescue team.

"All I could think of," Margrit told Vera, "was that if you were fed a meal worth eating and if you slept in a real bed, I would have to be content never to see you again."

The Hermans then joined 128 other Jews in their safe house, waiting each agonizing day for the Soviet troops to arrive. Not long after moving into the safe house together, they were forced to find a space in the building's cellar because Allied and Soviet bombing had become so intense. "Food, delivered in the dead of night by Wallenberg's volunteers—sometimes even by [Wallenberg] himself—was scarce," recalled Vera. "Yet morale was high as our hearts soared at the prospect of survival."[36]

The Hermans' protected house was on Vacsy Street in Pest, just two hundred yards from the Danube, which arced in a giant, gentle bend through the city. "We could see it from the house," Vera remembered. "One time, my father saved a Jew who was shot down on the banks of the Danube. You see, sometimes the Arrow Cross played games. They shot six Jews and [arranged their bodies on the ice] to form a Star of David. One day, my father looked out our cellar's window and saw that one of the legs of the star was moving. So he crawled out there and pulled a young girl off the ice."[37]

During the bombings, all 128 people squeezed into the dank cellar. "It was very, very crowded, crowded to the point where we lay on our side at night and if someone wanted to turn over, the whole row had to turn over," added Vera. "Life became more and more desperate. But there were moments of joy." Time even for young love: "There was a fourteen-year-old boy who had a crush on me and gave me his last lump of sugar in that cellar. I guess he was in love with me. It was a schoolboy crush."[38]

The frightened Jewish boy sat beside Vera, who was growing weaker by the day, and tried to distract her from her hunger and anxiety. Each night, she would settle down between her parents and hug them tight and try to find sleep. Perhaps, one day soon, when she awoke, they would finally be safe.

12

Dinner with Eichmann

ONE EVENING THAT November of 1944, Wallenberg is said to have arrived at the front entrance of his apartment in Buda. To his surprise, according to several accounts, he found Adolf Eichmann, wearing a civilian suit, and an aide, possibly SS Sturmbann-fuhrer Herman Krumey, waiting for him.[1] Wallenberg, it has been claimed, had invited Eichmann to dinner but forgotten the date.[2]

All that summer and fall, Wallenberg had nurtured his contacts among the SS and Arrow Cross—they were crucial if he was to exert maximum influence. On September 29, he had written to his mother: "A few days ago, I had invited some very interesting big game, namely Himmler's representative [possibly Adolf Eichmann]. Unfortunately, something came up at work at the last minute and prevented him from coming. He is quite a nice man who, according to what he himself says, will soon shoot himself."[3]

Wallenberg, the story goes, greeted Eichmann and his aide warmly, inviting them into his apartment, where he prepared cocktails for his guests and then said that he had to make a quick telephone call.[4] It was to his diplomatic colleague, Lars Berg, who would later vividly describe that night's events in a memoir published in Sweden in 1949.[5]

"I've got Eichmann here," Wallenberg told Berg, "and I've forgotten that I invited him to dinner. Can you set up something this quickly?"

Berg and a fellow Swedish diplomat, Gote Carlsson, lived not far away in a large mansion, owned by a wealthy count who had been accused of being part Jewish and had fled Hungary, leaving several servants, exquisite furniture, wines, and crockery in Berg's care. The Hungarian count's cook, Magda, was still on the premises and happy to prepare a lavish meal.

It was a short walk to the mansion where Berg and Carlson were living. The meal was magnificent. At first, Eichmann and Wallenberg talked about the war in general. But then Wallenberg cleverly changed the topic. Eichmann was acutely class-conscious and uncomfortable in formal situations such as dinner parties and diplomatic receptions. But now, according to Berg, he appeared to relax, perhaps enjoying Wallenberg's company and excellent wine.[6]

After dinner, Wallenberg offered Eichmann coffee and brandy in the mansion's large sitting room. Wallenberg was careful to seat Eichmann and Krumey so that they were facing curtains that covered an east-facing window. Eichmann sat in an overstuffed armchair, brandy snifter in hand. Then Wallenberg told Carlsson to open the curtains. Carlsson did so as Wallenberg turned out the lights. A fierce Soviet barrage lit the horizon to the east with explosions. "The effect was tremendous," Carlsson recalled. "The horizon was bright red from the fire of thousands of guns as the Russians closed in on Budapest."[7]

The scene, as recalled by Berg, was cinematic indeed. The dinner guests could hear the retorts of the guns as the room lit up with each explosion and was then cast back into darkness. Wallenberg stood near the window as Eichmann sat in his armchair, quaffing the brandy. He then began to engage Eichmann in a conversation about National Socialism.

"It's not really a bona fide ideology," said Wallenberg. "It's just the political incarnation of a single basic human emotion, hate. How can it last?"

Eichmann apparently tried to defend National Socialism, spewing clichés no doubt gleaned from *Der Sturmer* and other Nazi newspapers and propaganda leaflets, with their poisonous catchphrases about the Jewish-Bolshevik menace and world Jewish conspiracy.

Lars Berg listened closely as Eichmann, the Holocaust's most notorious figure, and Wallenberg, arguably its greatest hero, then discussed the Nazis' racial theories. "Wallenberg, who on this occasion had no special wish to negotiate with Eichmann," recalled Berg, "started a discussion about Nazism and the likely outcome of the war. Fearlessly and brilliantly, he picked Nazi doctrine apart, piece by piece, and foretold the total defeat of its adherents. Eichmann could scarcely conceal his amazement that anyone should dare to attack him and criticize the Fuhrer, but he soon seemed to realize that he was getting the worst of the argument. His propaganda phrases sounded hollow compared with Raoul's intelligent reasoning."[8]

But it was also clear that Eichmann was no careerist fellow traveler, like others in the SS, who had hitched his fortunes to the Nazis for profit and power. He was fanatical in his loyalty to both Hitler and the SS, still utterly committed to carrying out his Fuhrer's avowed mission of solving the "Jewish problem" once and for all. And now he was tantalizingly close to doing just that.

Wallenberg was still at the window.

"Look how close the Bolsheviks are," Wallenberg allegedly told Eichmann. "Your war is almost over. Nazism is doomed, finished, and so are those who cling to this hatred until the very last. It's the end of the Nazis, the end of Hitler, the end of Eichmann."

"Alright, I agree with you," Eichmann admitted. "Soon, very soon, this comfortable life will end. No more airplanes bringing women and wine from France. The Russians will take my horses, my dogs, and my palace on Rose Hill. They'll probably shoot me on the spot."

There was little doubt about that.

"For me, there's no escape, no liberation," added Eichmann. "There are, however, some consolations. If I continue to eliminate our enemies until the end, it may delay our defeat—even for just a few days. And then, when I finally do walk the gallows, at least I'll know I've completed my mission."

"Why don't you call off your people?" asked Wallenberg. "Why not leave now while you still can?"

Eichmann was beginning to lose his temper. "Budapest will be held as though it were Berlin."[9] With that, Eichmann got up to leave.

"I want to thank you for an exceptionally charming and interesting evening," he said, shaking Wallenberg's hand.

Berg watched as Eichmann then lowered his voice. "Now don't think we are friends," said Eichmann. "We're not. I plan to do everything I can to keep you from saving your Jews. Your diplomatic passport won't protect you from everything. Even a neutral diplomat can meet with an accident."[10]

NINETEEN-YEAR-OLD THOMAS VERES had been working for Wallenberg since October, when the Arrow Cross had taken power. It was Per Anger who had introduced the aspiring photographer to Wallenberg, and Veres quickly had become part of Wallenberg's team of Section C workers.

Veres later recalled that on November 28, he was at Section C, taking photographs to be used on the Schutzpasses, when he was called to the telephone. "They've rounded up all the protected laborers and taken them to the Jozsefvaros freight station," someone said at the end of the line. "They're packing them into boxcars. Hurry!"

The laborers had been preparing trenches and defenses and clearing rubble. But now Eichmann had convinced the Arrow Cross government to let him send them to build defenses around Vienna instead. And Eichmann had somehow found a train to take them there. His own men would oversee the deportation this time. The tracks leading to Austria had been fixed.

Without a thought for his safety, Veres grabbed his Leica and made his way to the Jozsefvaros train station. "Everybody, especially those on the Nazis' hit list, thought lying low was the best plan," he recalled. "Keep quiet; keep out of sight. Don't get involved. Yet here I was on a raw November morning, heading for Jozsefvaros station."

Veres saw Hungarian police and Arrow Cross thugs in green shirts, wielding machine guns, surrounding the station. "Anyone in his right mind was trying to get out. Wallenberg expected me to find a way in."

Veres put his camera in his pocket. Then he approached one of the policemen. "I'm a Swedish diplomat!" said Veres, trying to sound like Wallenberg. "I must go in to meet Raoul Wallenberg!"

The policeman didn't look convinced, but he allowed Veres inside. Thousands of Jewish men were being pushed onto boxcars. Veres spotted Wallenberg in his long trench coat, wearing his fedora hat, not far from his Studebaker car and his driver, Vilmos Langfelder.

Also with Wallenberg that morning was another member of the special rescue group, the Schutzling Protokoll, that Wallenberg had recruited: twenty-year-old student Janos Beer, who had been a friend of Veres since childhood. "What Wallenberg said was gospel among us," recalled Beer. "He was a very good organizer. People believed in him because he was so successful. He was very modest. He was also very brave, there's no doubt about that. But he was not reckless. He knew exactly what the dangers were. He gave the impression to anybody who worked with him that if you were in trouble he would be there for you."[11]

Wallenberg saw Veres and walked over to him.

In a low whisper, Wallenberg told him: "Take as many pictures as you can."

It was extraordinarily risky to do so. Veres was Jewish. If he were caught taking pictures, he would be instantly bundled onto a cattle-wagon or more likely shot on the spot by some drunken Arrow Cross youth itching to try out his new tommy gun on a Christ-killer. Nevertheless, he got to work, first making sure his camera was hidden. He climbed into the Studebaker, pulled out a penknife, slit a hole in his scarf, and wrapped it around his Leica so that the hole was over the camera's lens. Trying to keep his nerve, he then got out of the Studebaker and made his way through the railway depot, his finger pressing down on the shutter release when he thought he could capture a good image.

By now, Wallenberg had opened a briefcase and pulled out his black book of life, as he called the thick ledger filled with names and photographs of protected Jews. Veres had taken many of the images.[12]

"All my people get in line here!" he cried. "All you need to do is show me your Schutzpass!"

No one dared move, so Wallenberg approached the lines of terrified Jews and chose a man at random. "You, yes, I have your name here. Where is your paper?"

The man did not have a Schutzpass. Instead, he pulled a letter from his pocket. It saved his life. "Fine," said Wallenberg. "Next!"

Wallenberg soon stood in front of one of the boxcars.

"Open it!" he snapped at an SS guard. "There may be men inside holding Swedish passes."

An SS officer was quickly on the scene.

"Anyone with a Swedish pass can come out, but if anyone tries to bluff I'll shoot him on the spot."

Men got off.

"Which of you has documents in Hungarian proving that you once held a valid Swedish pass?" asked Wallenberg.

Men began to move forward.

"Present these documents to me at once!"

Some men pulled out scraps of paper, anything with writing on it would do. One man had no paper. "Once I was in Uppsala, at the university," he told Wallenberg.

"He has no pass, no paper," said the SS officer.

"Name a street in Uppsala," Wallenberg ordered the man.

The man said something.

"That's right!" said Wallenberg. "It's obvious that this man is under Swedish protection. Next!"[13]

Speed was of the essence. Wallenberg had to save as many men as possible before the SS or Arrow Cross decided to intervene. Veres worked quickly too, and the photographs he took that day remain the only visual evidence of Wallenberg saving lives.

"Now back to Budapest, all of you!" shouted Wallenberg.

The men walked out of the station. When they were safely on their way, Veres and Wallenberg calmly got into the Studebaker. Langfelder waited at the wheel. "The danger that we'd been in didn't hit me until then," recalled Veres. "This man, a Swede, who could have waited out the war in safety, was marching into train yards and asking others to do the same!"[14]

Janos Beer was also in the car. "It occurred [to Wallenberg] that the people he rescued had not eaten all day," he recalled, "and, instead of calling it a day and going back to the Legation, he asked [Langfelder] to head for the safe house to make sure that the group of men would be met by food, a warm soup. Wallenberg had not eaten either; we brought sandwiches but Tom Veres inadvertently sat on Wallenberg's sandwiches in the car. But Wallenberg could only be concerned about the people he just rescued; a small event which, however, underlined for me this great man's humanity."[15]

According to Beer, Wallenberg saved as many as a hundred men that morning.

Later that day, Wallenberg told Langfelder to drive him across the city to the Deli station in Buda so he could say goodbye to a young woman he had come to admire very much: Baroness Kemeny, the Arrow Cross foreign minister's wife, who had lent her support that fall to his operation. For doing so, she had been denounced to Interior Minister Vajna as a foreign agent working for Wallenberg. Vajna had apparently ordered her arrest. But then the Hungarian premier, Szalasi, had told her husband, Baron Kemeny, that she could leave Budapest within twenty-four hours rather than be jailed. "I must save the life of my unborn child," she reportedly told Wallenberg before she left Hungary for good. "That's my only excuse for abandoning you."[16]

THE NEXT MORNING, November 29, 1944, Wallenberg returned to Jozsefvaros station. He had learned that the SS planned to deport another batch of protected Jewish laborers—Eichmann had somehow managed to requisition yet another freight train to take them to the border. This time, Wallenberg arrived just before the train was due to leave from Jozsefvaros station. Again, he set up his table, opened his briefcase, and began to call out names. There were the usual long lines of men waiting to be deported.

Janos Beer and Veres were once more working for Wallenberg that morning. Veres later remembered finding Wallenberg, seated at a table, reading out common Hungarian names from his ledger, his book of life. Veres started taking pictures again. But then thirty-one-year-old SS

Captain Theodor Dannecker arrived to deal with the infuriating young Swede. The curled-lipped Dannecker, a former lawyer from Munich, had resolved many difficult situations for Eichmann over the years, recently clearing out Jews from Bulgaria and persuading apparently reluctant officials in Rome to send Italian Jews to Auschwitz.

Janos Beer, who was walking alongside the wagons, telling men with Schutzpasses to form in a line before Wallenberg, saw Dannecker arrive.[17]

"All of you released by the Hungarian government, back into town! March!" ordered Wallenberg.

Dannecker drew his pistol.

"Nein!" said Dannecker, and then held up his gloved hand.[18]

Wallenberg protested. Did Dannecker want to start an international incident?

But Dannecker wasn't swayed. "He maintained that the previous day, Wallenberg had taken people under false pretenses," recalled Janos Beer. "He didn't have the right to take them now. Wallenberg had communicated with the German Embassy. He had the right, but for the SS, whatever happened in diplomacy was not very important."[19]

Beer saw Dannecker point his pistol at Wallenberg.

Dannecker said he was going to shoot. He looked like he meant it. Wallenberg turned toward Beer. "He was absolutely calm," recalled Beer. "It was time to go."[20]

Reluctantly, Wallenberg drew back from Dannecker and made his way out of the station, accompanied by Beer and Veres. All three were soon sitting in the back of Langfelder's Studebaker. As they left the station, Wallenberg looked over his shoulder, back at the train station, at Dannecker and his black-clad SS men, and managed a smile. "I don't think we'll come back here for a while."

Later that morning, Wallenberg was reportedly ushered into the office of Veensenmayer's deputy, thirty-five-year-old SS Brigadierfuhrer Theodor Horst Grell, to whom he bitterly complained about Dannecker's actions—they were an outrageous violation of his diplomatic immunity. But like Dannecker, Grell was unmoved. "My advice to you, Mr. Secretary, is to worry more about the real Swedes living in Budapest," he said. "These Jews aren't Swedes. However, if you insist on becoming involved in things that don't concern you, then I cannot, unfortunately, protect you from the consequences."

Wallenberg persisted. "Several weeks ago," he protested, "a German military truck demolished one of my official cars. Since then, other of my cars have been the victims of similar 'accidents.' Is this what you mean by 'the consequences'?"

"I suggest that you return to peaceful Sweden, Mr. Secretary. There, the military vehicles are in less of a hurry. They can take more care not to endanger pleasure trippers such as yourself. I would advise you to take my advice. Good day."[21]

WALLENBERG HAD MANAGED TO SAVE three hundred men by Veres's estimation, but in that week alone Eichmann had deported seventeen thousand in the labor brigades from the station. Most would die of starvation and disease before the war's end.

The continuing murder of Budapest's Jews and the steady escalation in atrocities finally began to unnerve and depress Wallenberg. According to several of his workers, he appeared increasingly tired and drawn, deep circles framing his sad eyes. One morning, a dispirited Wallenberg told a Swedish Red Cross worker: "Even while we speak, somewhere, someone else is being murdered by the Arrow Cross . . . Laws no longer exist here; anything can happen. Sometimes one can't get from one street to the next . . . Anyway, reality doesn't matter any longer, illusion does."[22]

It was crucial, Wallenberg realized, to exert constant pressure on the Arrow Cross, which he did almost daily through carefully worded, sometimes even obsequious letters to key officials. He also insinuated that they might require his presence as a useful witness at inevitable war crimes trials.[23] In some cases, this combination of veiled threat and polite but constant complaint was effective. But increasingly it met with indifference and annoyance. The Arrow Cross was not the Wehrmacht or even the SS, who at least feigned abiding by certain rules.

In late November, Wallenberg visited Interior Minister Vajna's office and told him that he had learned that his Arrow Cross government was planning to place all of Budapest's Jews in sealed ghettoes. This would make it far easier to kill them in a massive pogrom. "If the Jews are endangered, Hungarians all over the world will pay dearly," Wallenberg told Vajna, "particularly Hungarians sympathetic to the Arrow Cross."

Vajna was unmoved.

"But Mr. Secretary, there are no Hungarians abroad who are sympathetic to us. And as for the others, I couldn't care less what happens to them."[24]

Wallenberg also failed to win over other Arrow Cross officials who had hardened their stance toward neutrals as the Soviets neared and their Arrow Cross government appeared further than ever from official recognition by Sweden, Switzerland, and others. The dictates of international law were not for Szalasi and his men. Wallenberg and his fellow diplomats, such as Lutz, were now seen as nothing much more than Jew-lovers meddling in Hungary's internal affairs.

One morning, Foreign Minister Baron Kemeny paid a visit to Wallenberg's offices. He told Wallenberg that he was giving him an ultimatum; unless the Arrow Cross were recognized by Stockholm within three days, all protected Jews would be handed over to Vajna for immediate deportation.

Wallenberg did his best to buy more time, telling Kemeny that three days was not long enough. Reports from the Swedish Legation to Stockholm about Kemeny's government were not too complimentary, he explained. If Kemeny were to make a few noteworthy humanitarian gestures, Wallenberg could guarantee that the reports would soon be more sympathetic. But it would take more than three days.

It seemed that soon all of Budapest's Jews would be deported en masse as Kemeny, Vajna, and others in the Arrow Cross government wanted. But then Reichsfuhrer Heinrich Himmler, of all people, came to Wallenberg's aid, apparently ordering an end to mass deportations to the death camps. Budapest's Jews would have to stay where they were: either in two ghettoes, where conditions were rapidly deteriorating, or in the many protected houses run by the Swedes and the Swiss.

LATE THAT NOVEMBER, Himmler summoned Eichmann to his mobile headquarters, a heavily guarded train stationed in the Black Forest near Triberg. Thirty-six-year-old SS Colonel Kurt Becher, Himmler's so-called economic specialist in Hungary, was present at the ensuing meeting. Becher had overseen the highly successful pillaging and appropriation of Jewish wealth and industries earlier that year in Hungary, mostly through extortion. He had also met with Wallenberg at least six times, though there is no known record of what they had discussed. According to one source, Becher had offered to "provide his protection and exit visas for four hundred Jews with Swedish passports in exchange for only 400,000 Swiss francs."[25] But Wallenberg had been unable to negotiate because his funds could not be used for paying ransoms.[26]

Suave and cunning, Becher later testified, while fearing for his life, that he had told Himmler that Eichmann had repeatedly tried to get around his orders in Budapest, hence the summons to Triberg. The death marches were a case in point—Himmler had ordered an end to them but Eichmann had continued to send mostly women and old people—few able-bodied male Jews were left in Budapest—to the Austrian border. "I had told Himmler that Eichmann simply did not take his orders seriously and would only carry them out if they were expressly confirmed by SS Major General [Heinrich] Muller," Becher recalled.

The meeting between Himmler, Eichmann, and Becher must have been a tense affair. Eichmann was far too dogmatic and unsophisticated in his methods compared to cool-headed and calculating operators such as Becher. The lower-middle-class Austrian, badly educated, was politically tone deaf, unable to see like Becher how profit-taking and escaping prosecution for war crimes were all that counted now as Germany headed toward apocalyptic defeat. Notably, unlike Becher, Eichmann had made no effort to secure the support of Jews who could later vouch for him and save his neck.

"Himmler talked to Eichmann [in a manner] I would call both kindly and angrily," recalled Becher. "I remember one thing that Himmler said to Eichmann in this connection: He shouted at him something like, 'If until now you have exterminated Jews, from now on, if I order you, as I do now, you must be a fosterer of Jews. I would remind you that in 1933, it was I who set up the Head Office for Reich Security, and not Grup-penfuhrer Muller or yourself, and that I am in command. If you are not able to do that, you must tell me so!"[27]

According to Becher, Eichmann was soon dismissed. But Himmler could not have been too upset with his protégé—he would award Eich-mann the Cross of War Merits, First Class, with Swords. At last, the "Master" would be recognized for his work. It would be his only reward for carrying out history's greatest genocide.

13

December 1944

T HEN WINTER DESCENDED. Snow fell from the ash-gray skies, dusting the ice floes on the Danube, the domes of the central synagogue, and the deserted streets and avenues. With each dawn, the sound of Soviet guns seemed to get louder and piles of Jewish bodies yet higher, like the mounds of garbage the drunken Arrow Cross no longer collected.

One night in early December 1944, as the snow fell, Tom Veres was working late at Wallenberg's Section C offices on Ulloi Street, a stone's throw from the central synagogue, now used as a horse stable by the Arrow Cross. Suddenly, a gang of Arrow Cross youths burst into the offices. The youths arrested Veres and everyone working alongside him.

Veres was terrified. He was carrying false papers stating that he worked for the Red Cross, and if they were discovered he was sure he would be shot on the spot. The green-uniformed Arrow Cross screamed and shouted at Veres and Wallenberg's other aides and workers. They were then marched toward Arrow Cross headquarters several blocks away. Veres ripped his false papers into small pieces and ate them as he trudged through the snow. When he arrived at the headquarters and was bustled inside, he heard the Arrow Cross start to shout and curse each other. They wanted to place Veres and the others in a cellar, but there was not enough room for them all to fit. "Put them on top of each other," one of the Arrow Cross thugs shouted. "They're gonna die anyway."[1]

Veres and the others were taken instead to another building, where they were made to stand against a wall and told they would soon be taken to the Danube to be shot. A man beside Veres asked: "Do you know which way's the Danube?"

"Once the shooting starts," replied Veres, "you'll know we'll be there."[2]

At that point, they heard a familiar voice.

"These are my people," Wallenberg shouted. "You cannot touch them." There was a heated discussion, but Wallenberg managed to get his way. Soon, Veres and Wallenberg's other people were hurrying back to his offices on Ulloi Street. Wallenberg had saved Veres and several dozen other Jews' lives. But how much longer would their luck hold?

By December 9, several weeks after Stalin had demanded the immediate seizure of Budapest, the Russian army's offensive had finally reached the Danube at Vac, a few miles north of the city, and the siege of Budapest began. Just the previous day, a courier had left for Sweden carrying Raoul's most recent dispatch for the Foreign Office. Wallenberg's last known report to Sweden confirmed that "as far as can be ascertained, only 10 Jews with Swedish safe conducts have up to now been shot in and around Budapest." It was a staggeringly low number given the circumstances.[3]

The courier also carried Raoul's last known letter to his mother, Maj:

Dearest Mother,
I don't know how to atone for my silence, and yet again today all you will receive from me are a few hurried lines via the diplomatic pouch. The situation here is hectic, fraught with danger, and I am terribly snowed under with work . . . Night and day we hear the thunder of the approaching Russian guns. Since Szalasi came to power, diplomatic activity has been very lively. I myself am almost the sole representative of our embassy in all government departments. So far I have been approximately ten times to the Ministry of Foreign Affairs, have seen the deputy premier twice, the minister of the interior twice, the minister of supply . . . I was

on pretty close terms with the wife of the foreign minister. Regrettably, she has now left for Meran [sic]. There is an acute lack of food supplies in Budapest, but we managed to stockpile a fair amount in advance. I have the feeling that after the [Russian] occupation, it will be difficult to get home, and I assume that I will reach Stockholm only around Easter. But all that lies in the future. So far, nobody knows what the occupation will be like. In any event, I shall try to get home as soon as possible. I had firmly believed I would spend Christmas with you. Now I am compelled to send you my Christmas greetings and New Year wishes by this means. I hope that the longed for peace is not too distant.[4]

At the end of the letter, Wallenberg scribbled: "Love to Nina and her little one."[5]

WALLENBERG DID NOT TELL his mother that his concerns were now overwhelming. Life was increasingly precarious for his staff of four hundred or so employees, almost all Jews who lived with their families in ten buildings that belonged to the Embassy and were thereby supposedly protected. With foresight, Wallenberg had arranged for them to be inoculated against epidemics such as typhoid and cholera, which would soon sweep through the city as the Soviet siege grew ever more ferocious. But the fear that they might all be killed, at any moment, grew with each new night and day.

Neutral diplomats were also now targets. The Swiss diplomat, Carl Lutz, was arrested and beaten. The Arrow Cross also broke into Swedish Embassy buildings and seized Lars Berg and others, who were lucky to either escape or be later released after much negotiation. "Our greatest worry was Wallenberg's safety," recalled Per Anger, who now carried a gun. "The Arrow Cross men [such as Kurt Rettman] hated him openly and intensely. He learned several times that they intended to murder him."[6]

If the Arrow Cross didn't kill the neutral diplomats, Russian bombs and shells might. Veesenmayer, Hitler's representative in Hungary, had already made the Germans' intention clear, declaring that Budapest could be "de-stroyed ten times, so long as Vienna could thereby be defended."[7] 60,000 German and Hungarian defenders would fight to the bitter end against more than 180,000 Soviet and Romanian troops.[8] The scene was set for an epic battle that would eventually rival that of the siege of Stalingrad. 800,000 people, including at least 120,000 Jews, were now trapped in Budapest. They would all end up victims or traumatized survivors.

EICHMANN HAD VOWED TO STAY in Budapest until the last German died defending the city. But as the Soviets encircled the city, he and his killing squads prepared to flee. During his last hours in Budapest, he al-legedly called senior Arrow Cross figures to a meeting and apologized to them for not liquidating all Hungary's Jews. Hungary had been the only country in Europe where he had not succeeded in his goals. But time had run out for him. Yet they still had the chance to finish what he had begun. If they wanted to be effective, they should ignore the demands of the neutral diplomats.

The war could still be won, stressed Eichmann. Hitler had secret weapons that would soon be unleashed, and then, when the Soviets had been defeated, Eichmann would return to Budapest.[9]

By December 22, the Soviets were almost in Buda itself. Katushka rockets lit the sky above the Hotel Majestic with streaks of fire and ex-plosions. The shellfire was continuous. Searchlights crisscrossed the city. That night, Eichmann got into the back of his black Mercedes and told his driver to take him across the Danube, and into Pest. He had one more piece of unfinished business with the city's Jewish Council.

Earlier that evening, one of Eichmann's assistants had been ordered to make contact with the Council, which had its headquarters in the Gen-eral Ghetto, where just 243 buildings housed over seventy-five thousand people—so many that they were forced to sleep on staircases, living four-teen to a room, if they could find one.

An SS officer had told a porter called Jakob Takacs to make sure the Jewish Council gathered at nine o'clock. Eichmann would arrive at that time to meet with them. Sure enough, at 9 p.m., the SS arrived in three staff cars and pulled up outside the Jewish Council headquarters on Sip Street. Eichmann and two aides stepped out of a car. Guarded by an SS man with a submachine gun, Eichmann strode toward the porter's lodge.

Takacs heard Eichmann knock.

"Well, where are they?" asked Eichmann.

Takacs was terrified. Eichmann looked drunk—his eyes were bloodshot.

"The Jewish Council members," Eichmann said. "Where are they?"

"I was told to get them here for nine o'clock in the morning," lied Takacs.

Eichmann raged that a call had been made, and it had been agreed that they would be there at nine o'clock. Takacs said he thought he had meant nine in the morning. Hearing the commotion, Takacs's sister arrived just in time to see Eichmann pull out his revolver. He said he would shoot brother and sister if they did not gather the Jewish Council members straight away. Takacs said this was impossible because the members were spread out in various houses. It would take all night to get them together. One of Eichmann's aides then pistol-whipped Takacs until he collapsed, blood from facial wounds running across the floor.

Eichmann then turned to Takacs's sister.

"Tell your brother when he comes round," said Eichmann, "that if the entire council is not here at nine in the morning, lined up for inspection, I will have both of you shot."[10]

The next morning, fearing for their lives, the Jewish Council assembled, along with a heavily bandaged Takacs and his sister, and waited nervously for a vengeful Eichmann to reappear. The council's diary entry for that day, December 23, 1944, reads: "An hour or two, full of anxiety, passed, and at last it was learned that the Eichmann detachment had left Budapest most urgently during the night."[11]

EICHMANN HAD FLED, managing to escape through the last gap in the front lines.[12] It was not a moment too soon for the last remaining Jews in the city. But now the Germans were the least of their worries. Knowing that time was fast running out for their regime, the uncontrolled Arrow

Cross street gangs turned their rage on the defenseless, captive Jews. In a city renowned for its subtle charms and rich culture, barbarism became the norm and evil was personified. Just as there had been nothing banal about the mass murders by Eichmann and his men, now there was very little that was mundane about Budapest's most psychopathic fascists. According to Hungarian historian Christian Ungvary: "Practically all party activists were obliged to take part in tortures and executions, which served as a so-called loyalty test."[13]

While Verdi's *Aida* played to packed audiences at the grand Opera House in the heart of the city, grotesque characters roamed from the rubble-strewn streets, where posters warned that anyone caught helping Jews would be shot on the spot, to the fetid courtyards, where horse carcasses lay rotting, to the Danube embankments, where hundreds of Jews were slaughtered at dawn, their bodies dumped into the river to be washed away into oblivion. Each day now, between fifty and sixty bodies of Jews who had been shot through the base of the skull—execution-style—were brought to a central hospital.[14] One twenty-three-year-old Hungarian woman, Wilmos Salzer, had a penchant for burning naked Jewish women with candles. Another Hungarian sociopath, Kurt Rettman, delighted in shooting Jews on sight. "It's a pity to go through all the bother of deportations and closing the Jews into ghettos," Rettman had said in November. "If we just shoot every Jew, the problem is solved."[15]

Perhaps the most notorious figure was Father Andreas Kun, a Minorite monk who wore a black cassock and carried a giant crucifix and snub-nosed revolver. By his own admission, Kun personally killed more than five hundred Jews that winter. He would also order his mostly teenaged followers to line up Jews on the banks of the Danube, and then, as they took aim, he would cry out: "In the holy name of Jesus, fire!"

All that the Jews who Wallenberg had saved could do was hope and pray. At his main office in Ulloi Street, almost two hundred protected Jews waited for the Russians, desperately willing them to arrive before the Arrow Cross decided to raid the protected building and kill them all. Among those living in the cramped conditions, squeezing into the basement shelter each night, were Marianne Lowy and her husband, Pista; Janos Beer and several of his fellow Schutzling Protokoll volunteers; and Erwin Koranyi's sister, Marta.

The question on everyone's mind on Christmas Day of 1944 was not if but when the Arrow Cross would try to break into safe houses. On Christmas Eve, Arrow Cross gunmen had entered a Red Cross children's home and shot children, some of them toddlers, in an act of unimaginable cruelty that stunned even Wallenberg and his fellow rescuers. Christmas had only made the Arrow Cross more determined, it appeared, to murder the surviving Jews in Budapest who were most vulnerable.

Twenty-year-old Janos Beer was heartened to see that the German Wehrmacht still respected Swedish neutrality, but he was under no such illusions about the Arrow Cross. "A German Wehrmacht unit came to Ulloi Street and put a machine gun on the balcony," he recalled. "They were told that this was a Swedish Embassy, and they took the machine gun down and walked out. Very soon, several of them were found dead. But it still showed that some Germans would honor international law."[16] The Germans knew that there had to be some rules or chaos and anarchy would make the defense of Budapest all the harder. But the Arrow Cross didn't appear to care.

At 1 Jokai Street, where Erwin and Alice Koranyi had taken sanctuary, the fear was the same: that drunken gangs of teenage killers would force their way into the building and begin firing. The street fighting outside was now so intense that only those who craved nicotine ventured out of the fetid basement, where smoking was not allowed. "The Russians closed the ring around Budapest on Christmas Day," recalled Erwin. "We could hear the sound of artillery, a constant rumbling. Then came an attempt at a truce. The Russians sent four men with a white flag, asking for the German surrender [the terms were excellent]. There was no point carrying on the killing. The answer from the Arrow Cross and the SS was to shoot all four of them. Not long after, there was total silence, not one shot was fired. The elite troops were withdrawn, and the Russians sent in their garbage. It came from a huge criminal jail. Murderers, thieves— they volunteered for frontline duty. The deal was that they would be in the front line until the end of the war, but whoever survived would be a free man."

The hellish noise of war began again. "There was an enormous shelling and then airplanes strafed the streets at low level, dropping stick bombs chained together." Now the fighting was not house to house but room to room, with Germans on one floor, Russians on another, and so on through building after building. It could take two days to clear a house.

Movement around Pest was extremely dangerous, especially for Jews, even if they had valid papers. The Arrow Cross no longer accepted any form of identification papers, maintaining that they were all forged, and had come up with a brutally simple method of checking to see if young men like Erwin were Jews.

"Pull down your zipper and show your cock," they ordered.

If a man or boy was circumcised, recalled Erwin, "that was it . . . brrrrppppp . . . You were finished right there and then, no questions asked."[17]

14

The Inferno

THE RIVER FLOWED, gray and imperious, through the increasingly shell-shattered city that Europeans had once called the Queen of the Danube. Along the banks of the Danube, ice formed, blood-stained in places from the Jews who had been shot and thrown into the river.

On January 6, 1945, from the top of Castle Hill in Buda, photographer Tom Veres and Wallenberg watched the Soviet artillery fire light up the horizon above the Danube. With them were three heavily armed Budapest policemen, who had been assigned to them for their protection.

"How long do you think it will be now?" asked Wallenberg.

Veres wasn't sure, but he knew it could be a matter of only days, not weeks, before the Soviets arrived. He would later remember that Wallenberg looked exhausted, his face pale and haggard. He was sleeping very little.

Mortars and shrapnel fell close by. They decided to return to their car in case they were caught in the open. Langfelder pulled away. In the backseat, Wallenberg sat beside Veres, squeezed between the policemen, whose guns poked out the window.

"This reminds me of the time I was kidnapped by bandits in the States," Wallenberg told Veres. "I had been hitchhiking from Chicago back to school in Ann Arbor, and these four guys picked me up, drove me into the forest, and pulled guns. They robbed me of about fifteen dollars."

Wallenberg smiled.

"Although my life was in less danger then," he added.[1]

A few days later, Veres was called to the phone at the Swedish Legation offices on Ulloi Street. A man who managed the Gerbeau Palace,
the apartment building where Veres's parents lived, was on the line. He
told Veres that his parents had been seized by the Arrow Cross. Veres
begged the man to tell him precisely what had happened to his parents,
but the man could not. Thankfully, Veres knew where Wallenberg was
now in hiding—in a vault at the Hazai Bank in Pest. It took him two days
to cross Pest, through the ruined streets, and get to the bank on Harmincad Street, where he found Wallenberg.

Wallenberg sympathized but said there was nothing he could now do.
It was too late. It would be six months before Veres discovered what had
happened to his parents. Like thousands of others that winter, they had
been shot and their bodies dumped into the swirling Danube.[2] Veres
himself would survive that winter and eventually establish himself as a
successful commercial photographer in New York after the war.

Fighting back his dismay at the slaughter of more and more of the
Jews he had saved and protected, Wallenberg continued to work tire-
lessly in the first days of 1945, snatching only a few hours' sleep each
night, rolled up in his sleeping bag on the floor of a bank vault, in a basement of some protected house, or in some other hideaway that only
Langfelder and Wallenberg's closest aides knew about.

Knowing that many Arrow Cross commanders had fled Budapest
along with Eichmann, Wallenberg reportedly ventured one morning into
the Arrow Cross headquarters in Budapest's central town hall. He took a
translator, Laszlo Hajmal, with him, having learned that the remaining
Arrow Cross members had seized Dr. Peter Sugar, one of his most effective aides in Section C. Langfelder drove Wallenberg and Hajmal to the
building, where Wallenberg came across Gyula Sedey, the city's chief of
police, taking refuge in the hall's air-raid shelter.

Wallenberg took the opportunity to confront Chief Constable Sedey
about the lack of food supplies to the Jews in the central ghetto, where
acute starvation was now widespread.[3]

Sedey had recently declared that the Jews there were to receive rations of just nine hundred calories a day. And even this small amount was usually stolen by the Arrow Cross.

Wallenberg angrily accused Sedey of sentencing to death the Jews of the central ghetto. They had barely enough food to last a day. If Sedey refused to supply them, they would die. According to Hajmal, who took notes as Wallenberg spoke, Sedey tried to defend his actions, saying he was unable "to allocate more food to *any* of Budapest's inhabitants."

"The other people in Budapest are not in the same position as the Jews!" shouted Wallenberg. "You have a special obligation to the Jews because you've imprisoned them in a ghetto. Jailors have a moral responsibility to feed their prisoners. I demand that you tell me now exactly how you propose to supply food to the ghetto."

Sedey was taken aback. He apparently stuttered an incomprehensible answer. Wallenberg had Sedey on the defensive, so he pushed one of Sedey's aides out of a chair and began to type an order on Sedey's official stationery. He then read out what he had typed to Sedey. It was an order from Sedey commanding the rationing board to provide adequate food to the ghetto. If anyone died of starvation in the ghetto, the rationing board would be to blame. Wallenberg ordered Sedey to sign it and then grabbed the paper.

"As soon as I leave here, I plan to go to Arrow Cross military headquarters at Varoshaz Street to inquire about [Sugar]. If I don't return here afterward, you'll know that they've taken me prisoner as well."[4]

"But how could you possibly think that they'd harm you, a neutral diplomat?"

"Arrow Cross men struck [Carl Lutz,] the Swiss charge d'affaires," replied Wallenberg. "Now you know where I'm going, and if I don't return, my government will hold you responsible."[5]

Wallenberg soon arrived at the Varoshaz Street headquarters. Arrow Cross guards stopped him. He showed his papers but they were not impressed. "You'll have to show us a written authorization from [Imre] Nidosi [the Arrow Cross commandant] if you want to leave the building alive," he was warned. Wallenberg and Hajmal headed to the basement anyway. They heard screams. Arrow Cross teenagers were torturing Jews in nearby cellars. The torture had started in the building's laundry, but its drain had become blocked with clotted blood.[6]

Wallenberg searched in vain for Nidosi and then quickly left with Hajmal, fearing that they would be killed if they stayed any longer in the bloodstained basement, where the continuous torture, rape, and disfigurement were harrowing evidence of the limits of his power to intervene.

Wallenberg had not found Sugar, and he felt the failure acutely.

"Everything was in vain," he reportedly told Hajmal. "I've failed, and I'm afraid we'll never see him again."[7]

Wallenberg was right. Sugar was one of several of Wallenberg's aides who would be seized in the coming weeks by the Arrow Cross and, in all likelihood, tortured in the Varoshaz cellars and then murdered, their corpses thrown into the Danube so they would disappear without a trace.

There was no need for crematoria in Budapest.

"YOU SHOULD DISAPPEAR AS SOON AS POSSIBLE."

This was the unequivocal warning given by Arrow Cross official Pal Szalai to Wallenberg on January 7, 1945. In recent weeks, Szalai had become an important source of information for Wallenberg. The Arrow Cross's liaison with the city police, Szalai now met with Wallenberg almost daily to provide warnings and briefings on what the Arrow Cross planned next. Uniquely, it seemed, he was no anti-Semite and had become disillusioned with the Arrow Cross leaders, most of whom had fled Budapest and set up camp far from the Soviets' guns.

"The Arrow Cross leaders who might have kept order have fled or gone underground," explained Szalai. "The worst elements have taken over, and Vajna is under their influence. They've also taken over the Foreign Ministry. If you go there to make diplomatic protests, you may never come out alive. You can also anticipate that the Arrow Cross will now attack individual members of the Swedish Legation; they'll send even more violent search parties to the Swedish houses."[8]

Wallenberg's greatest fear now was not for his own safety but that his work could be undone overnight in some savage pogrom. The Germans might repeat what they had done in Warsaw, destroying the ghetto and tens of thousands of lives. When Wallenberg learned from Szalai that this indeed seemed imminent, he acted quickly, making sure the Germans knew exactly what would happen if they attempted such an atrocity.

Pal Szalai later claimed, while on trial for his life, that he passed on a note from Wallenberg to German General August Schmidhuber, now in command of German forces in Budapest. The note promised that Schmidhuber would be held personally responsible for any massacre and hanged as a war criminal when the war was over.

Szalai gave the following testimony at a postwar trial of Arrow Cross murderers:

> Two days before the liberation of the ghetto, late one afternoon, a police officer came hurrying into my office in the town hall and told me that five hundred German soldiers and twenty-five Arrow Cross men had assembled in the Hotel Royal building. Together with another two hundred policemen, they intended to commit mass murder of all the inhabitants [of the ghetto] with machine guns that night . . . At the town hall air-raid shelter there was an SS general, commander of the Feldherrnhalle division. His name was Schmidhuber. I immediately asked for an audience with him. I warned him: "According to Wallenberg's statement, unless he prevents this vile act, he will be held responsible and will be held accountable not as a soldier but as a murderer."[9]

Wallenberg's warning may have influenced Schmidhuber's decision to forbid the liquidation of the ghetto. In Szalai's case, his cooperation with Wallenberg undoubtedly saved his neck: He was the only Arrow Cross' senior official who was set free, in 1946, in recognition of his work with Wallenberg. His fascist colleagues were hanged in public before massive crowds.

THE JEWISH CENTRAL HOSPITAL, where Erwin and Alice Koranyi worked, was by January 7 overflowing with the sick, dying, and severely wounded, some of whom had been shot and then miraculously fished out of the Danube by Wallenberg's volunteers. The fact that some Jews survived the shootings along the Danube irked the Arrow Cross, one of whose officers remarked: "The trouble is not that this was done but that some were left alive, because so long as they aren't completely exterminated, they'll all turn into vindictive swine."[10]

In the maternity ward of one hospital, motherless babies began to starve to death. According to one account: "In despair, the nurses clutched the babies to their breasts so they might enjoy the comfort of a warm human body before fading away. After a while, the nurses found themselves producing milk, and the babies were saved from starving to death."[11]

The streets were now strewn with stiff corpses, turning Pest into a veritable charnel house. So many dead Jews were dumped on benches in the once beautiful Varosliget Park that it took several days to remove them.[12] All the morgues in the city were full, so hundreds of bodies were soon stacked up like cordwood in the courtyard of the Central Synagogue.[13]

ERWIN KORANYI NOW SLEPT EACH NIGHT facing the door so that he could respond more quickly if the Arrow Cross stormed the protected building where he and Alice were now living, at 1 Jokai Street. It was in the early hours of Friday, January 7, when they were both suddenly woken by shouting and the sound of gunshots. An Arrow Cross gang was threatening to throw a hand grenade at the closed front door of No. 1 Jokai Street. A terrified man opened the door, and the thugs ran into the building. Within minutes, they disarmed the police, who had been ordered to defend the building in case of just such an attack. The Arrow Cross then ordered everyone into a courtyard "within three minutes." They shot a few people who could not move fast enough, including a man in a wheelchair. Then they began a systematic search of the building.[14]

Erwin's sister and mother were able to sneak away and hide in a cabinet in an office. There they prayed in the darkness. Erwin was still in a fourth-floor apartment with Alice, desperately looking for some hiding place, when the Arrow Cross began to clear the building floor by floor, shooting anyone they found. He and Alice crawled out a bathroom window that led to an outside light shaft. A thin metal crossbar served as their only foothold above a hundred-foot drop.

Erwin would vividly recall, with the precision of a doctor, what happened next, during perhaps the most intense hours of an extraordinarily dramatic life: "We heard yelling and occasional revolver shots. Our hands were numb from the strain and the January cold as we clung to the edge of the windowsill with white knuckles. Our hands froze, but sweat was running down our backs and our mouths were parched. We could hear each other's heartbeats in that undertow of anxiety. Who was the one just killed? . . . The palpitation became the marker of time."[15]

The hours crawled by, as if time had slowed down just to taunt them. Still they clung to life. Erwin needed to wipe his nose but could not. His muscles ached, sinews stretched taut. They tried not to think of the dark drop below them. "Good that I used to be a gymnast," Erwin told himself. But he had only so much strength, and he had to give more and more of it to support Alice. Small pieces of cement began to crumble from the edge of the metal foothold, plunging down. How much longer could it hold? Then Erwin realized that the Arrow Cross had departed— the building was silent.

Alice and Erwin crawled back inside the protected house. To their amazement and profound relief, they found Erwin's father, who had been hiding in a folded bed. Then they discovered Erwin's mother and his sister, Marta.[16] In all, 20 people had succeeded in hiding in the building. The rest, a total of 266, had been taken away. Most would be killed. "Marta's fiancée was among those seized," recalled Erwin. "He was taken to the Danube to be shot. But at the last minute, one of the Arrow Cross asked for strong men to chop wood. One of the strong men chosen was Marta's fiancée."[17] Instead of chopping wood, he was told to pick up the dead Jewish bodies all around him and throw them into the Danube. But at least he had been spared.

That night, Alice and Erwin found shelter in an empty apartment in the neighborhood. The next morning, they crossed the city to Wallenberg's offices on Ulloi Street. It was a much larger building than 1 Jokai Street and had several air-raid shelters below it. Erwin's parents and his sister hid in one of them. In another, Alice and Erwin huddled together on a straw mattress. They had not eaten but were so physically and emotionally drained that they quickly fell asleep.

At 7 that evening, loud shouting and screams again awakened them. Arrow Cross soldiers were flooding the building and were soon standing in the air-raid shelter where Alice and Erwin had taken refuge. The soldiers ordered the 150-odd people in the shelter to line up. Everyone was searched, and many were kicked and hit with guns. Then they were all ordered to march outside with their hands above their heads. "They told the Jews not to bother about taking any personal belongings with them," recalled one of Wallenberg's staff, Tibor Vayda, who managed to hide. "They wouldn't need anything where they were going. The Arrow Cross claimed that the air-raid shelter was not part of the embassy, and that they could do with the Jews in the shelter as they pleased."[18]

On the fourth floor, Marianne Lowy watched in horror. She had asked her husband, Pista, to accompany her to obtain flu vaccine from a doctor who worked in deplorable conditions in the bombed-out upper stories of the building. But Pista had been distracted, staring into a shard of a broken mirror as he tried to shave.

A few feet from Marianne was a brilliant violinist called Victor Aitay. "We rushed to the window," recalled Marianne. "A long line of people was being marched out from the basement." Among them were Marianne's husband, Pista Reiss, and Alice and Erwin Koranyi. "I was certain that I'd seen the last of my husband," added Marianne. "Whenever the Arrow Cross got hold of Jews, they simply marched them off to the banks of the Danube and shot them into the river."[19]

The winter night was bitterly cold. Soon, Alice and Erwin and the others found themselves at the entrance to the Maria Teresa barracks. They were herded down narrow wooden stairs to a basement.[20] A teenaged, red-haired Arrow Cross soldier was sleeping on the floor, a submachine gun on his chest. The youth woke up.

"Take them to the Danube," he murmured to other Arrow Cross youths, and then fell back to sleep.

Alice and Erwin and the others were soon out on the street, marching again with hands above their heads, toward the local Arrow Cross headquarters, at 41 Ferenz Ring. On its first floor, they were pushed against a wall and their coats taken away. "We stood in our shirtsleeves," recalled Erwin. "We knew that eventually we would have to shed the rest of our clothing, all but the underwear. Soon, but not yet. Questions were being asked by one of the Arrow Cross soldiers, who was seated behind a small table. A search for more valuables, and more abuse."[21]

Erwin was now close to collapsing from exhaustion. He stared at Alice. She, too, looked like she was "a hundred years old." Fatigue had left deep lines on her face; her thin, pointed nose was now prominent. "A narrow, barely blue blood vessel arched up under her pale skin on the side of her neck, and where her jawbone protruded, a fine but visibly rapid, fluttering pulse betrayed her frightful expectation at parting so abruptly from her young life."[22]

Alice turned to face Erwin.

He would never be able to forget what she said next.

"I'm pregnant."[23]

Erwin held her close.[24]

Then they were on the move again.

The Arrow Cross told them they were going to shoot them all and dump their bodies in the Danube.

MEANWHILE, BACK ON the fourth floor of Ulloi Street, Victor Aitay, who operated the telephone switchboard, called a secret number and managed to get a message to someone working on Wallenberg's staff at Section C.

IN THE BREAST POCKET of Erwin Koranyi's jacket was half a cigarette. But the jacket had been taken away. It was all he could think about as he faced the Arrow Cross executioners.

Mortars landed in nearby streets.

Erwin wanted it all to end.

What if I jump into the Danube before the Arrow Cross opens fire? Would I stand a chance? Maybe it's better to get it over with . . .

Erwin was "impatient" to die.[25]

Alice then saw a large American car pull up nearby. A man in a dark-blue suit, wearing a fedora, stepped out of the car. He was holding up a megaphone.

Alice stared at Wallenberg. He was unarmed, shouting that he wanted his Jews back. They did not belong to the Arrow Cross. They were his. "It was extraordinary because everybody could kill him," Alice recalled. "Why not kill him? Killing was everywhere."

It was around 2 a.m. as Alice and the others watched, barely able to believe what they were seeing.

"These are Swedish citizens! Release them immediately and return their belongings to them!"

To Alice, it seemed as if God had answered her prayers. "For an instant," she recalled, "I thought: 'God has come to save us.' To our astonishment, the executioners obeyed Wallenberg. He seemed very tall indeed—and strong. He radiated power and dignity. There was truly a kind of divine aura about him on that night."[26]

Erwin saw several policemen, who were clearly working for Wallenberg. "The policemen were talking to the Arrow Cross commander. What was happening? One of the high-ranking police officers was Pal Szalai, with whom Wallenberg used to deal."[27] The police were armed. They began to take guns from the Arrow Cross youths. Among the policemen was a man in a leather coat, Karoly Szabo, whom Erwin recognized. Then some of the policemen told Alice and Erwin and the others to form a line and walk back to the Ulloi Street building.

More than two hours had passed since Marianne Lowy had seen her husband and the others marched away. She was still on the fourth floor when she looked through the window and saw, to her amazement, a line of people trudging back under the protection of armed Hungarian police. Snow drifted down. She looked among the gray-faced survivors. There, unbelievably, was Pista. "If that was not a miracle, I don't know what is," she would later recall. She rushed down to greet him, overwhelmed by joy and relief. "It was like getting life back."[28]

Meanwhile, Erwin Koranyi's sister, Marta, spotted Erwin and Alice among the returning Jews. She cried as she kissed her brother and Alice.

All the returnees were given some bread.

Someone struck a match and the stump of a cigarette was lit. Erwin took it, filled his lungs with nicotine, and exhaled.

It was hard to believe, but he was still alive.

ANARCHY AND CHAOS ruled the streets. But Wallenberg's presence still counted.[29] Each evening, even though he was effectively on the run, Wallenberg would visit his protected houses and check on those he had saved. Thirteen-year-old Vera Herman was still hiding in the cellar of one of the protected houses with her parents, Emil and Margit. Several times, she saw Wallenberg arrive late at night and spend a few minutes playing with the young children in the cellar. "I think it was a relief from all the stresses and the tensions," she recalled. "He loved children. His first goal was to save children."

Vera could feel little except a constant aching hunger and a lingering fear. "There is a numbness that takes over. We went on day after day until we became a well-oiled machine, but numb. Then to see Wallenberg—it gave me an absolutely indescribable feeling of hope and of wonder. It was remarkable to see someone who thought your life was worth saving."[30]

Wallenberg also found time each night to check in on his workers in Section C. The section had gone underground, moving from one building to the next, often a few hours ahead of Arrow Cross thugs intent on stopping the manufacture of Swedish protective passes. Because his staff might be seized at any moment, Wallenberg had insisted that they all wear sturdy boots, which were donated by a shoemaker, Miksa Boschan, who was later murdered by the Arrow Cross. "I witnessed the death marches to Hegyeshalom," Wallenberg explained to his staff. "I saw how, after a few kilometers of marching, the shoes of men and women, which were not suitable for long marches, fell apart and thus the fate of the deportees was sealed. We never know whether there will be a repetition of these marches; everybody should be prepared for it."[31]

One night, recalled twenty-four-year-old Agnes Adachi, who worked for Section C, she and her fellow Jews were based in a grand villa in

Buda when Wallenberg showed up. To Adachi's shock, Wallenberg announced that they were next to a building occupied by the SS.

"No talking," he said, "and, please, write lightly."

Adachi and the others would create the passes and then divide them among themselves and deliver them to Jews in hiding throughout the city. These deliveries were very risky: They would be shot on the spot if caught. But as Adachi recalled, "It was impossible for us to be afraid with Wallenberg as our leader because we thought that if he could take such risks, then so could we. His calm relaxed us, and I can remember thinking, 'Boy! It would be easy to fall in love with a man like this.'"[32]

That night, Adachi gathered the passes, five hundred of them, and wished everyone in the room a good evening. Then she set out for Pest, on the other side of the Danube. All she could hear, she later recalled, was the sound of her "footsteps in the crisp snow." She managed to deliver the passes, which included some for several of her friends.

On another night, remembered Adachi, she was present when Wallenberg answered an urgent phone call and was told that eight Arrow Cross thugs had raided a house on Katona Street full of his protected Jews, most of them women and children, including several infants.[33] Wallenberg immediately contacted the Foreign Ministry of the Arrow Cross.

"How can you do this?" he protested. "This house is protected by the government—your government!"

He was told that his "Swedes" would be returned, but he knew this was probably a delaying tactic and rushed with Thomas Veres and others to the house.

The entrance was open.

Behind the windows and iron gates of protected houses nearby, Jews looked on, faces etched with fear—they had "felt the proximity of death only a very short time before."

Wallenberg ran inside only to find an Arrow Cross officer searching for anyone who might have tried to hide. He told Veres to ask the officer where the protected Jews in the house had gone.

"In the Danube," said the officer.

"Why?" shouted Wallenberg.

"They were dirty Jews."[34]

There was nothing more to be done. Wallenberg had not made it in time.[35]

Worse was to come. The next raid was on a Swedish-protected orphanage, which Wallenberg visited most days. Agnes Adachi recalled that he arrived there and found that all but one of the children had been taken away and killed. "This was the first time we saw Raoul really desperate," she remembered. "He went down on his knees and cried. After a long while, he got to his feet and said that he would fight on."[36]

A few nights later, recalled Adachi, Wallenberg arrived at the Section C offices and asked for volunteers. He had learnt that the Arrow Cross was executing Jews on the banks of the Danube.

"How many of you can swim?"

Adachi raised her hand. "Best swimmer in school."

"Let's go."

It was a black night. There was no moonlight, no stars.

The Arrow Cross did not hear Wallenberg and his group of rescuers approach. Adachi and other swimmers, with ropes around their waists, soon stood on an embankment. Doctors and nurses waited nearby in cars. There were others to help pull Adachi and her fellow swimmers back out of the Danube. "I never thought twice about what I was about to do," remembered Adachi. "I stood fully dressed with coat, boots, and hat at the edge of the water, waiting for the sound of the gun so that we could synchronize our jumps with the bodies falling. Four of us, three men and me, jumped in and then pulled people out. We pulled fifty people out. But then we were so frozen that we couldn't do it anymore."[37]

Adachi would not see Wallenberg again. After her freezing night on the banks of what would forever be the Red Danube in her memory, she fell so sick that she was unable to continue her grueling and dangerous, though profoundly satisfying, work for Section C.[38] She would survive the siege and make a new life in America after the war, becoming a librarian in Queens, New York.

HOUR BY HOUR, the Soviets closed in, having now encircled Budapest. On January 10, with Soviet forces only a mile from the Danube, Wallenberg met for the last time with his friend and colleague Per Anger. Anger begged him to stay with the other Swedish Embassy officials who had moved to Buda, on the western bank of the Danube, but Wallenberg refused to leave Pest, where more than one hundred thousand Jews still lived in two ghettoes and dozens of protected houses. He would not abandon those he had saved. Anger recalled how he "pleaded insistently" with Wallenberg to suspend his operation: "The Arrow Cross men were especially on the lookout for him, and he ran great risks by continuing his aid work. But Wallenberg would not listen to me."[39]

Anger asked Wallenberg if he was afraid.

"Sure, it gets a little scary, sometimes," replied Wallenberg, "but for me there's no choice. I've taken on this assignment and I'd never be able to go back to Stockholm without knowing inside myself that I'd done all a man could do to save as many Jews as possible."[40]

Anger's fellow diplomat, Lars Berg, would recall that Wallenberg was daring and fearless when he stepped in to rescue Jews. "I like this dangerous game," he told one aide.[41] But otherwise he was "not at all a brave man by nature. During the air raids, he was always the first one to seek shelter, and he was badly affected when the bombs sometimes fell a little too close to us. But when it was a question of saving the lives of his protégés, then he never hesitated a second."[42] According to the Hungarian writer, Jeno Levai, who interviewed many of Wallenberg's protégés after the war: "Wallenberg was not born a death-defying, brave hero. He was fully aware of this. With his characteristic self-deprecating humor and exaggeration, he always called himself a *Hassenfuss*—a timid rabbit. It is undoubtedly true that he was afraid for his young life—and he had every right to be."[43]

WALLENBERG HAD BY NOW made his base a large safe house on Benczur Street, under the protection of the Red Cross, which had so far not been raided by the Arrow Cross. The house was close to the front line and the most imminent threat was a direct hit from heavy Soviet shelling, which now seemed some days to continue around the clock. Within days, if not hours, the area was sure to be liberated by the Soviets, hence its attraction to Wallenberg, who wanted to contact them as soon as possible so he could urge them to speed their advance and begin supplying food and medicine to Budapest's Jews. He had been only just dissuaded from trying to cross the front line by some of his staff and trusted police contacts, who had told him it would be tantamount to suicide.

The Benczur Street house was already home to several wealthy Jewish industrialists and other prominent Jews. Remarkably, contemporary accounts reveal that a German colonel—according to Lars Berg, it was SS colonel Kurt Becher—had provided protection for the premises, having dined with the refined occupants several times, much preferring the company of the cultured Jews to the uneducated criminals of the Arrow Cross. According to one account, Becher, with whom Wallenberg was in regular communication, had actually posted an SS guard outside the house to fend off attacks by the Arrow Cross.[44]

Wallenberg had devised a detailed plan to help the Jews after the Soviets had liberated Budapest. He hoped to help them find jobs, reunite with families, and get new housing. He told aides he wanted to meet as soon as possible with the Russians so he could implement the plan, hopefully with their help. If they did not want to provide material support, he would use American funds from the War Refugee Board.

On January 12, 1945, Wallenberg left the Benczur Street safe house despite heavy street fighting. He visited his offices on Ulloi Street and signed his last batch of Schutzpasses.[45] Then he paid a visit to the town hall, where he met with his Arrow Cross informant, Pal Szalai. "After the Russians take Buda, I hope you'll make your way to my Ulloi Street office," he told Szalai. "From there, we'll go together to visit Malinovsky. Afterward, I'll take you with me to Sweden to introduce you to the king."[46]

Wallenberg then headed to the Swiss Legation, where he met with a Hungarian Jew, Miklos Krausz, who had helped Wallenberg's rescue efforts and also assisted Lutz.[47] He told Krausz he was there to pick up some money and documents. That night, the Russians advanced to

within a mile of Benczur Street. Only a few hundred yards now separated the central ghetto from the Red Army. Intense shelling continued
through the night, forcing Wallenberg and all those hiding in the
Benczur Street two-story house to seek refuge in the basement.

The following morning, January 13, 1945, Wallenberg was still huddled in the basement when he saw its walls start to shake. He could hear
the Soviets drawing closer, battling their way through neighboring streets
and the sewers and corridors that linked many basements and cellars of
Pest. There was a loud banging. Bricks in the cellar wall were knocked
loose, and fifteen Russian soldiers burst through the wall, covered in
plaster and dust.

The Soviets soon realized they had liberated a basement full of Jews.

"We also are Jews," one of them said, "but don't tell anyone because
there are a lot of anti-Semites among us."

"I am a Swedish diplomat," explained Wallenberg, who then showed
the soldiers his official papers.

"You'll have to speak with my commanding officer," said one of the
men.

A few hours later, soldiers returned with two senior Soviet officers.
Wallenberg told the Jews in the house, "I'm going to accompany them,
but I don't think I shall be away for the night."

Later that day, Wallenberg visited the office of his Section C, where
he met with the publisher, Karl Muller, who had introduced him that fall
to Baroness Kemeny. Muller, a decorated Jewish veteran of the Great
War, had forged a close relationship with Wallenberg over the last six
months. He told Wallenberg that he had just narrowly escaped the Arrow
Cross, and had that day returned from Buda where, he said, conditions
were as terrible as ever for the surviving Jews.

Wallenberg told Muller that he would go to Buda to see for himself
and do what he could to help. Muller advised against this, saying that Arrow Cross units in Buda had been given photos of Wallenberg. Now
more than ever he was a marked man, having recorded Nazi and Arrow
Cross atrocities.

Wallenberg seemed undeterred.

"My life is one life," he told Muller, "but this is a matter of saving thousands of lives."[48]

Over the next two days, the Red Army apparently questioned Wallenberg several times. The Soviet secret police, the NKVD, also interrogated him. Repeatedly, Wallenberg asked to meet Marshal Rodion Malinovsky, the Red Army commander whose troops had now liberated much of Pest. He hoped with his help to organize the supply of medicine and food to the Jews still living in Pest. Gabiella Zekany, a secretary to Major General Leonid I. Brezhnev, commander of the Special Political branch of Russia's 18th Army, later claimed to have witnessed an interrogation of Wallenberg. "At the beginning, the Soviet officer was rather cordial," she alleged, "but at some point in the interview, he began to suspect that Wallenberg, who after all did speak excellent German, was really a German, perhaps a spy. At this point, the officer dismissed me and said that he had to check Wallenberg's identity."[49]

On January 16, Wallenberg made what was probably his last intervention on behalf of Hungary's surviving Jews, arriving just in time to save Mrs. Janos Kandor and around fifty other people who had found refuge in a Swedish Embassy building at 20 Revai Street.

A police guard had been posted at the entrance, but he was no match for the group of Arrow Cross who had stormed the building. "They collected all wedding rings, small chains, all remaining food and forced us into one corner of the courtyard," recalled Kandor. "Then we were lined up in front of a machine gun."

Kandor stood with her husband, eleven-year-old son, and seven-year-old daughter.

Three Arrow Cross men stood by the machine gun, yelling obscenities. "You vermin—while we're protecting the country, you're hiding here. Now we'll take care of you."

Kandor waited to die with her family, listening to the whistle and roar of bombs falling nearby. Then she saw a group of people rush into the courtyard. They were led by Wallenberg. "He seemed to me like an angel of mercy," recalled Kandor. "He was shouting that this was an extraterritorial building. Little by little the shouting ceased, the Arrow Cross picked themselves up and left without taking what they gathered, the food, the rings. We could not believe our own eyes. He was victorious again, with his belief and his willpower. Then he left quietly."[50]

A few hours later, Wallenberg packed extra supplies of food and fuel in his Studebaker and made other final preparations for a journey to the Soviet military headquarters in Debrecen. He intended to make the trip with his driver, the young engineer Vilmos Langfelder, and another Jewish assistant, Gyorgy Szollos. According to Szollos, the men had hidden "a great quantity of gold and jewels in the car's fuel tank." In a briefcase, along with important documents, he carried "a very large amount of money."[51]

Wallenberg apparently believed it would be useful should he need to bribe any Russians en route.

THERE WERE SEVERAL EYEWITNESSES to Wallenberg's last hours in Budapest.

On the morning of January 17, 1945, Wallenberg visited a Hungarian Jew who ran a safe house protected by the Swiss. Wallenberg said he was heading for the Russian headquarters in Debrecen, 125 miles to the east. "I seem to have formed a good relationship with the Russian military," added Wallenberg.

Wallenberg and Langfelder then drove back to the Benczur Street safe house, where Wallenberg checked on the well-being of the Jews he had saved. Laszlo Peto, who worked as Wallenberg's liaison officer with the Jewish Council, later said he begged Wallenberg not to leave so soon because of snipers and ferocious room-to-room fighting in nearby buildings. According to Peto, Wallenberg pointed through a window. His car was parked in the street below. Two heavily armed Red Army soldiers were sitting on motorcycles beside it. "They have been ordered especially for me," said Wallenberg.[52]

Wallenberg then left with the escort. His next stop was the Swedish-protected hospital in Pest that he had kept supplied with medicines throughout the siege. At the entrance to the hospital, Wallenberg slipped on a patch of ice. As he picked himself up, he spotted three Jewish men leaving the hospital. Free at last, they still wore yellow stars on their over-coats. Wallenberg smiled. "I am happy to see that my work has not been completely in vain."[53]

Then Wallenberg visited the Swiss Legation on Szabodsay Square. He located Miklos Krausz, who had worked closely with him and other neutral diplomats, and told him he was going to drive to Debrecen to talk to General Malinovsky. Krausz later recalled telling Wallenberg that it was unwise to do so and that he should stay in Budapest. "We now have 150 armed policemen guarding the ghetto," said Krausz. "And anyway, why do you want to leave just now, at the very moment the Russians are liberating the city?"

"Debrecen is where the Russians and Hungarians have their head-quarters," Wallenberg replied. "I think I'm the best person to explain the Swedish houses and passes to them as well as to persuade them not to mistrust the liberated Jews."

This seemed foolhardy to Krausz. He had always thought Wallenberg was a little naïve. He asked Wallenberg how he was going to convince the Russians to do what he wanted. Wallenberg pointed out that the Swedes had been responsible for protecting Russian property in Hungary throughout the war. He was certain that the Russians would "respect the suggestions" of a Swedish diplomat.

"I think it's a waste of time," said Krausz, "and dangerous, too. You'll be traveling on open roads and there's still a great deal of fighting every-where."

Wallenberg could not be dissuaded.

"If Buda is liberated before I return from Debrecen, please tell [Swedish Ambassador] Danielsson where I've gone."[54]

Laszlo Peto, the young volunteer for Wallenberg's Section C, remem-bered Wallenberg being in a "great mood, a brilliant mood."[55] Peto joined Wallenberg and Langfelder for a short trip to a Swedish-protected house on Tatra Street, which had been freed the night before by the Soviets. The Russian escort stayed in the street. Peto and Wallenberg met with a man called Rezso Muller, who was responsible for the occupants of the house. Wallenberg handed Muller 100,000 pengos and told him to use it to buy food and whatever was needed for housing the Jewish occupants.

He'd be back from Debrecen in about a week. Wallenberg then left with Langfelder and Peto in the Studebaker, headed for Debrecen, escorted by a Soviet officer on a motorbike with a sidecar. But they had only gone a few streets when Langfelder made an uncharacteristic error and crashed into a truck carrying tense Soviet soldiers.

One of them jumped down and pointed a gun at Langfelder and Wallenberg. According to Peto: "[The] Soviet soldiers were probably being taken to the front, as we heard the sound of a fierce battle from the direction of the inner city. After the collision, the soldiers jumped from the truck, shouting loudly. They surrounded our car and started abusing Langfelder . . . They wanted to take him along, but a Russian captain explained that he was escorting a foreign diplomat, and thus Langfelder was released. We noticed that only the mudguard of our car had suffered damage."[56]

Peto then decided at the last moment to stay in Budapest and try to find his parents.[57] "Wallenberg understood," recalled Peto. "He drove me to the corner of Arena Street and Benczur Street. There, after a warm farewell, I wished him all the best for his trip, which under the circumstances appeared extremely hazardous."[58]

Peto watched the Studebaker until it disappeared from his sight.

THE FOLLOWING DAY, the Red Army arrived at the edge of the central ghetto, smashed down fencing, and walked through its squalid streets. Some soldiers told survivors that they should leave their hiding places, for now they were safe. Starved and dirty figures slowly staggered into the daylight after weeks in dark and dingy cellars. At the sight of them, some Soviet soldiers, veterans of slaughter on the Eastern Front, burst into tears, and then ripped the yellow stars off some of the Jews' coats.[59]

"Now you are free!"[60]

RAOUL WALLENBERG HAD RISKED HIS LIFE to save Hungary's last Jews. But he was not in Budapest to celebrate their survival with them. Instead, he and Langfelder were being escorted under Soviet guard toward Debrecen. At a checkpoint on the outskirts of Budapest, NKVD officers wearing green uniforms with red shoulder boards allegedly arrested them and hustled them into a Soviet car.

Langfelder and Wallenberg were then placed, reportedly with four armed guards, on a train bound for Moscow. They passed through Romania, where they were permitted to exit the train and eat at a restaurant, the Luther, in the small town of Iasi. As the train then rumbled toward Moscow—the journey took several days—Wallenberg filled his time writing a detective story. He and Langfelder were apparently told that they were in protective custody and did not yet consider themselves to be prisoners as such, although Wallenberg would soon be registered with the Soviets as a "prisoner of war."[61]

THE RED ARMY FOUND 97,000 Jews alive in Budapest's two Jewish ghettos. In total, it has been estimated that around 124,000 Hungarian Jews in the city had survived the Nazi extermination effort. According to the Swedish diplomat Per Anger, Wallenberg saved at least 100,000 of them. Others say far more conservatively that he can be credited with perhaps 20,000, and even this figure was achieved through working with many others at the Swedish embassy, although it should be remembered that he was the central figure, the driving force of its rescue efforts.

Wallenberg did not act alone in Budapest, and that has tended to be forgotten in some of the hagiographic accounts of his activities. Other than the formidable Charles Lutz (whom some claim saved more lives), those who worked alongside him in Budapest and have since been proclaimed "righteous among nations" include Friedrich Born of the Swiss Red Cross; Giorgio Perlasca, charge d'affaires of the Spanish Legation; Monsignor Angelo Rotta, the Papal Nuncio in Budapest; and Peter Zurcher and Dr. Harald Feller of the Swiss Embassy. But of all the neutral diplomats, Wallenberg was the one who had placed himself in the most danger, directly in the firing line, in the crosshairs of the SS and Arrow Cross.[62]

Part Four

THE
COLD WAR

15

Liberation

THEY WERE NOW LIVING like hunted animals, hiding in their basement, listening to the ever-louder sounds of war reverberating through the brick walls. As Raoul Wallenberg left Hungary by train with a Soviet escort, thirteen-year-old Vera Herman still huddled beside her parents in the freezing cellar of their Swedish-protected house in Pest, close to the Russian front lines. One day that January of 1945, she watched in amazement as sewer covers in the cellar started to move and then rose into the air. "All of a sudden, we saw these men in their white Siberian uniforms, happy and handsome," recalled Vera. "We had made it! There was a lot of screaming, carrying on, embracing of the soldiers. They were kind, wonderful. They spent the night playing the balalaika and singing to us. They gave us kids chocolate. We were lulled into a false sense of security."[1]

Not far away, the Soviets finally arrived on Ulloi Street, where Wallenberg's main office and three protected houses were situated. Marianne Lowy, her husband, Pista, and almost three hundred protected Jews were crowded into a central courtyard, listening to the German batteries firing at the Soviets at close range to try to halt their advance. Retreating German soldiers dropped hand grenades into a nearby cellar full of Jews as a final "farewell."

Marianne saw Russians appear in the building. Then the Germans returned, and a savage battle for the building began. "In the midst of it," one report later confirmed, "crouching and crawling under tables and straw mats, there were three hundred protected Jews, including pregnant women and lactating mothers. Their bodies were pressed close together. They were covered with gunpowder and smoke, from the grenades used in the battle."[2]

Marianne and the other Jews tried to get to safety, but it wasn't until they had endured several hours of brutal combat, with bullets flying over their heads and ricocheting off walls, that they managed to escape across the Russian lines by crawling backwards on all fours to a large cellar at 22 Ulloi Street. There, the Russians treated those who were wounded and provided bread and food.

ENTIRE BLOCKS OF PEST had disappeared into fields of broken bricks and rubble. Conditions throughout the city were horrific. The cold and damp had penetrated everywhere.[3] There was no food and water. The dead were too numerous to bury. "The stiff dead bodies, partly covered by snow, were stacked up like so many timbers," recalled Erwin Koranyi, "often the last-minute horror frozen onto their motionless faces and cold, open mouths. Fine ice crystals gathered on the eyelashes, rendering them statue-like, as if they had never been alive. At least they had been spared the lengthy nocturnal walk in their underwear to the shore of the Danube."[4]

The water, far from being blue, was ice cold and a dirty brown. The dark currents carried frozen blocks of ice, some still stained with blood, and floating bodies, hands tied behind their backs with cord or wire. No one will ever know the exact number, but it has been estimated that the Hungarian Arrow Cross murdered at least twenty thousand people along the banks of the Danube in the less than three months that they held power.[5] Almost all were Jews.

Someone had recently told Erwin that they had seen the "shadow of death" on his face. Now, when he looked around, he could see it on others' faces, but he dared not tell them. "Survival was such a fragile plight," he remembered.

Alice and Erwin spent each night now in the basement of 1 Jokai Street. Erwin had managed to scrounge some bread and they were given

meat cut from a dead horse. One evening, Erwin climbed to the
bombed-out upper floors so he could smoke. He looked out onto Revai
Street. A German Tiger tank stood nearby.[6]

Erwin found some shelter by a wall and fell asleep. The next thing he
knew, dawn was breaking and the tank was gone. He could see the horizon flaring with orange artillery bursts. Erwin then saw two men in the
street. One was a Hungarian officer walking with his arms in the air, in
front of a small man, dressed in a Soviet uniform. The Soviet was wearing an olive-green jacket and a hat with earflaps over his ears, the hammer and sickle clearly visible on his uniform. He was pointing a
submachine gun at the Hungarian and shouting at him.

The Soviets had arrived at last.

Then another soldier was standing beside Erwin.[7]

The Soviet soldier stuck a gun in Erwin's ribs.

"Give me watch!"[8]

The man already had four watches but wanted another. Erwin did not
have a watch, and so the man moved on. Then Erwin found Alice and
told her that the Soviets had arrived. "We were liberated from death itself," he remembered. "It was as if life had begun again after a vicious,
bad dream."[9]

They decided to move farther into Soviet-held territory, scared that
the Germans might retake the neighborhood. In one street, they came
across a soldier holding a basket full of bottles of champagne. "Good
friend," said the soldier, as he gave Erwin one of the bottles. Erwin stood
there in the whistling wind, unshaven, a rope holding the remnants of
his winter coat closed at the waist, shoeless in the snow, and holding a
bottle of expensive French champagne. Then another Soviet soldier appeared nearby, swearing at him and brandishing a revolver.

Erwin handed over the champagne. "It was a surrealistic experience,"
remembered Erwin. "But the liberation was a miraculous joy, a flurry of
delight. Later in my life, I always associated it with the melody of the
New World Symphony—the drums imitating the bombardment and the
main motif expressing the hope."

Where next? Erwin and Alice started out for Jokai Street, where they
hoped to find his relatives. To their great joy, they discovered that Erwin's

parents and sister, Marta, had survived. "Our immediate family was one of the very rare ones," recalled Erwin, "in which both parents and children survived."[10] Then Alice's brother, George, emerged from somewhere in the ghetto, terribly emaciated but alive. But he had no news about any of Alice's other relatives.

MANY OF THE BRUTALIZED SOVIET SOLDIERS who had liberated parts of Budapest now wreaked vengeance on the city and its women. "There are enough women and they don't speak a word of Russian," wrote a Soviet soldier in a letter. "So much the better: We don't have to try and persuade them—we just point the pistol at them, the order 'lie down' settles the matter, and we can move on."[11]

The rape and pillage would last until the spring in some parts of Buda. It seemed that every female was to be automatically seized as Soviet booty, to be defiled at will, and all bourgeois objects, such as antique carpets, were to be defaced and defecated upon. There were rumors that Malinovsky had given his men a free reign in Budapest for three days as a reward. Whatever the truth behind their rampage, its result was indisputable—a lifelong loathing of all things Russian among many Hungarian women. Those who resisted the drunken Soviet embrace or the more common pistol to the head were often raped with extreme violence and then killed.

Marianne Lowy recalled how fortunate she was not to be gang-raped as so many of her peers were. A fellow Jewish survivor from the Ukraine had warned her that the liberating Russian soldiers would rape every woman, but if Marianne said she was *klapetz*—pregnant—she might be left alone.[12] "Russian foot soldiers started to trample into our basement," she remembered, "and everybody was lined up. I noticed that the Russians were just sorting out women and taking them into another room."[13]

"You, come here!" a Soviet ordered Marianne.[14]

Marianne said she was *klapetz* and was passed over. She then slipped away to a nearby cubicle, where she hid under a cot for more than twenty-four hours until the Russians had finished raping the other women. Finally, she crept out of the basement and up steps until she was outside, able to at least breathe fresh air. "The streets were an incredible sight," she recalled. "There were dead horses, probably from the cavalry, literally piled up on street corners. And people were tiptoeing out from corners and basements, sneaking up to the dead horses, cutting off hunks of horsemeat to feed themselves."[15] More than thirty thousand horses had been left behind in the city during the siege and killed. Without their meat, thousands would no doubt have starved to death.

Marianne made her way through the shattered streets of Pest toward her childhood home, hoping her relatives might do the same, if any had survived. She finally reached the elegant apartment building where she had grown up. Her parents were there. After an intensely emotional reunion, when things had calmed down a little, Marianne noticed that an oil painting of her, aged six, still hung on a wall. "All around the frame were bullet holes—soldiers had taken aim at it," she recalled. "I had been their bull's-eye but, amazingly, the painting had not been touched. All their bullets had missed. To me, it would always symbolize survival."[16]

WOMEN EVERYWHERE IN LIBERATED PEST now lived in terror of the Russians. Vera Herman would later recall that a teenage girl in her own cellar was killed shortly after their liberation. "The Russian youth who did it was drunk. I don't know how he killed her, but he killed her."[17] Thankfully, Vera's father, Emil, was clever enough to make sure his wife and daughter, after enduring so much, did not now join the tens of thousands of women who became victims of Soviet soldiers' sexual aggression—an estimated ten percent of all females in Budapest, aged as young as ten and as old as ninety, some of whom were raped more than twenty times. "My father found some jelly and he smeared me and my mother with it," Vera remembered, "and then he found some bandages and bandaged us. The Russians—even when drunk—could be warm and sympathetic by nature. They looked at me and my mother and said 'balnia, balnia'—she's sick, she's sick. So they left us alone, stayed away."[18]

Vera's father Emil was the only Slav in the cellar. All the other survivors were Hungarians. When the Russians asked for someone to interpret for them, Emil decided to volunteer, but after just a day working
with the new masters of Eastern Europe, he had had enough.

"We have to get out of here," Emil told Vera and Margit.[19] "I did not
survive this hell to become a Russian undercover agent."[20]

EMIL HAD SEEN what the Russians were doing—rounding up civilians
and sending them to holding prisons; the NKVD picked up off the street
many ordinary Hungarians, even postmen, simply because they were
wearing a uniform. General Malinovsky had reported erroneously that
he had taken some 110,000 prisoners and therefore now ordered that
at least 50,000 men be seized so that he could deliver the correct
number.[21]

Emil Herman was right to be wary of the green-uniformed NKVD,
who had now replaced the Arrow Cross and Gestapo as agents of repression and terror in Hungary. It is estimated that only a third of those arrested would survive the Soviet gulags, where as many as 2.3 million
people languished in 1945.[22]

Erwin Koranyi was lucky to escape the dragnet. "I was 'officially invited' to visit the northern Soviet Union twice but I declined," he recalled with bittersweet humor. "The Russians declared the number of
German POWs to the Red Cross, but then they killed them, so they decided they needed to get the numbers back up. They didn't care who it
was—they picked up people on street corners: postmen, bus conductors,
anyone in a uniform."

Erwin was seized on a street one day along with a score of other men.
"They gathered us in an inner courtyard," he remembered. "They brought
more and more people in. I saw one man go over to a guard and give him
a bottle of some kind of alcohol. The guard told him he could leave, and
then I saw the guard hide the bottle among some rubble. When he
turned his back, I stole it. A while later, I offered him the bottle and he
took it, let me go, and then I ran for my life."[23]

But it wasn't long before Erwin was again caught out on the streets and herded with hundreds of others to the central railway station, from where he was certain he would be shipped to Siberia. He had escaped deportation to Auschwitz during the Holocaust thanks to Raoul Wallenberg, but now there was no one to rescue him. "I felt really hopeless. We were about to be taken away. Then I saw a Russian officer. The Russian had curly hair and looked like a Jew."

Erwin approached the officer.

"Do you speak Yiddish?" he asked.

"Yes."

The officer realized that he was talking to a fellow Jew and allowed Erwin to leave the station.

Erwin was fortunate indeed. An estimated seventy-five thousand of his fellow Hungarian civilians would be arrested, sent to camps in Hungary and then to the wilds of the vast Soviet gulag archipelago. Hundreds were Jews who had survived Eichmann's attempts to kill them only to perish in a Soviet death camp. Added to these innocents were the hundreds of thousands of already captured Hungarian troops. The reasons for arrest were usually not given and were sometimes simply ridiculous: one sixteen-year-old, George Bien, was picked up with his father because he owned a radio.[24]

ALTHOUGH MOST OF PEST had now been liberated, it felt no safer to survivors—especially the women—than when the Nazis and Arrow Cross had controlled the city. Bishop Jozef Grosz would later describe conditions as "hell on earth. Women, from girls of twelve to mothers in the ninth month of pregnancy, raped; most men deported; every home looted; the city and its churches in ruins; in the restaurants and stores, horses; in the streets, cemeteries . . . thousands of unburied bodies . . . This is how things must have been in Jerusalem when the prophet Jeremiah uttered his laments."[25]

Everyone who could leave what was, after all, still a war zone now tried to do so. When Vera Herman and her parents were sure that the

Germans were not going to counterattack and retake the area of Pest where they had hidden, they started walking toward the countryside, away from the bullet-riddled, Russian-patrolled streets of the destroyed city. They did so despite fierce fighting and terrible weather. "It was snowing and hailing," recalled Vera. "The bullets were flying all around us. But we kept on going."[26]

They were headed toward the past, back to Czechoslovakia, which they had fled in 1939, almost six years before.

ERWIN AND ALICE KORANYI STAYED in Budapest for a week after their liberation and then decided, like the Hermans, to leave the city, where fighting had only intensified as the Soviets finally reached the Danube; the siege, ever bloodier, would continue for another month as the Germans fought to the bitter end in Buda.

In all, 80,026 Soviet soldiers died to take Budapest—one in two of all those who fought in Hungary. In the defense of the city, 48,000 Hungarian and German soldiers also lost their lives.[27] Less than 1,000 German troops managed to break out of the besieged city and reach their own lines, but at enormous cost—an estimated 17,000 German troops were massacred as they tried to escape by forewarned Soviets. "The escape routes showed an apocalyptic picture," Hungarian military historian Christian Ungvary has written, "with mountains of bodies, human remains carved by Soviet tanks, and paving stones covered in blood and pieces of flesh. Bodies were piled up in pyres several meters high."[28]

To escape such hellish scenes, Erwin and Alice walked through the bitter winter weather toward the town of Szeged, a hundred miles to the south, to a medical school they had attended before the Nazis had occupied Hungary. They were both determined to return to their studies so they could become qualified doctors.[29] Erwin would later recall that it was around this time that they heard that Wallenberg had been killed, shot by the Germans just before the Soviets arrived. Then Erwin heard another rumor—the Soviets had arrested Wallenberg.

Alice and Erwin kept walking, along the iced roads and through snow-storms. They passed many Russian soldiers along the road to Szeged, but Alice was not molested.

"Thankfully, nobody wanted me," she recalled.[30]

16

The Fall

BERLIN HAD CHANGED since Eichmann had last worked there. It was now a fast-spreading ruin, bombed day and night by the Allies. Jittery Berliners who could still manage moments of gallows humor joked about learning Russian. Amid the fields of rubble, posters warned: "Looters will be punished with death." The entire population, it seemed, had taken to shelters. News on all fronts was grim. Hardly anyone now believed Goebbels's increasingly surreal propaganda.

Only die-hard Nazis such as Eichmann and some of his men placed any hope in Hitler's miracle weapons arriving in time to prevent total Gottedammerung. Theodor Dannecker, who had threatened to kill Wallenberg, was as fervent a Nazi as ever, and now blamed the German Volk—people—for failing to stop the Red Army's advance. "I believe in the eternal Germany and the higher mission of our Fuhrer Adolf Hitler," he blustered, echoing the beliefs of Eichmann and others who still refused to accept that their world was falling apart.[1] Dannecker would commit suicide in an American prison camp in Bad Tolz before the year was out.[2]

That January of 1945, Eichmann met in Berlin with his Gestapo boss, forty-four-year-old Bavarian Heinrich Muller, still one of the most feared men in Nazi Germany.

Like many other SS officials, Eichmann had just been given a certificate stating that he had worked the last few years for a civilian firm, not as history's most efficient "desk murderer." Apparently, Eichmann was outraged by the attempt to whitewash his time with the RSHA and the years he had dedicated to implementing the Final Solution, and had requested a meeting with Muller to air his grievances.

Muller was a small man with thin lips and piercing eyes, utterly devoted to the Fuhrer.[3]

"Well, Eichmann, what's the matter with you?" the Gestapo chief asked.

"General, I don't need these papers."

Eichmann reportedly patted a Steyr army pistol, holstered at his waist. "This is my certificate," said Eichmann. "When I see no other way out, it will be my last remedy. I have no need for anything else."[4]

After his meeting with Muller, Eichmann spoke in person with Heinrich Himmler, whom he found in an optimistic mood.

"We'll get a treaty," Himmler told him, slapping his thigh. "We'll lose a few feathers, but it will be a good one."

Eichmann later recalled his last days in Berlin: "Serious work was out of the question. Uninterrupted air raids were creating greater and greater devastation. I spent more time looking around in the ruins than at my desk. I was only interested in . . . building a defense line that would cost the enemy as much blood as possible. That was all I thought about. I had the field of rubble around my office on Kurfursten Street transformed into a defense position, with streetcar tracks, tank traps, and nests of sharpshooters."[5]

As the Soviets began to surround Berlin, Eichmann also met with forty-two-year-old SS General Ernst Kaltenbrunner, his chief in the RSHA. Kaltenbrunner was the embodiment of the perverted, Nazi brute: a hulking Austrian with small eyes set back in an inscrutable, scarred face that rarely showed any emotion other than anger. His nicotine-stained hands reminded one of his colleagues, the SS Intelligence Chief Walter Schellenberg, of a gorilla's.[6]

Kaltenbrunner made it clear that he had little time for Eichmann. In fact, Eichmann's fellow mass murderers in the Gestapo wanted nothing to do with him. He was now an "apocalyptic memento of their own sins."[7] "The department heads and Kaltenbrunner," recalled Eichmann bitterly, "took to eating lunch every day in our building. I was never invited."

In late March, Eichmann received an order to destroy all his files and records, including documents showing the origins of the Final Solution. "That took several days," Eichmann remembered. "At about that time, I said to officers under me, who were sitting around dozing dejectedly, that in my opinion the war was definitely lost, and that I was looking forward to the battle for Berlin. If death didn't come to me, I'd go looking for it."

As the Soviets fought ever closer to the center of Berlin, Eichmann gathered his closest advisers—Krumey, Wisliceny, Dannecker, and others—in his office on the heavily bombed Kurfursten Street and said a gloomy goodbye to them. "If it has to be," he told them, "I will gladly jump into my grave in the knowledge that five million enemies of the Reich [Jews] have already died like animals."[8]

Then, in early April, Eichmann was ordered to report to Heinrich Himmler, who told Eichmann that he was planning to negotiate with the Western Allies. He wanted Eichmann to ship all the "prominent Jews" from Theresienstadt to a safe place in the Tyrol as quickly as possible, so he could use them as hostages in his negotiations.

On what would prove to be his last visit to Theresienstadt, Eichmann met with the camp's Jewish Council. "Let me tell you something," Eichmann allegedly told the Council. "Jewish death lists are my favorite reading matter before I go to sleep." With that, Eichmann is said to have picked up several lists of inmates from a table and walked out of the meeting.[9]

Now that Germany's defeat was inevitable, Eichmann and all those who had carried out the Final Solution were toxic. Association with him was potentially fatal as Allied military police and counterintelligence began to scour Germany for those guilty of war crimes.

"They'll be searching for you as a war criminal, not us," the commandant of Theresienstadt, Anton Burger, warned Eichmann. "You'll be doing your colleagues a great service if you make yourself scarce."[10]

Eichmann took Burger's advice, heading toward Austria. On April 17, 1945, he was almost killed when a squadron of enemy planes dropped bombs on a village as he passed through. "The explosions were so bad I stuck my nose in the ground and kept it there," recalled Eichmann. "My driver and I took advantage of a brief pause between the two waves. It was a miracle. The car started right up, we didn't even have a flat tire. We made it."[11]

Eichmann continued south. The Austrian Alps soon loomed in the distance. There, near the village of Altausee, high in the mountains, he planned to make a last stand with other Gestapo and SS stalwarts, fighting to the very end. En route, he stopped at his home in Linz, where he said goodbye to his plump, dark-haired Czech wife, Vera, and his three sons: Klaus, nine, Horst, five, and Dieter, aged three. Eichmann reportedly handed Vera four cyanide capsules and a stash of cash. "If the Russians arrive and discover who you are, you have no alternative; you must commit suicide," he told her. "If the French arrive first, use your own judgment, but if the British or Americans arrive, first throw the capsules away."[12] He would not speak to her again for seven years.[13]

In Altausee, Eichmann found slab-faced Ernst Kaltenbrunner in a log cabin high in the mountains. Kaltenbrunner was nonchalantly sipping cognac as he played solitaire.

"I was just carrying out the Fuhrer's orders when I sent Jewish transports to concentration camps for extermination," Eichmann told Kaltenbrunner.

"That was your big mistake," Kaltenbrunner answered. "You, the executor of those orders, will have to give your life for them."[14]

Kaltenbrunner than asked: "What are you going to do now?"

Eichmann said he was going to lead resistance in the mountains.

"That's good," replied Kaltenbrunner. "An Eichmann in the mountains will never surrender—because he can't." The implication was clear: If Eichmann gave himself up, he might be shot on the spot, as many SS men were by enraged Allied soldiers now aware of the unparalleled inhumanity of Auschwitz, Dachau, Buchenwald, and so many other Nazi camps that had been recently liberated.[15]

Kaltenbrunner laid out another card.

"The game is up."[16]

Among the motley crew of SS men loitering around the village of Altausee was Eichmann's former colleague Wilhelm Hottl. Hottl later recalled meeting Eichmann and some of his aides at the Donner bridge near Altausee. The gray limestone Loser Mountain towered six thousand feet above them. "Eichmann was a nervous wreck and was supporting himself with a stick. He complained that Kaltenbrunner had asked his adjutant to hand over a wad of British banknotes to him. He was furious. 'To hell with that. I don't need money. I've got my own. I want orders! I want to know what we do now!'"

Eichmann told Hottl he was going to try to reach a remote village called Bad Ischl on foot because the route there by road was blocked by retreating Wehrmacht units. Hottl never saw Eichmann in person again.[17] "Somehow the air became cleaner when he left," recalled Hottl.[18]

Not long after, according to Eichmann, he received orders "to prepare a line of resistance in the Totes Gebirge [mountains] and convert to partisan activity." For Eichmann it was "a worthwhile job," and he went about it with his characteristic enthusiasm. "Anybody else would have refused, but I had known those mountains well in my youth, and besides, I saw possibilities of survival because it's a region with enormous amounts of game and lots of cattle in the summer." But his enthusiasm soon wilted. "I received a message from Kaltenbrunner by courier: 'Reichsfuhrer's orders: No one is to fire on Englishmen and Americans.' That was the end."[19]

Eichmann apparently gathered his men, pulled out a large stash of cash, and handed over five thousand reichsmarks to each of his most trusted aides, making them sign receipts for the money, ever the efficient bureaucrat. Then, with a colleague whom he had known since the early thirties, Rudolf Janisch, he headed toward Salzburg. "We were in scruffy civilian clothes," Janisch recalled. "No sooner were we back on German soil than we ran straight into an American patrol. The blood group tattoos underneath our arms gave us away as SS henchmen."[20]

It was early May 1945 when Eichmann was taken into custody, adopting the guise of SS Untersturmbannfuhrer Otto Eckmann, just one of countless German prisoners-of-war now filling huge camps that sprang up among the ruins of the Third Reich.

It later emerged that an American lieutenant interrogated the "architect of the Final Solution."

"What is your name?"

"Otto Eckmann," said Eichmann.

"Rank?"

"Second lieutenant, 22nd Waffen-SS Cavalry Division."

"Born?"

"March 19, 1905. Breslau."[21]

The year was one earlier than his true birth date, and Breslau was convenient because the Soviets had occupied it after massive bombing that would, Eichmann hoped, have destroyed local records.

The lieutenant asked a few more routine questions, and then Eichmann returned to his work party.

The following month, June 1945, Eichmann was moved to another camp. He was now one among several million German POWs, as yet unrecognized but terrified of being discovered. He later claimed that he wanted to inject himself with an overdose of morphine but didn't because he couldn't find a hypodermic needle.[22] One thing was certain: Like his countrymen, Eichmann had reached rock bottom—*Nullpunkt*. His life no longer had any purpose. His mission to liquidate European Jewry had ended in rejection by his superiors and in humiliation. Raoul Wallenberg had been right in his prediction the previous November. Nazism had indeed been defeated, but at the cost of tens of millions of lives.

"Righteous Gentile"—Raoul Wallenberg at work in Budapest, 1944. (*Thomas Veres; courtesy U.S. Holocaust Memorial Museum*)

The Envoy—Wallenberg's passport photograph, June 1944.

Adolf Eichmann—Architect of the Final Solution, in uniform (*left*); and receiving justice on trial in Israel, 1961. (*Courtesy Israeli Security Agency*)

Eichmann's victims—Some of Budapest's last surviving Jews being rounded up in October 1944 after the Arrow Cross had come to power. (*Bundesarchiv*)

Eichmann's villa in Buda, as seen in this photograph taken in November 2008. The terrace overlooked the international ghetto in Pest. (*John Snowdon*)

View of Budapest from Eichmann's villa in Buda. (*Author photo*)

Hitler's envoy to Hungary, SS diplomat Edward Veensenmayer, served only two years of a twenty-year sentence for his direct involvement in the murder of hundreds of thousands of Hungarian Jews.

Eichmann's aides—SS captain Dieter Wisliceny (*below left*), hanged in 1948 for his role in the Final Solution; and the man who pointed a pistol at Wallenberg, SS captain Theodor Dannecker (*below right*), arguably Eichmann's most ruthless aide. He later committed suicide in American custody in 1945.

Jewish women being herded through the streets of Budapest, October 1944. Many would soon be sent on death marches to Austria. (*Bundesarchiv*)

The infamous selection process, often presided over by Dr. Josef Mengele, at Auschwitz. Over 450,000 Hungarian Jews were killed at the death camp in just six weeks during the summer of 1944. (*National Archives*)

Jewish women and children from a Hungarian transport just arrived at Auschwitz. (*Yad Vashem*)

Prison laborers in the quarry at Mauthausen, the camp in Austria where Eichmann gathered his men before setting up his final operation in Hungary. (*U.S. Holocaust Memorial Museum*)

Some of the many thousands of Jews killed by the fascist Arrow Cross along the banks of the Danube during the winter of 1944–45.

Some of the hundreds of Jewish corpses dumped by the Arrow Cross near Budapest's Dohanyi Street synagogue.

Wallenberg's close friend and colleague, diplomat Per Anger, on the roof terrace of the Swedish legation in Budapest. (*U.S. Holocaust Memorial Museum*)

Carl Lutz, the formidable Swiss diplomat who worked closely with Wallenberg and himself saved tens of thousands of lives. (*Swiss Archives of Contemporary History*)

Wallenberg meets with some of his 400-odd staff in Section C of the Swedish Embassy. (*Thomas Veres; courtesy of U.S. Holocaust Memorial Museum*)

Schutzpass issued by Wallenberg, July 1944. Wallenberg would issue thousands of these protective passes. (*Courtesy Erwin Koranyi*)

Some say he saved over 100,000 lives—Raoul Wallenberg at his desk, in Section C, 1944. (*Thomas Veres; courtesy U.S. Holocaust Memorial Museum*)

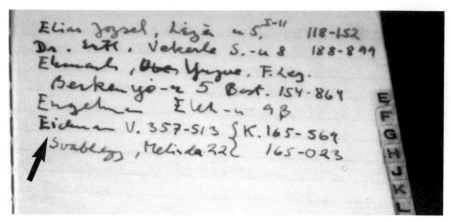

Wallenberg's address book, seized by Soviets in 1945. Note the three contact numbers for Eichmann. *(John Snowdon)*

Wallenberg's day-book, 1944. On Saturday, August 5, Wallenberg met with Erwin Koranyi at 4 pm. On Monday, August 7, at 10 am, he had a meeting to negotiate the release of five prisoners, including Erwin's wife, Alice. *(Courtesy Erwin Koranyi)*

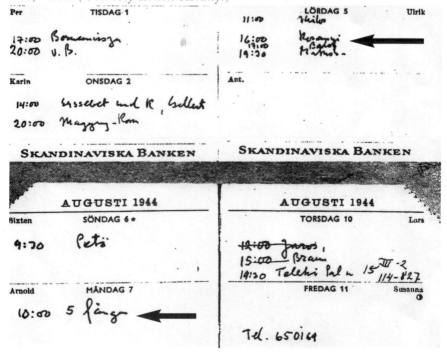

A famous photograph, taken secretly, by Thomas Veres. Wallenberg negotiates with Arrow Cross officials for the release of Jewish forced laborers in Budapest in November 1944. Wallenberg has his hands clasped behind his back. *(Thomas Veres; courtesy U.S. Holocaust Memorial Museum)*

Jewish forced laborers saved by Wallenberg, November 1944, Budapest. *(Thomas Veres; courtesy U.S. Holocaust Memorial Museum)*

Alice Breuer, aged 18, April 1944, just after the Nazis occupied Budapest. (*Courtesy Erwin Koranyi*)

One of 100,000—Holocaust survivor Alice Breuer, rescued twice by Wallenberg, seated in her home in July 2009, Stockholm. (*John Snowdon*)

Alice Breuer and Erwin Koranyi graduate with medical degrees, Innsbruck, 1950. Both have since enjoyed long and distinguished medical careers.
(*Courtesy Erwin Koranyi*)

Erwin Koranyi, Alice Breuer's first husband, at his home in Ottawa, February 2010.
(*Tony Eprile*)

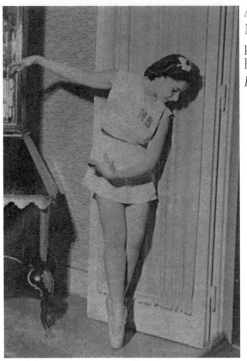

Aspiring actress and dancer Marianne Lowy practices her pirouette in her Budapest home. (*Courtesy Marianne Lowy*)

Marianne Lowy, aged 14, in Budapest. (*Courtesy Marianne Lowy*)

Susan Tabor, saved by Raoul Wallenberg during the death marches of November 1944. *(Author collection)*

Alive because of a young Swede— Margit Herman, mother of Vera Herman, in New Jersey after her family had settled in the United States. *(Courtesy Vera Goodkin)*

Vera Herman was Margit's only child. *(Courtesy Vera Goodkin)*

Raoul Wallenberg's parents, Fredrik and Maj von Dardel, in Stockholm in the 1970s after having searched for their son for over three decades. *(Courtesy Guy von Dardel and Nina Lagergren)*

The siblings—Wallenberg's half-brother and half-sister, Guy von Dardel and Nina Lagergren, continued the quest for their long lost brother after their parents' deaths. *(Courtesy Guy von Dardel and Nina Lagergren)*

17

Lost Hero

RAOUL WALLENBERG and Vilmos Langfelder's train shunted into Moscow on January 31, 1945. Moscow was now the epicenter of a nation that was utterly committed to waging total war and that had lost more than ten million men on the Eastern Front alone. Many Red Army soldiers and Muscovites worshipped Stalin as never before now that victory was finally in sight. Red banners and flags hung everywhere. Stalin's face was emblazoned on huge posters, gazing down on the weary civilians and men in olive green Red Army uniforms who trudged through snow-filled streets.

Wallenberg and Langfelder were given a tour of Moscow's magnificent underground system, a true marvel of Stalinist proportions, and then escorted on foot to a large, floodlit building at the center of the city—the infamous Lubianka prison, headquarters of the NKVD. Inmates had a dark joke about its rooftop enjoying the best view in Moscow because it stretched all the way to Siberia.

The Hungarian and the Swede's final destination must have come as a profound shock if the Soviets had not told the men where they were headed. Indeed, Wallenberg's naivety about the Russians, if he still had any, must now have evaporated as he was registered in the prison and his few possessions placed in a manila envelope. He and Langfelder may have had a few seconds to wish each other luck and say goodbye. They had for many weeks been inseparable, sharing the darkest days and nights in Budapest's history as they had desperately awaited the Soviets, who had now become their jailers. They would not set eyes on each other again. As with other new arrivals at Lubianka, they were made to take a cold bath before being led along dimly lit corridors toward cells whose walls were painted a gloomy dark green.

Wallenberg was placed in cell 123 on the fifth floor of the prison. Two prisoners already occupied the cell: Otto Scheuer, an Austrian, and Gustav Richter, who had worked at the German Embassy in Bucharest. According to these two men's subsequent testimony, Wallenberg was terribly concerned that his arrest would destroy his reputation, and by extension that of the Wallenbergs back in Sweden.

"In the circumstances," Richter reassured him, "it is certainly no cause for embarrassment. I don't think it will damage your good name."[1]

Meanwhile, back in Sweden, Soviet sources indicated to Wallenberg's family that he was alive and well in Moscow, just one of many Western diplomats who had been taken into protective custody as the Red Army swept inexorably toward Berlin. In February 1945, seventy-three-year-old Alexandra Kollontay, the Russian ambassador in Stockholm, told Maj von Dardel that her son was being held by the Soviets. Kollontay, the world's first female ambassador (to Norway in 1923), was a wily veteran of the 1917 revolution and a favorite of Stalin's, hence her survival of the Terror in the 1930s.

Kollontay also allegedly told the wife of the Swedish foreign minister that it "would be best for Wallenberg if the Swedish government didn't stir things up." Possibly because of these two statements, Kollontay was then recalled to Russia.[2] She was not dispatched to the gulag, like so many others exposed to the decadent West, but she did remain silent about Wallenberg from then until she died aged seventy-nine in 1952, a year before Stalin's death.

That February in Budapest, where fighting still raged in the hills of Buda, the NKVD interrogated Wallenberg's associates, among them Paul Hegedus, who had worked closely with Wallenberg.

Hegedus later gave a vivid account of his interrogation.

"Who is Wallenberg, and what was he doing in Budapest?" he was asked.

"He came here to save Jews," replied Hegedus.

"Lies! Raoul Wallenberg was a German spy. Why else would he have come here if he wasn't in the pay of German espionage? All this so-called work to save Jews—that was just a cover for the spying that the Swedes were doing for the fascists. Wallenberg helped the fascists and the Arrow Cross by giving them protective passes."

"[Wallenberg] may have given a few passes to his enemies," replied Hegedus, "if by doing so he could stop thousands of Jews being deported. In any case, the fascists could easily make their own passes by stealing them from Jews and changing the names."

During a later interrogation, a different intelligence officer told Hegedus: "It was not just Wallenberg; [Lars] Berg was a spy too, and the whole Swedish Legation. They were all German spies. Why else would they stay in Budapest after the Nazis and Arrow Cross came to power? Do you really think any sensible person would believe that people would stay in this town, under siege, just for 'humanitarian purposes' when they could have returned to their nice peaceful neutral country!"[3]

Others who had worked with Wallenberg were also arrested and questioned at length about Wallenberg's contacts and actions. Lars Berg himself was interrogated several times by the NKVD. They told him that they believed both he and Wallenberg had run a spy ring for the Germans in Budapest.[4] According to another colleague, Gote Carlsson, the NKVD refused to accept that Wallenberg had been in Budapest for humanitarian reasons. Carlsson was told: "It is totally illogical for someone like Wallenberg to leave peaceful Sweden to come and risk his life in Budapest to save strangers."[5]

THE ORDER TO ARREST WALLENBERG had undoubtedly come from the top—if not Stalin then one of his inner circle who may have wanted to use Wallenberg and other neutral diplomats as bargaining chips in dealings with Western and neutral nations.

The Swiss diplomats Harald Feller and Peter Zurcher, who had worked alongside Wallenberg in Budapest, were also incarcerated in

Moscow at this time. Wisely, both vehemently denied dealing "in politics or intelligence work." They eventually returned to Switzerland in exchange for Russians who were sent back to the motherland.[6]

Wallenberg was in a more difficult position. A Soviet intelligence chief, General Alexander Belkin, later claimed that the Soviets had received information that Wallenberg was "an established asset" of the German, British, and American intelligence services.[7] Wallenberg's pocket diary, which was taken from him upon entry into Lubianka, may have been used to support Belkin's assertion. In great detail, it listed Wallenberg's appointments with Nazi and Arrow Cross officials in Budapest.

In an address book, Wallenberg had also jotted in blue ink three contact numbers for Eichmann and his office address in Buda. That Wallenberg had deliberately curried favor with all parties in Budapest as part of his rescue efforts seems not to have occurred to the Soviets. Instead, they had already dismissed any notion that Wallenberg was in Budapest solely for humanitarian reasons, convinced that his rescue activities were simply a front.[8]

ACCORDING TO THE Hungarian historian Christian Ungvary, Wallenberg's imprisonment in Moscow may have had another explanation: He knew the truth behind one of the most closely guarded cover-ups of the twentieth century—the Katyn massacre of April 1940, when the NKVD secretly killed more than twenty thousand Poles. Around eight thousand were officers taken prisoner during the Soviet invasion of Poland in 1939; the majority were Poles arrested for being "intelligence agents, gendarmes, saboteurs, factory owners, lawyers, priests, and officials."[9] Each was shot in the back of the head, allegedly on Stalin's direct orders. In spring 1943, the Germans found more than four thousand bodies in the Katyn forest. The Soviets denied any involvement, blaming the Germans; and in 1945, the Allies were inclined, for political reasons, to believe them.

Wallenberg was apparently aware that a Hungarian forensic pathologist called Ferenc Orsos had inspected the scene of the massacre in 1943 and sent details to Budapest. His report and other documents pertaining to the most shameful Soviet atrocity in Poland were then kept in the Hungarian General Credit Bank. Wallenberg is said to have known of the documents, as did Bela Varga, president of the Hungarian National Assembly in 1945, and Zoltan Miko, a resistance leader.

The NKVD also seized Varga and Miko. Miko would be executed on August 15, 1945. His assistant, Vilmos Bondor, was asked over and over during interrogations what he knew about certain documents. Bondor was sentenced to twenty-five years in prison. Varga escaped execution only after being warned by his interpreter, a Soviet colonel, to say that he knew nothing if asked about Katyn.[10]

IN EARLY MARCH 1945, officials and staff such as Berg, Carlsson, and Per Anger at the Swedish embassy in Budapest were escorted to Moscow, where they met with the Swedish ambassador, Stefan Soderblom. Soderblom was anxious that the Swedes could damage Swedish–Soviet relations if they spoke out about the horrific Soviet rape and pillage that had swiftly followed the liberation of Budapest. According to Per Anger: "Soderblom displayed evident nervousness at our arrival. Had he feared that the Russians, instead of allowing us to travel to Sweden, would shunt our train onto the tracks to Siberia?"[11]

Just before the diplomats were sent back to Sweden, Soderblom took Anger aside at a train station in Moscow.

"Remember, when you get home," Soderblom warned Anger, "not one harsh word about the Russians!"[12]

On March 8, 1945, Soviet-controlled radio in Hungary announced that Gestapo agents or the Arrow Cross had killed Wallenberg en route to Debrecen. Some officials in Sweden and Soderblom in Moscow were inclined to give the report some credence, even though on January 16, 1945, the day before Wallenberg had left Budapest, Vladimir Dekanozov, Soviet deputy commissar for foreign affairs, had informed the Swedish Embassy in Moscow that Raoul Wallenberg had been taken into Soviet custody.[13]

Wallenberg was far from dead. That March, while his colleagues waited in Moscow to return home, he was moved to a new cell in Lubianka, where he met two prisoners: Wilhelm Roedel, who had worked at the German Embassy in Bucharest, and Hans Loyda, a Czech who had been an interpreter for the Wehrmacht. As soon as Wallenberg entered the cell, they knew who he was thanks to descriptions they had been given by Langfelder, with whom they had already shared a cell. Wallenberg was pleased to hear that Langfelder was still alive and apparently well, and he asked that his cigarette ration be given to him.

Langfelder never received it. He was no longer in the prison. The Russians have never divulged his fate, but it is probable that he was shot like so many others—in the back of the head, NKVD-style—and his body cremated.[14]

On April 12, the American ambassador in Moscow offered Soderblom assistance in finding and releasing Wallenberg. Soderblom declined the offer. In a report to the Ministry of Foreign Affairs on April 19, he then neglected to mention the American approach.[15]

Had Soderblom and the Swedish government loudly demanded the release of Wallenberg at this point, he could perhaps have joined his fellow Swedes as they returned via Finland that April to Stockholm. But Soderblom and his colleagues did not. And for that, Wallenberg's parents and immediate family would never forgive them. "It would seem natural that our government, who had sent him on a dangerous mission," says his sister Nina Lagergren today, "should have stood behind [Raoul] at the most important time, after the war, but instead he was abandoned."[16]

Wallenberg was left behind bars in Moscow, one of tens of thousands of people seized by the rapacious NKVD and SMERSH in Eastern Europe in 1945. The Soviets undoubtedly knew that the Swedes would not make too much of a fuss about Wallenberg and other citizens apparently lost in the Soviet Union after the war. *Rysskrack*—fear of Russia—was, according to the Hungarian-born journalist, Kati Marton, "the strongest emotion in postwar Sweden."[17] What mattered most to Swedes like Soderblom, it seemed, was their precious neutrality, from which many in the Swedish establishment, notably the Wallenberg banking dynasty, had profited handsomely.[18]

Wallenberg's cousins, Jacob and Marcus, had had a particularly good war thanks to their dealings (which they had tried to conceal) with Nazi corporations.[19] In fact, these über-bankers, arguably the most cynical and calculating of all neutral capitalists during World War II, had bene-fited so much from their Nazi connections that General Lucius Clay, in charge of the American occupied zone in postwar Germany, demanded that the Wallenberg brothers be prosecuted as war criminals.[20]

In coming years, the brothers would do little to help their cousin, much to Wallenberg's parents' dismay.[21]

LARS BERG STOOD ON THE SHIP'S DECK with other Swedish colleagues from the embassy in Budapest. They looked at the approaching wharf and a small crowd that had assembled to welcome them home. It had been a long and harrowing journey via Moscow from Hungary, where as far as the embittered and disillusioned Berg was concerned, nothing now remained except "ruins and terror." As the ship, which had brought them across the Baltic from Finland, neared the dockside, Berg could see his relatives waving and cheering, and one family that was "still and silent"—Wallenberg's mother, Maj, and his stepfather, Frederick von Dardel.

Berg's mother cried tears of joy when she took him in her arms. Then Berg spotted Wallenberg's mother close by; she too was crying, not tears of joy but of "deepest sorrow."[22] Her small figure seemed particularly frail and forlorn to Berg that morning of April 18, 1945, as he stepped onto Swedish soil.

Maj had been told that Raoul would not be among those returning, but she had not believed it.[23]

Now, clearly, it was true—Raoul had not come home after all.

"Where is Raoul?" she asked. "I had hoped he was with you."[24]

WALLENBERG HAD BEEN LEFT BEHIND in the gulag, a phantom that some of his own countrymen appeared only too willing to forget.

It is known that Wallenberg was moved that April of 1945 to Lefor-tovskaya prison, where he stayed until sometime early in 1947. He shared a cell, Number 203, on the fourth floor with a fellow political prisoner, a German Embassy official called Willi Roedel.[25]

Wallenberg and Roedel were allowed just twenty minutes exercise a day in the overcrowded prison shaped like a K. The only way they could communicate with other prisoners was through tapping on pipes and walls with a toothbrush. The inmates used many different codes; the most basic involved knocking once to signify the letter *A*, twice for *B*, and so on. According to Roedel, Wallenberg spent a great deal of time knocking on the walls and pipes, using German and French. Three prisoners later recalled messages he tapped: German diplomats called von Rantzau, Rensinghoff, and Wallenstein, whose cell was below his.[26]

When Wallenberg explained one day through tapping that he wanted to send a letter to Stalin, Wallenstein suggested that he begin it with these words: "Agreez, Monsieur le President, l'expression de ma tres haute consideration."[27]

Wallenberg wrote the letter and handed it to a prison guard. It is not known if Stalin received it.

SWEDISH AMBASSADOR Stefan Soderblom's time in Moscow was coming to an end. To his great delight and surprise, Marshal Joseph Stalin had granted him an audience before he was to return to Sweden. In a report made public many years later, in 1980, Soderblom described the June 15, 1946, meeting with Stalin, which lasted less than ten minutes, in vivid detail.[28] He was clearly starstruck by the yellow-eyed marshal of the Soviet Union, whom he described as "fit and in vigorous health. His short but well-proportioned body and his regular features made an especially agreeable impression. His tone of voice and demeanor gave an impression of friendliness."[29]

Soderblom briefly explained the humanitarian activities of Swedish diplomats in Budapest. "Among those who saved twenty-five to thirty thousand Jews was a Swedish diplomat, Wallenberg," he added, "who was in the protective custody of Russians when he disappeared without a trace."[30]

Stalin apparently asked Soderblom to spell out Wallenberg's name and jotted it down on a pad of paper.

Then came words that Nina Lagergren, Wallenberg's sister, believed sealed her brother's fate.

"I am personally convinced," said Soderblom, "that Wallenberg fell victim either to a road accident or to bandits."[31]

Stalin placed the scrap of paper with Wallenberg's name on it in his pocket. Soderblom then asked for an official statement from the Russians to the effect that all possible action had been taken to find Wallenberg. "This would be in your own interests," Soderblom reportedly explained, "as there are people who, in the absence of an explanation, would draw the wrong conclusions."

Stalin is said to have smiled knowingly and puffed on his pipe. The meeting was over.[32]

ACCORDING TO SOVIET RECORDS, Wallenberg was still very much alive in 1946 as Soderblom returned to Stockholm.

During an interrogation early the following year, Wallenberg was told that he was "a political case."

"If you think you are innocent," an interrogator added, "you must prove it. The best proof of your guilt is that the Swedish government and the Swedish Embassy have done nothing for you."[33]

"I have asked many times to be allowed to contact the Embassy," Wallenberg replied. "I am asking again. Or let me get in touch with the Red Cross."

"No one is at all interested in you. If the Swedish government or the Embassy cared about you, they would have contacted you ages ago."

Wallenberg wanted to know what the Soviets intended.

The answer must have been chilling: "For political reasons, you will never be sentenced."[34]

The last message his cell's neighbors received from Wallenberg, in the spring of 1947, was just as bleak: "They are taking us away."[35]

Wallenberg's last known communication was two knocks on the wall with his fist.

Before he was taken away, Wallenberg had reportedly said that the Soviets wanted to make him disappear into "darkness and fog."[36] And that is exactly what happened to the man who is said to have saved more lives than any other during the Holocaust.

18

Brave New Worlds

THE COLD WAS INESCAPABLE. It pursued Alice and Erwin, day and night, chilling them to the marrow, slowing but not stopping them as they trudged on blistered feet in late January 1945 through deep snow and bitter winds, determined to reach the university of Szeged in southern Hungary. "The rumbling of blasts slowly died away and no more angry, billowing smoke columns could be seen on the horizon," remembered Erwin. "Here and there, the ditches along the highway were filled with burnt-out equipment." As Erwin and Alice trudged on, hungry and close to collapse from exhaustion, they saw "discarded Hungarian military uniforms that were frozen stiff and crackled like glass when stepped on."[1]

Finally, on February 6, 1945, they arrived in Szeged, a hundred miles south of Budapest, and found a place to stay so that they could resume their studies. They soon discovered that many of their former friends at the university had not survived the Holocaust.

As they returned to their studies, the trauma of the last year began to burrow deeper and deeper into their bruised psyches. Alice sank into an ever-darker depression at the thought of what might have happened to her family and friends. "I loved her with all my heart, but she could not help the change within herself," remembered Erwin. "As the distance between us began to grow, I too experienced a heaviness."[2]

Soon, Alice could not sleep. Her cheeks were hollow, and dark circles appeared under her eyes. She barely reacted to a gentle embrace. Then, one night, she began to bleed. It was the fifth month of her pregnancy. Erwin quickly got her to a hospital, but Alice miscarried.

From that moment on, their relationship would never be the same. Erwin tried to find something, anything, to lift Alice's spirits. All he could think of was chocolate. So he sold some textbooks and went to the local black market with a Russian officer he had befriended. The Russian officer took out his revolver, placed it on a scale, and said to a black market vendor: "Match it!" Erwin returned to Alice's bedside with enough chocolate to feed the entire ward.[3]

But no amount of black-market chocolate could cheer Alice. Her depression only deepened when she and Erwin returned late that spring of 1945 to Kormend, the town on the far western border where she had grown up, part of a large and joyous family in a flourishing Jewish community. Alice learned that her sister, Ibi, had last been seen in a concentration camp near the Baltic Sea, probably Stutthof, where she had died just before liberation. Her father, although very sick with dysentery, had been liberated in Bergen-Belsen. But the very next day he had died. Her mother, Cecil, was thought to have been murdered soon after arriving at Auschwitz, one of Eichmann's hundreds of thousands of Hungarian victims. "Of the once-flowering little Jewish community of Kormend," recalled Erwin, "totaling perhaps three hundred Jewish people, only Alice, her brother, George, and three [boys] survived."[4]

THE PAST WOULD NOT DIE. At medical school that summer, it came back to haunt Erwin with a vivid vengeance: He started to suffer from terrible nightmares, and would wake up in a cold sweat. But he tried his best to carry on with his studies, ever more determined to become a doctor. "There was no further news of Wallenberg," he recalled. "By then we knew that he was in a Soviet prison, although the Kremlin kept denying it. Perhaps he was mistreated by the Soviets without [their] being aware of his identity, and consequently it was too embarrassing to let him go— so they had to kill him to hide their blunder? But surely the Swedish government would do something. Wallenberg had a powerful family in Sweden."[5]

Back in Budapest, there were worrisome signs that the Soviets were not to be trusted when it came to safeguarding Jews who had survived the Holocaust in Hungary; less than 5 percent of the those sent to death camps had returned, often to find that their neighbors or others had moved into their homes. Now, it was "not the Jews but the Hungarian proletariat" that had suffered most under the Nazis. Incredibly, there were cases of Jews being murdered, even after returning from the camps to their former communities.

One day, as they studied, Erwin and Alice heard shouting on a street outside. They looked out of a window and saw three men.

"Jews to Auschwitz!" they shouted. "Kill the Jews."[6]

Erwin was so furious that he lost control and ran outside and assaulted them. A crowd quickly formed, and then a policeman arrived. Some of the crowd attacked Erwin. The policeman did nothing to stop them, and Erwin was badly beaten.

IT WAS ALSO DURING THAT SUMMER of 1945 that Alice and Erwin's marriage ended. Erwin still loved Alice, and he would never stop doing so. But she wanted to be alone. So much suffering and tragedy had created a chasm between them—her family had died, his had not. "Lici decided to be on her own," Erwin would later write. "The separation was unexpected, and it was tremendously painful for me. I suffered for the longest time and did not know how to ease the agony. And to complicate matters further, Alice became ill. She kept losing weight, had an elevated temperature, slept poorly, waking up frequently with night sweats, and developed a 'smoker's cough' that kept getting worse."[7]

Alice was diagnosed with tuberculosis. There was no known cure. Erwin could not sleep for worry and began to drink heavily. His panic attacks and nightmares got worse. He felt he had to do something, anything, to try to stay sane, so he chose to return to Budapest and confront his demons. "I decided to cure myself," he recalled, "by facing the devil. I rented a room in the just-reopened Majestic Hotel, Adolf Eichmann's former headquarters. I thought that by doing so I would be able to break the power of evil. But my experiment turned out to be a disaster.

I woke up in the middle of the night with a nightmare and a panic attack. I had to open the window to breathe, but in doing so, I had seen the dark abyss, the yawning black shaft, and it took all my strength to tear myself away from the fascination of a tempting oblivion."[8]

Alice was moved to a sanatorium in Buda. Although Alice and Erwin's marriage was over, Erwin stayed true to his vow to look after Alice. He visited her, bringing whatever delicacies he could find on the black market and sharing his class notes with her so she could stay interested in her studies. The stresses and losses of the last year had wrecked her immune system, and Erwin was terrified that she would quickly waste away. He already felt empty, his spirit stolen, by their separation. The only thing that animated him was visiting her in the sanatorium. Then he realized, in a sober moment, that he was being consumed by self-pity. He stopped drinking, but he was still beset by sudden anxiety attacks. He cut his fingernails short to stop himself from scratching his forehead constantly while asleep. He did not know that he was suffering severe post-traumatic stress disorder, which had no name then. The disorder would stay with him for the next twenty-five years.

SUMMER BECAME FALL, and the leaves began to turn. Erwin continued to visit Alice. Slowly, her health improved. After seven months, a remarkably short time for people suffering from TB, she was well enough to leave the sanitarium. Meanwhile, the political situation had changed quickly in Hungary. Stalinism was in full force. All across the country and the newly acquired Soviet satellites, the inhuman power of the informer's lie now tore friends and families apart as more and more people were arrested for "political reasons." Hasty show trials and the mass imprisonment of "dubious bourgeois" soon would be in full sway—thousands would be executed and more than 350,000 sent into internal exile or to prison camps under arch-Stalinist dictator Matyas Rakosi.

HAVING SURVIVED THE WAR, Emil Herman decided that he did not want his family to grow up under another oppressive, dehumanizing ideology—communism. In 1947, he and his wife, Margit, and daughter, Vera, now fifteen, decided to leave Stalinist Czechoslovakia for America. They were on an American quota and managed to gain the necessary papers to emigrate. However, due to the acute shortage of doctors in the country, the Czech authorities saw Emil's wanting to leave as a betrayal. It was uncertain whether they would in fact allow him to do so.

One October day, Emil and his family arrived at the airport in Prague. Vera and her mother wore jewelry and Emil carried some cameras, all of which they hoped to sell in America. They had not been allowed to take their savings out of the country.[9] As they tried to board their plane, Emil was stopped and strip-searched. Officials found a small gold piece in his pocket. He was taken aside for questioning while Vera and her mother took their seats on the plane. "At that point, we did not know whether they were going to let him go or not," Vera recalled. "He could easily have been accused of smuggling. We knew that if he didn't get on that plane, he would have been stuck for good and would have been disgraced."[10]

The pilot on the plane was anxious to leave.

"The propellers are running," he told Margit. "I have ten more minutes; then I have to take off with him or without him."

Eight minutes later, Vera saw the pilot reach down through the open door. Vera thought he was moving the steps to the plane. But then, to her immense relief, she saw her father board. Not long after, the Swedish American Airlines plane taxied away and then took off.[11] A few hours later, the Hermans arrived in Wallenberg's birthplace—Stockholm— where they stayed for one night in the Grand Hotel. Vera marveled at the view from the hotel's third-floor window, gazing at hundreds of well-dressed, prosperous Swedes riding light-blue bicycles to work, and then she gorged on oranges and bananas, which her father bought in a local market. Not one building in Stockholm bore a bullet hole.

On October 28, 1947, after a stormy ten-day crossing of the Atlantic, the Hermans' boat, the *Gripsholm*, approached the port of New York. Vera stood with her nervous parents on deck, looking in awe at the Statue of Liberty—for yet another generation of European émigrés a welcome symbol of a land where individual freedom was celebrated rather than feared. "After the [boat] docked, we were all scrambling for a glimpse of the New World," recalled Vera. "When I finally had my turn at the porthole, my stomach was tied up in knots, and I felt overwhelmed, as if there were no ground to stand on."[12]

The date of her arrival was Czech independence day. "I was sixteen and didn't understand a word of English," she remembered. "I went to school two weeks later. My problem was that I was sixteen going on forty-five. The other kids thought I was a rarity. They had never seen a foreign student. They were wearing bobby socks and saddle shoes. I came to school in heels and hose."[13]

The following year, 1948, the war for Israeli independence broke out. Vera's father, she recalled, "said that he did not have it in him to mount the kind of struggle that it would take to make a new beginning in Israel. It was then about building a new country from rock and sand while at war, a constant state of war. He was a very brave man, but he just said he did not have it in him. We did not know at the time that already in his late forties, his heart was not much good. He covered it up. He had this inner fatigue. He could manage the struggle here but not in Israel."[14]

BACK IN HUNGARY, more and more people were trying to escape across the border to Austria. But doing so was riskier than ever before. The Iron Curtain was now a deadly reality: minefields, barbed wire, armed guards ready to shoot on any pretext, and sniffer dogs now marked where East met West in Europe. Just months away from graduation, Alice and Erwin Koranyi were in a terrible bind. Should they leave while they still could, and not finish their medical degrees, or stay and wither away under Stalinism? "The choice was unfair and wicked," recalled Erwin. "The decision was tearing us apart, but we could not live under a dictatorship again."[15] Once more, Erwin turned to his contacts in the underworld and discovered that it was possible to buy one's way across the border. But it was expensive and very dangerous. The minimum punishment if caught was eight years in prison.

Erwin could afford the smuggling fees for only one person. So he urged Alice to go ahead of him. He would never forget watching as she pulled out a small case and packed and unpacked it over and over, trying to fit in enough to last a lifetime. Two days after leaving with a smuggler in his car, Alice called. She could not say much, but she had made it safely to Austria.

Now it was Erwin's turn. But he had spent all his money trying to get Alice out, so he decided to risk being shot by crossing the border alone and on foot. He did not say goodbye to his parents. Instead, he told them he was going to a party. Nor did he pack anything, wanting to travel light. He put his most crucial medical papers in one pocket and a pharmacology book in another, and then took a bus to a village near the border. As the bus left Budapest, he looked out at the familiar city landmarks with "bitterness in [his] heart." He would never see the city again.[16]

That night, Erwin headed across country. Soon he was at the Ipoly River, swollen with snowmelt. He forged across, the water above his hips, and then through swamps on the other side. A day later, he crossed into Austria through a pine forest, "inhaling the resinous cold air," and then made his way to Vienna, where he discovered to his shock that Alice had decided to go to Italy to finish her studies and had set out alone. But as she tried to get into Italy through the Brenner Pass, Italian guards had arrested her and sent her back to Austria. She was now in a displaced persons camp in Salzburg, "morally defeated."[17]

Erwin found Alice, and they went to Innsbruck, where a medical school had agreed to allow them to complete their degrees. They got a little money from the American Joint Distribution Committee and donated their blood for extra cash to buy food and textbooks. Among their fellow students was a young man called Laci Revesz, a Jewish émigré from Romania, who soon became Erwin's roommate. Along with Laci, Alice and Erwin graduated a year after arriving, in June 1950.

Meanwhile, Erwin had learned that his parents, his sister, Marta, and Pipez had been allowed out of Hungary and had gone to Israel, arriving with nothing but a sense of freedom. "I missed my family," he recalled. "So when I finished the course, I decided to go to Israel."[18] Alice stayed behind with Laci Revesz in Germany and soon found a job at the Max Planck Institute in Cologne.

In Israel, Erwin had a joyous reunion with his family in Haifa. He took a job in Eilat, a godforsaken desert town with just four hundred employees of a construction company, but soon decided that living in a hut in the middle of a desert was not good for his health or his finances. He returned to Europe, where he drifted aimlessly for several months. At some point, he discovered that Alice had meanwhile become engaged to Laci Revesz, who had managed to get to Sweden and was now trying his best to get the papers for Alice to join him there.

It must have been painful to acknowledge that Alice had decided to live with another man. But any pangs of jealousy he felt were probably forgotten when Erwin found Alice in Cologne. She had lost a lot of weight, and had large, dark circles around her eyes. "I was shocked," he remembered. "The shadow of death had taken over her face." Erwin insisted on taking her to a nearby hospital. He found work and visited her every day. Thanks in part to Erwin supplying her with large doses of Vitamin E, Alice made a slow recovery. Then, one day, her immigration visa arrived from Sweden.

Alice left for Sweden to be with Laci Revesz, and Erwin applied for an immigration visa to Canada. He arrived there in October 1952 and found work in a Montreal mental hospital. Soon, he was earning enough to put something aside each month for his parents in Israel, who were struggling in the nascent country to make ends meet. Then, in 1954, they sent shocking news. On his sixteenth birthday, Pipez had celebrated with friends on a kibbutz. "They danced and sang and drank orange juice," recalled Erwin. "When the time came, the *Kumitz* ended. They took a truck to return home, but the truck sped away prematurely. Pipez fell off. He did not move. Soon it was clear that he had died instantly of head injuries."[19]

In his wallet, they found a picture of Alice.

THE HERMANS EVENTUALLY SUCCEEDED in establishing new lives in America. But it was a difficult transition. Emil had to begin almost from scratch. "He rode ambulances in Harlem for a pittance and served as house physician in old peoples' homes for meals and a couple of dollars," recalled Vera, "studying late into the night for all his tests. But he never uttered a word of regret or even nostalgia. He made a decision in favor of democracy and never looked back."[20]

At age fifty, Emil qualified as a doctor in the United States and then worked as a psychiatrist for twenty years. In 1972, his health rapidly declined. He collapsed one day and was able to recover sufficiently, recalled Vera, to "consume his last dinner with gusto, praising my mother's cooking, as well as her looks, and inviting her for a walk around the block, where they were seen smiling, holding hands. Then his time ran out."[21]

Margit, widowed at sixty-eight, tried to build another new life for herself. In 1973, she began to volunteer at the Helene Fund Medical Center in Trenton, New Jersey, and worked for the next twenty-three years in its gift shop. Before she died in 1995, her only child, Vera, whose life she had saved through her immense courage and determination, was able to spend a great deal of time with her. Margit's beauty was "unaltered by ninety-two years of living," Vera recalled, "including [her] Holocaust experiences and the stresses of twenty-three years of widowhood."[22]

Gradually, but faster than her parents, Vera had also adapted to her new home in the United States. She excelled academically, eventually gaining a master's degree from New York University, where she met her husband, a postgraduate chemist named Jerry Goodkin. They have been together ever since. Their first daughter, Kathleen, was born in 1958, and was joined by Deborah in 1960. Vera then devoted herself to her family and teaching, gaining a doctorate in 1982 and eventually becoming a professor of French and English at Mercer County College in New Jersey, where she would retire in 1997, a much-loved teacher and mentor.[23]

19

Going After the "Master"

L IKE WALLENBERG, Adolf Eichmann also disappeared in the immediate aftermath of the war. Captured in 1945 by the U.S. Army, for two years he used a false name as he was shuttled from one vast POW camp to another. In 1947, he escaped American custody and worked as a laborer under various guises. Then in 1950, with the help of Italian archbishop Alois Hudal, who ran a ratline for Nazi war criminals, he obtained a false passport and made his way to Argentina. He was but one of many wanted Nazi killers who successfully found refuge in the 1950s under the fascist regime of Juan Peron. Eichmann began a new working-class life in the Buenos Aires suburbs, finding jobs in various factories, and then lived for a period on a remote ranch, where he was a rabbit farmer.

Back in Europe, dedicated Nazi hunters, notably Simon Wiesenthal, were convinced that Eichmann was still alive, although his trail had gone cold, and were determined to bring him to justice. But what did their quarry look like? One of the biggest problems facing Wiesenthal and others seeking to find Eichmann was how to obtain a photograph of their wanted man. Without a decent likeness, if not a photograph of Eichmann, it would be impossible to identify him, let alone arrest him and bring him to trial. To complicate matters, Eichmann had been careful to destroy any photographs, going so far as to seize negatives in which he appeared. "He consciously wanted to remain 'the man in the shadows,'" recalled his closest associate, Dieter Wisliceny. "Whenever he needed photographs for identification papers, he had them taken by the Gestapo Photographic Laboratory. I myself took two pictures of Eichmann."[1] Eichmann had told him to hand over the negatives.

The best way to get to the "Master," reasoned Nazi hunters such as Wiesenthal, would be through the many women in his life, starting with his wife.[2] In early 1946, a handsome, charming Holocaust survivor, Manus Diamant, went to Bad Aussee, near Linz, where Vera Eichmann was still living with her and Eichmann's sons. He spent a month there and then returned to Vienna, having befriended Eichmann's three sons but having failed to confirm that Eichmann was still alive.

Then came a breakthrough. In February 1947, fellow Nazi hunter Tuvia Friedman learned that Joseph Weisl, Eichmann's long-standing driver, was in prison in Vienna. During a subsequent interrogation, Weisl told Friedman about one of Eichmann's mistresses, a Frau Missenbach: "She was quite a woman, and he spent a lot of time in Doppel because of her. He probably gave her several hundred thousand marks, which was taken from Jews."

"Where does Frau Missenbach live now?" asked Friedman.

Weisl picked up a pen and drew a map of the area near Linz where she was now living.

"She must have a photo of Eichmann," said Weisl. "I saw one there myself once. She was very proud of him. She knew him from the time he was an ordinary SS enlisted man, and she grew prouder as he kept on getting higher ranks all the time, until he became a lieutenant colonel."

"How many times did you ever take a picture with Eichmann?"

"Never," said Weisl. "He didn't take pictures with me. I was just a driver."

A guard took Weisl back to his cell, and Friedman returned to his Vienna office. The next day, Friedman sent Manus Diamant to Linz to meet with Wiesenthal, who encouraged Diamant to try to seduce Missenbach. "When you think it's the right time, you'll contact me," Wiesenthal told him. "I'll get the Austrian police to search her house for illegal ration coupons. She won't even miss the photo—if she's still got it."

WITHIN WEEKS, Diamant was getting on famously with Missenbach. One day, she showed him a photo album. He smiled as he looked at pictures of her as a baby, and then flicked through the album and stopped at a picture of a man in civilian clothing.

"Who's this?" he asked.

"Oh, a friend. He died, in the war."

Missenbach quickly turned the page.

At the earliest chance, Diamant phoned Wiesenthal.

"Bring your people."

The police made a thorough search and took the photograph. Prints were made and soon distributed around the world. "The photograph of Eichmann was taken in 1939, and he would certainly have changed by 1947," remembered Friedman. "But it was a clear, sharp reproduction. We were all very grateful that the blackness surrounding Eichmann had lifted. Now, at last, we would see the face of our quarry."[3]

Several years would pass, however, before the next break in the hunt for Eichmann. This time it would be Simon Wiesenthal, operating out of an office in Eichmann's hometown of Linz, who would make a crucial discovery, thanks to a passion for collecting stamps. Late in 1953, he met with an Austrian aristocrat in the Tyrol. They drank wine and talked stamps. Wiesenthal told him about his attempts to track down Nazi criminals. The Austrian baron told Wiesenthal that several Nazis in the Tyrol had returned to political power "as though nothing had changed."

The baron then told Wiesenthal about a friend of his, a German lieutenant colonel. In 1952, the German officer in question had gone to Argentina, where he now worked in Juan Peron's army as an instructor, as did many other brutal ex-SS men. "He just sent me a letter," the baron told Wiesenthal, and then handed over the letter. "I asked him whether he met any of our old comrades down there. Here is what he writes: 'There are some people here who we both used to know . . . Imagine whom else I saw and even had to talk to twice: dieses elende Schwein Eichmann, der die Juden kommandierte [this awful swine Eichmann who commanded the Jews]. He lives near Buenos Aires and works for a water company.'"[4]

"How do you like that?" added the baron. "Some of the worst criminals got away."

Wiesenthal did not respond, worried that the baron might become suspicious. "This was no Altaussee rumor," recalled Wiesenthal, "this was fact."[5]

It was the first time that there had been definite confirmation that Eichmann was alive. But the trail soon went cold. Several more years would pass before Eichmann would be finally run to ground.

THE TAPE RECORDER'S SPOOLS TURNED, sometimes into the early hours, week after week, as Adolf Eichmann explained his role in history's greatest genocide. Eichmann's confessor was an ex-SS officer, Wilhelm Sassen, who had agreed to help Eichmann publish his memoirs anonymously. Sassen was half-Dutch, half-German and had served in the Waffen-SS during the war.[6]

The pair talked at Sassen's home over a five-month period during 1956 and eventually recorded sixty-seven tape reels, which produced a script of 695 pages, covering the Final Solution and Eichmann's role in it. Eichmann had been introduced to Sassen by none other than Otto Skorzeny, with whom Eichmann had become reacquainted in Argentina. Skorzeny had served three years in prison before being acquitted of war crimes. The man who had been instrumental in the Arrow Cross putsch of October 15, 1944, was now a close adviser to Juan Peron, and was even rumored to have slept with Eva, Peron's legendary wife.

Eichmann rambled for hour after hour, at one point telling Sassen that Hungary "was the only country where we could not work fast enough, where I was under pressure all the time trying to mobilize transportation and assembly centers for the deportees. Such was the tempo forced upon us by the Hungarian government. In Denmark, our experience was the exact opposite . . . Both were extreme exceptions to the rule generally encountered in the other countries of Europe."[7]

Eichmann finally grew disillusioned with Sassen when he read what he claimed were doctored transcripts of their conversations, and the joint venture fell apart. Then in 1958, two years after parting ways with

Sassen, Eichmann decided to put down roots in Argentina and bought a small plot of waterlogged land in the poverty-stricken, desolate Bancalari district of Buenos Aires. With his three teenage sons, Eichmann built a house at 14 Garibaldi Street.

During 1956, his eldest son, Klaus Eichmann, had befriended an attractive young woman named Sylvia Hermann. Sylvia's father, Lothar, had fled Nazi Germany in 1938 after spending time in a concentration camp. Lothar Hermann often spoke with Klaus Eichmann when he came to visit his daughter. One day, he read an article about a war crimes trial in Frankfurt. Eichmann's name was mentioned in the article. Guessing that Klaus was none other than the son of Nazi war criminal Adolf Eichmann, Lothar wrote to the authorities in Frankfurt, who in turn passed on his letter to Fritz Bauer, the attorney general of Hesse.

Bauer was a former concentration camp prisoner who had fled first to Denmark and then Sweden, before returning to Germany after the war. He passed on Lothar Hermann's letter to the Israeli Foreign Ministry. Walter Eytan, the director general of the Israeli Foreign Ministry, then arranged a meeting with Isser Harel, who headed Mossad, the skilled and much-feared intelligence service set up to track down and kill enemies of Israel such as Eichmann. It was eventually decided that Eichmann should not be assassinated but brought back to Israel to stand trial.

In early 1960, Mossad contacted Hermann and Operation Eichmann began in earnest. It was imperative that Mossad agents sent to Buenos Aires knew for certain that they had found their man. Simon Wiesenthal was painfully aware that the photographs Mossad had of Eichmann, thanks to Manus Diamant, were now twenty-four-years old. New ones were needed if the Israelis were to positively identify the right man. Wiesenthal came up with an ingenious solution: Recent photographs of Eichmann's brothers would give Mossad an idea of what Eichmann now looked like.[8]

Wiesenthal duly arranged for photographers to take pictures of Eichmann's brothers at a funeral. Mossad could then compare their faces with that of Eichmann. "They did a fine job," recalled Wiesenthal. "Hiding behind a large tombstone at a distance of about two hundred yards, they made sharp pictures of the members of the funeral procession, although the light was far from perfect. That night, I had before me enlarged photographs of Adolf Eichmann's four brothers: Emil Rudolf, Otto, Friedrich, and Robert."[9]

Wiesenthal then sent the photos to Mossad. In April 1960, Mossad agent Zvi Aharoni arrived in Buenos Aires and staked out the house at 14 Garibaldi Street. He soon saw a man who fitted Mossad's profile of Eichmann. When he then tried to find out who owned the house, he discovered that it belonged to a certain "Veronica Catarina Leibel de Fichmann." The last name's similarity to Eichmann gave him away. "When I saw that," Aharoni recalled, "I knew I'd cracked it."

For several days, Aharoni and his agents monitored Eichmann's comings and goings and soon discovered that he was a creature of habit. Each evening, around 7:45 p.m., he would get off a bus and walk to his home. It was decided that the Mossad agents would seize Eichmann as he did so. The date was set for May 11, 1960, Eichmann's wedding anniversary.

At 7:40 that evening, Aharoni was in place in a car on the street where Eichmann's bus stopped. The bus arrived on time, but there was no sign of Eichmann. Had their cover been blown? The agents waited for a quarter of an hour, growing increasingly nervous. Then another bus stopped and Eichmann got off.

Eichmann had his hand in a pocket.

"Maybe he's got a gun!" hissed one of the agents, who was sitting nearby in a black sedan.

Eichmann came closer and closer. As he passed the black sedan, one of the agents walked up to him and blocked his path.

"Momentito, Señor!"

Eichmann instantly realized something was up and tried to make a run for it. The agent jumped on him, and the two of them rolled in the gutter. Eichmann shouted for help and "howled and screamed."

When the agent tried to pull Eichmann to his feet, "he let out a piercing scream . . . the primal cry of a cornered animal."[10]

So that no one would hear Eichmann, an agent revved up the car's engine. Eichmann was then pushed into the car, where he immediately went quiet and stopped struggling. He was breathing heavily. He didn't say a word but was clearly very angry.

Aharoni drove off.

"Keep quiet and nothing will happen to you," he told Eichmann in German. "If you struggle, you'll be shot!"

There was no reaction.

"Can you hear me?" yelled Aharoni. "What language do you speak? Que lengua habla?"

Still no reply.

Aharoni thought Eichmann was unconscious. Perhaps he'd killed himself with poison. But then, after they had driven a few hundred yards, Eichmann suddenly said something. He was calm, and it sounded almost as if he were talking to himself.

"I am already resigned to my fate."

Aharoni made sure he was not being tailed. Later that evening, having crossed Buenos Aires, he arrived in front of a Mossad safe house. Eichmann was hustled into the house and then into a small room.

"Sit down!"

Eichmann did so.

"Undress!"

Eichmann took off his coat, tie, and shirt.

"Lift your left arm."

Eichmann did so slowly. There was a telltale scar in his left armpit. Unlike other SS fugitives, Eichmann had removed his blood type SS tattoo himself in a German POW camp, not through surgery.

One of his captors pulled out a cap worn by SS officers and put it on Eichmann's head. Another agent looked at a picture and passed it to the other agents. They nodded. Then yet another Israeli agent entered, carrying X-ray plates. He was a doctor and carefully examined Eichmann's collarbone and skull, both of which were once fractured. Eichmann was asked to write a few words. His handwriting was then examined.

"You are Karl Adolf Eichmann."

"Are you Americans?" asked Eichmann.

"You are Karl Adolf Eichmann."

"You must be Israelis." Fear showed in Eichmann's eyes. "The others are not interested in me," said Eichmann. "Ich habe die ganze Zeit gezittert dass es so kommen wird. [I have always feared this is how it would happen.]"

The agents then placed Eichmann on an iron bed, with one leg shackled to the bed frame. When an agent began peering and prodding around in his mouth, Eichmann said that after so many years they needn't expect him to still be on the alert and to have poison hidden in his teeth. In spite of his protest, his false teeth were removed and a thorough search made of his clothes and shoes.

"If you cooperate and don't try anything foolish," one of the agents told Eichmann, "you will be given a fair trial and the benefit of legal counsel."

"All right," Eichmann said. "I will cooperate."[11] He was now trembling with fear.

"You can quite easily understand," said Eichmann, "that I am agitated at the moment. I would like to ask for a little wine, red wine if it's possible, to help me control my emotions."

One of the agents agreed to Eichmann's request.

"As soon as you told me to keep quiet, there in the car, I knew I was in the hands of Israelis," said Eichmann. "I know Hebrew: I learned it from Rabbi Leo Baeck: 'In the beginning God created the heavens and the earth . . . *Shma Yisrael* . . .'"

· Eichmann's captors were stunned by Eichmann's use of their holy language. According to Mossad Chief Isser Harel: "The obsequious tone he used addressing his captors was enough in itself to disgust them, but when he pronounced the sacred words that millions of Jewish lips murmured three times a day and at the moment of ultimate dread, they were shaken to the core."[12]

Eichmann was now a prisoner of the Jews, a race he had vowed to destroy. To his surprise, during the ten days and nights that he was in Mossad's custody in Argentina, he was neither molested nor insulted. Nevertheless, he was convinced that his captors would kill him sooner or later. "Every time we gave him something to eat," recalled one of the agents, "he thought we were about to poison him; if we took him out to walk in the courtyard, he was afraid we would shoot him. We thought we were dealing with a man of particular intellectual qualities. But before us stood a nobody, a coward who cooperated all down the line, who never gave us any problems and sometimes even offered to help us."[13]

It seemed that all Eichmann now cared about was his family. It was the one thing about which he showed genuine emotion. He told one of his captors of his worries about his wife and children.

"I didn't leave them any money," Eichmann said. "How will my wife and sons live?"

"No harm will come to them," one of his captors replied. "They'll manage all right without you. But tell me, please, you who worry so much about your children, how could you and your colleagues murder little children in the tens and hundreds of thousands?"

Eichmann looked upset.

"Today, I can't understand how we could have done such things," he confessed. "I was always on the side of the Jews. I was striving to find a satisfactory solution to their problem. I did what everybody else was doing. I was conscripted like everyone else—I wanted to get on in life."[14]

On May 19, 1960, Eichmann was disguised as a crewmember of El Al Israel Airlines and taken on board a plane bound for Israel.[15] Dressed in airline uniforms, the Mossad agents and their prisoner had managed to get through the Argentine passport control undetected. The agents' doctor had assured them that Eichmann could be kept drugged in such a way that he could walk and keep his eyes open but not speak. Later that day, the El Al aircraft touched down in Israel.

At 4 p.m. on May 23, 1961, Israel's prime minister, David Ben-Gurion, stepped up to the rostrum in the Knesset to address the packed chamber. "I have to inform you that a short time ago, Israel's security forces located one of the biggest Nazi criminals, Adolf Eichmann," he announced. "He is already in detention in this country and will shortly be brought before court here under the law of 1950 on the punishment of Nazis and their accomplices."[16]

There were cries and gasps and then thundering applause.

The following day, fifty-five-year-old Adolf Eichmann found himself standing before Berlin-born police superintendent Avner W. Less, who would lead the criminal investigation into Eichmann's many crimes. "Suddenly, there stood before me a very ordinary looking man," recalled

Less, "not much taller than me, skinny rather than slim, certainly no Frankenstein monster, nor a devil with cloven hooves and horns."

For more than 275 hours, Less would question Eichmann in painstaking detail. Before each interrogation, Eichmann would stand to attention, as if he were facing an SS disciplinary hearing. Less was surprised at first by how poor Eichmann's German was. "Official language is the only language I know," Eichmann would later admit.

At one point, Less asked Eichmann if he had any regrets.

Eichmann looked at Less in astonishment and said that remorse was "something for little children."[17]

Eichmann's trial began after eight months of investigation.

Criminal case 40/61 opened on April 11, 1961, with Eichmann sitting in a bulletproof glass box, wearing spectacles and showing no obvious emotion as Moshe Landau, president of the court, read out charges in Hebrew against him. Simon Wiesenthal was one of many onlookers who were surprised by Eichmann's appearance: "Everything about Eichmann seemed drawn with charcoal: his grayish face, his balding head, his clothes. There was nothing demonic about him, he looked like a bookkeeper who is afraid to ask for a raise."[18]

The journalist and academic Hannah Arendt, who was covering the trial for the *New Yorker,* famously noted that: "The trouble with Eichmann was precisely that so many were like him, and that the many were neither perverted nor sadistic, that they were, and still are, terribly and terrifyingly normal." Eichmann had personified the "banality of evil."[19]

For those in the courtroom who had survived his genocide, by contrast, nothing was normal about the man whose crimes they heard catalogued for the first time. To them and those still alive today who were saved by Wallenberg, Eichmann was the very incarnation of evil, and Arendt's assessment could not have been more profoundly wrong.

Central to the prosecution's case were Eichmann's actions in Hungary, which had proved that far from being a cog in a machine and a bureaucrat who had just been "taking orders," he had disobeyed Himmler's instructions and tried to kill Hungary's last Jews until he was forced to flee Budapest before the Soviet advance.[20] Told to stop his genocide,

Eichmann did the opposite. Witnesses from Hungary such as Joel Brand, whom Eichmann had sent on a fruitless and tragic mission—a cruel distraction as it turned out—were able to face their former tormentor and testify to his crimes in Budapest. The "blood for trucks" deal and his experiences in Budapest and then British custody would, Brand concluded, "haunt [him] until [his] dying day. It is much more than a man can bear."[21]

The judges at the trial finally decided that Eichmann was a Jew-hating Nazi fanatic whose "hatred was cold and calculating, aimed rather against the Jewish people as a whole, than against the individual Jew, and for this very reason, it was so poisonous and destructive in all its manifestations." Rather than confess and atone for his crimes in public, Eichmann had lied repeatedly during cross-examination in a vain attempt to escape conviction. "[This] attempt was not unskillful, due to those qualities which he had shown at the time of his actions—an alert mind; the ability to adapt himself to any situation; cunning and a glib tongue."[22]

At one point during the trial, Attorney General Gideon Hausner had spoken of Eichmann's greatest adversary, Raoul Wallenberg, by now missing for more than a quarter century. "One bold man," said Hausner, "who had the strength to act according to his conscience and belief. His deeds, like those of King Christian of Denmark, give rise to the somber thought: How many could have been saved, even in the countries of actual extermination, had there only been more like him among those who had the power to act, whether openly or in secret?"[23]

IT WAS 8:21 A.M. ON Friday, December 11, 1961, when the "Master" finally got his comeuppance.

Judge Moshe Landau pronounced the trial's verdict in Hebrew: "Beit din she dan otcha limita. [The court condemns you to death.]"

Eichmann stood with his back straight, poker faced, in his bulletproof box.

"You will be hanged by the neck until death ensues," declared Landau.

Eichmann—the "enemy of the human species"—had been found guilty on all fifteen counts.[24]

In a handwritten letter, Eichmann had already appealed to President Ben Zwi of Israel for clemency. But Zwi had publicly stated that "There can be no pardon for what this man has done."[25]

Israeli authorities were meanwhile flooded with letters from around the globe. Volunteers asked to be allowed to hang Eichmann. Many people suggested that Eichmann be killed in a gas chamber. Others recommended a far more prolonged, painful, and public end for the man who had protested throughout the trial that he was "not the monster I am made out to be."[26]

At 11:30 p.m. on May 31, 1962, a Protestant clergyman entered the condemned's cell.

"I am not prepared to discuss the Bible," snapped Eichmann. "I do not have time to waste."

While awaiting the verdict, Eichmann had earlier told the same clergyman, Reverend William Hull, "My brother is a lawyer at Linz . . . he wrote me that on the evidence submitted there was only one verdict possible, and that I should be set free."[27]

At ten minutes to midnight, guards led Eichmann to the execution chamber, where he was stood on a trapdoor. A noose hung from a beam above him.

The noose was about to be placed around Eichmann's neck when he suddenly spoke to the small group of witnesses before him.

"After a short while, gentlemen, we shall all meet again. So is the fate of all men."

Eichmann looked down. He seemed to be struggling to control his emotions.

"I have lived believing in God and I die believing in God."

There was another pause.

"Long live Germany. Long live Argentina. Long live Austria. These are the countries with which I have been most closely associated, and I shall not forget them. I greet my wife, my family, and my friends. I had to obey the rules of war and my flag."

The noose was placed over Eichmann's head.

One of the guards present, Shalom Nagar, recalled that he was standing a few feet from Eichmann, who refused to have his face covered and was still wearing a pair of checkered slippers.

Nagar pulled the lever on the gallows and Eichmann fell, dangling by the rope. His face was soon as white as chalk, his eyes bulging and his tongue dangling.

An hour later, Nagar and a colleague removed Eichmann from the gallows. "The rope rubbed the skin off his neck," recalled Nagar, "and his tongue and chest were covered with blood. I didn't know that when a person is strangled all the air remains in his stomach. So when I lifted him, all the air that was inside came out and the most horrifying sound was released from his mouth—'baaaaa'—I felt [that] the Angel of Death had come to take me too."

With the help of other guards, Nagar placed Eichmann's corpse on a stretcher and carried him to an oven. A fellow guard, who had survived Auschwitz, had ensured that the oven was working at the optimum temperature. Nagar pushed the stretcher toward the oven, but he was shaking so hard with nerves that Eichmann's corpse rolled from side to side. Finally, he was able to push the "architect of the Final Solution" inside the oven and close its doors.

Shalom Nagar was supposed to accompany the ashes to the port of Tel Aviv, but he was so affected by the experience that his boss had to send him home.

Eichmann's ashes were dumped in the Mediterranean. They would not poison Israeli soil.

Forty years later, Nagar told an Israeli journalist: "God commands us to wipe out Amalek [the enemy of the Jew], and 'not to forget.' I have fulfilled both."[28]

VERA HERMAN, like many of those rescued by Wallenberg, followed the Eichmann trial with intense interest. "There was so much pain that nothing could make up for it," she recalls, "but if anything came close, that was it—Eichmann's trial. It was a book ending for me. I was happy that he was executed, but it wasn't enough. You can only die one death and he should have died a million times."[29]

Erwin Koranyi also followed the trial from Montreal, where it made daily headlines. He realized now how common men like Eichmann had been in German society under the Nazis. Indeed, Eichmann had been but one of many who had belonged to the Hitler cult. "Hitler's genius was to understand that there is a balance between aggression and love. Hitler somehow instinctively grasped that if you fuel the aggression, then you automatically increase the love and dedication to the cause. Somebody must be hated terribly to do that."[30]

20

The Wallenberg Mystery

I N STOCKHOLM in the months after the war ended, Raoul Wallenberg's parents waited anxiously for the day when the Soviets would
send their son home. They celebrated his thirty-fourth birthday in
August 1945 and paid a tax bill for him that October.[1] But the weeks became months, and then two years, and still Raoul did not return. In
1947, Raoul's increasingly desperate mother appealed to Stalin directly:

> To Generalissimo Joseph Stalin:
>
> As mother of Raoul Wallenberg, legation secretary to the Swedish
> mission in Budapest, I plead with the powerful rulers of the Soviet
> Union for help in retrieving my beloved son. In short, my son's
> story is as follows: From July 1944 to January 1945, he fought with
> all his might and intelligence against the Nazi terror, which wanted
> to destroy the entire Jewish population of Budapest. When
> Budapest was liberated by the forces of the Soviet Union, my son
> was put under protection of the Russian military authorities in
> January 1945. This fact was officially communicated to the
> Swedish Foreign Office by the Foreign Ministry of the Soviet
> Union in January 1945. In February that year, this joyful message
> was further confirmed to me by Ambassador Kollontay. Since then,
> two and a half years have passed without the Soviet authorities
> communicating any further information about him. My trust in the

powerful Soviet Union is so great that, despite my anxiety, I have remained convinced that I would see him again. As I presume that the delay with his return home is due to misunderstandings by lower-level officials, I now turn to the ruler of the Soviet Union with a prayer that my son may be returned to Sweden and to his longing mother.

Respectfully,
Maj von Dardel[2]

Maj von Dardel gave the letter to the Swedish Foreign Ministry in Stockholm and asked them to pass it on to Moscow. But the letter never reached Stalin. An official stated caustically: "If this is just a matter of calming Mrs. Von Dardel, we can always conduct a mass at Minindel [the Russian Foreign Ministry]."[3] This dismissive attitude was shared by many Swedish diplomats including Dag Hammarskjold, the Swedish UN secretary general (1953–61), who complained wearily: "I do not want to begin World War Three because of one missing person."[4]

It was not until August 18, 1947, that Andrei Vyshinsky, the Soviet deputy foreign minister, made the first official Soviet statement about Wallenberg: "Wallenberg is not in the Soviet Union and he is not known to us." Refusing to believe Vyshinsky, Raoul's parents founded Wallenberg Action, an international pressure group whose mission was to try to find their son. Maj told her daughter, Nina, and son, Guy, to assume that Raoul was alive until the end of the century and not to give up hope.

According to researcher Susanne Berger, who has spent many years investigating Wallenberg's fate: "Fredrik and Maj von Dardel faced an impossible situation: While the Swedish government asked them to provide credible evidence for their son's presence in the Soviet Union after 1945, it refused them full access to all witness testimonies and documentation in the case, citing government secrecy laws."[5]

Five years passed and still Wallenberg's parents did not know what had happened to their son. On October 24, 1952, Raoul's stepfather wrote in his diary: "Raoul Wallenberg's fate has lain like a dark cloud over our existence." Both parents railed against the Swedish Foreign Ministry, which they believed had so cruelly abandoned their son. The strain of not knowing what had happened to him must have been immense. They reportedly withdrew socially, playing solitaire and painting in the few hours when they weren't trying to find him.[6] Increasingly, they felt ostracized from polite Stockholm society. "People are afraid to talk to me about Raoul," Maj admitted, "but they are also afraid not to talk to me about the one subject which I live for. So, really, it's much easier for them just to avoid me."[7] Their son's heroism was inspiring but also perhaps an uncomfortable reminder of how most of his countrymen, unlike their neighbors in Norway, had been content to stand by and do nothing as the world at their borders disappeared into flames.

SIXTY-FIVE-YEAR-OLD Fredrik von Dardel sat at a table in his living room. One day in March 1956, his seventy-one-year-old wife, Maj, watched as he wrote neatly in blue ink on a white piece of paper. Maj was seated by a telephone near a green-marble chest cabinet, where a picture of twenty-four-year-old Raoul stood beside some flowers.

Husband and wife were preparing a letter for Sweden's prime minister to hand to his counterpart in Moscow.

Dear beloved Raoul,

After many years of despair and terrible longing for you, we have finally reached the point where the heads of the coalition government, Prime Minister Erlander and Minister Hedlund, are going to Moscow to ensure that you will be allowed to return home. May they be successful, and may your suffering finally be at an end. We have never given up hope of seeing you again, even though all our efforts to contact you up to now, to our great regret and sorrow, have been in vain. The 11 years that have passed since your disappearance have been filled with despair night and day, but we have been sustained by the hope of one day seeing you

among us and again being able to kiss you and hold your hands
and hear your beloved voice . . . There is a room here waiting for
you when you return with the prime minister.[8]

Erlander arrived at the Kremlin that April and was soon shown into a
room, where he faced Premier Nikolai Bulganin, Foreign Minister
Vyacheslav Molotov, and sixty-two-year-old party secretary Nikita Khrushchev, Stalin's boorish successor. Khrushchev would be best remembered in the West for taking off a shoe and banging it on a podium, like
some frenzied peasant, at the United Nations in 1960.

Erlander reportedly tried to impress on the three Soviets, the most
powerful men in the communist world, why Sweden regarded the Wallenberg case as important. Khrushchev and Molotov listened to Erlander
as he pulled documents from his briefcase. But then Bulganin accused
Erlander of bringing up the case to harm relations between the Soviet
Union and Sweden.

"This is a waste of time!" he shouted. "We don't have time for this kind
of nonsense!"

"If you won't even accept the material that I have brought," Erlander
replied, "how can you be so sure that this whole affair is a falsification,
an unimportant sideshow cooked up to embarrass you?"

"I don't want to hear any more of this!" shouted Bulganin.

Erlander stood his ground.

"At the very least I must demand that you accept this material and appoint someone you trust to investigate it. If you refuse, I'll end my visit
now. I won't go to the south of your country as planned; I won't visit the
atomic power facility you have so wanted me to see."

Khrushchev took the file of documents Erlander had brought on the
Wallenberg case.

Bulganin then told Erlander: "It's a great pity that we have to waste so
much time on an affair such as this; however, as a gesture of our goodwill
toward Sweden, we will accede to your request that we accept this material about Wallenberg, and we will appoint someone to examine it. You
will have our reply as soon as possible."[9]

The Soviets took their time replying. Almost a year later, on February 6, 1957, Deputy Foreign Minister Andrei Gromyko gave a memorandum to Swedish Ambassador Sohlman in Moscow:

At the request of the government of the kingdom of Sweden, the competent Soviet authorities were charged with undertaking a thorough examination of the Wallenberg file received by the Soviet Foreign Ministry from Sweden in March, April, and May 1956. As a result, the authorities studied the archives for the registration of prisoners. They also examined the reports of interrogations, looking for a sign of the presence of Raoul Wallenberg. Similarly, they questioned those who may have been concerned in the circumstances mentioned in the Swedish dossier. No one interrogated recognized the name of Wallenberg. None of these efforts provided the smallest indication that Raoul Wallenberg had spent time in the Soviet Union.

However, in the course of their research, the Soviet authorities had the occasion to examine the files of prison infirmaries. They discovered in Lubianka a handwritten report which may refer to Wallenberg. This report is addressed to Abakumov, minister for state hospital service. It is dated July 17, 1947; "I am writing to inform you that the prisoner Walenberg [sic], known to you, died suddenly in his cell last night. He was apparently the victim of myocardiac infarctus [heart attack]. In view of your instructions to me to supervise Walenberg personally, I ask you to let me know who should conduct the autopsy to ascertain the cause of death. 17 July 1947. Signed: Smoltsov, Colonel, Chief of the Prison Infirmary." The same report contains a second manuscript note from Smoltsov: "Informed the minister personally. Order given to cremate the body without autopsy. 17 July 1947."

Smoltsov died on May 7, 1953. The above-mentioned facts lead one to conclude that Wallenberg died in July 1947. Evidently he was arrested, like many others, by the Russian Army in the area of fighting. That he was later detained in prison and that false information was given about him to the Foreign Ministry by the chief of state security over a number of years is one aspect of the criminal activity of Abakumov. As is well known, the latter was sentenced by the Supreme Court of Justice and executed for serious crimes.

The Soviet Union expresses its sincere regret in relation to these circumstances and assures the government of the kingdom of Sweden, and the family of Raoul Wallenberg, of its profound sympathy.[10]

RAOUL WALLENBERG'S PARENTS were not inclined to believe a word of Gromyko's communiqué. They persisted in their search, buoyed by several alleged sightings of their son in the gulag, through the sixties and well into the next decade. But still they found no hard evidence that their son was alive, despite the best efforts over the years of such high-profile supporters as Nazi hunter Simon Wiesenthal ("If before I die, I could embrace my own beloved son, this is all I ask," Maj had written to him); oil magnate Armand Hammer, who enjoyed back-channel relations with Brezhnev; Alexander Solzhenitsyn, dissident author of the greatest indictment of the gulag, *The Gulag Archipelago;* and nuclear physicist Albert Einstein, who had written to Stalin in 1947. (Stalin had reassured Einstein that he knew nothing about Wallenberg's whereabouts.)[11]

The Swedish government did not make the parents' search for their son any easier. In 1976, Fredrik von Dardel asked for all the documentation in his son's case to be made public. Instead, Sweden passed a law, according to the Wallenberg researcher Susanne Berger, "which simply shortened the then-valid fifty-year secrecy requirement to thirty years—rendering most of the relevant material still inaccessible. This included important information about other Swedes in Soviet captivity after 1945. Without this documentation, a proper evaluation of Wallenberg's fate became almost impossible."[12]

On February 6, 1978, a Swedish official visited Wallenberg's parents and later noted in his diary: "A very painful meeting with these two old people . . . That he is alive is taken for granted."

That April of 1978, Raoul's stepfather ended his journal, begun in 1956, with two words in English: "stone wall."[13]

Frustrated and exhausted, the parents finally could take no more heartbreak. In 1979, after decades of looking in vain for their son, they took their own lives. On February 12, Raoul's ninety-three-year-old stepfather died in his bed from an overdose of sleeping pills. According to the *Wall Street Journal*: "Raoul Wallenberg's mother, again widowed, lay on her sofa two days later and swallowed an overdose of barbiturates. [Their daughter] Nina Lagergren arrived shortly after. Her mother, still alive, asked Nina to promise that she and [her brother] Guy would keep fighting for their older brother—and presume him living, as she had long instructed, until 2000. Nina gave her word."[14]

Eighty-seven-year-old Jacob Wallenberg—Raoul's godfather and cousin—attended the funeral for Raoul's mother and father. "[Raoul's] childhood hero," the journalist Kati Marton later reported, "spent an unusually long time taking his leave of the couple's twin coffins. Some who were present felt Jacob was apologizing to them for his many years of indifference."[15]

Jacob died the following year.

RAOUL'S SIBLINGS CARRIED ON the search after their parents' deaths, hoping that in some corner of the Soviet gulag their brother might still be alive. Nina found some comfort in meeting people whom her brother had saved, including Vera Herman and Alice Breuer. "I felt a very strong emotional sensation looking at these lovely people," she recalled, "all so deeply committed in wanting to pay their debt to their savior."[16]

Around the world, Wallenberg's deeds had not been forgotten. Tens of thousands of survivors longed to know what had happened to the man who had saved them. Many now lived in America, having fled repression in their native Hungary. In 1979, California resident Tom Lantos ran for Congress and was elected. Lantos had escaped from a forced labor camp and had hidden in Budapest under Swedish protection. He had then escaped Hungary in 1947 after protesting against communism. He and his Hungarian wife, Annette, whose father was murdered by the Arrow

Cross, were determined to honor, if not find, their savior. One of Lantos's first actions as a congressman was to introduce a bill making Raoul Wallenberg an honorary citizen of the United States. The bill passed the House of Representatives by 396 to 2 and through the Senate unanimously.

At just after 2:30 p.m. on October 5, 1981, at a White House ceremony attended by Nina Lagergren and her brother, Guy von Dardel, President Ronald Reagan eulogized their lost brother.

"Raoul Wallenberg is the Swedish savior of almost one hundred thousand Jewish men, women, and children," said Reagan. "What he did, what he accomplished, was of biblical proportions. Wherever he is, his humanity burns like a torch. Sir Winston Churchill, another man of force and fortitude, is the only other person who has received honorary U.S. citizenship."

Reagan then added: "I heard someone say that a man has made at least a start in understanding the meaning of human life when he plants shade trees under which he knows he will never sit. Raoul Wallenberg is just such a man. He nurtured the lives of those he never knew at the risk of his own. And then just recently, I was told that in a special area behind the [Yad Vashem] Holocaust Memorial in Israel, Hungarian Jews now living in Sweden planted ten thousand trees in Raoul's honor."

Reagan turned to face Nina Lagergren and her brother.

"Mrs. Lagergren. Mr. von Dardel," said Reagan. "We're going to do everything in our power so that your brother can sit beneath the shade of those trees and enjoy the respect and love so many held for him."[17]

REAGAN'S SPEECH AND the very public recognition of Wallenberg's achievements at the White House encouraged many to believe that a breakthrough in the Wallenberg case might materialize. Surely the Soviets would respond to Reagan's statements with new details, perhaps even by releasing Wallenberg as an act of détente? But the months passed, the cold war stretched on, and Wallenberg's fate remained its most exasperating mystery.

Then, at last, there was an astonishing development. In 1989, after the Berlin Wall came down, the Soviet ambassador in Sweden called Raoul's brother and sister to a meeting in the Soviet embassy in Stockholm. The Soviets apparently wanted to close the book on Wallenberg, once and for all, and they invited the siblings to Moscow.

Glasnost was in full force. Doors finally seemed to be opening. Survivors talked of Wallenberg being freed. Vera Herman and others in the United States hosted a party for Nina in New Jersey that year, before she and her brother headed to Moscow at the invitation of the Russian foreign ministry.

On October 16, brother and sister stood in an office in the KGB headquarters in Moscow and watched a Soviet official place a wooden box before them.[18] It contained all that the Soviets could find, they said, of their brother's belongings, taken from him in 1945: the address book with Adolf Eichmann's three telephone numbers, a cigarette case, his diplomatic passport, and stacks of Hungarian banknotes and U.S. dollars. "To hold those things in my hand," recalled Nina, "was both a wonderful and a painful thing . . . a deeply emotional moment."

But she was not convinced that the Russians had revealed everything. "In that system, although people disappeared frequently, it didn't happen without any record being kept," she later said. "They must show us the proof, open up the files, be honest with us. For fifty years we have been trying to learn the truth, and it still lies out there somewhere."[19]

During the 1989 visit, a Soviet Foreign Ministry spokesman, Grennadi I. Gerasimov, apologized to Nina and her brother for his country's "tragic mistake."

"Your brother was swept up in the maelstrom of repression," he added.

The message from other officials was essentially the same as before: Wallenberg had died in 1947.

"We simply don't believe them," Nina told journalists in Moscow during the visit. "We are convinced our brother is still alive in a prison here."[20]

Back in America, even though cold war tensions were easing, those rescued by Wallenberg were bitterly disappointed by the outcome of the trip. "We had sent Nina off, saying 'bring him back to us,'" recalled Vera Herman. "Instead of her brother, she got a brown paper bag with his belongings in it."[21]

Brother and sister returned to Sweden, none the wiser as to what had happened to their brother, and carried on their soul-destroying search.

Guy Von Dardel was now obsessed. He even commissioned an FBI sketch of what his brother would look like at age eighty. He traveled to Russia fifteen times in 1994 alone, suffering scabies and hypothermia.[22]

THE YEAR 1994 ALSO SAW the publication of a sensational memoir, *Special Tasks*, by eighty-seven-year-old Pavel Anatolyevich Sudoplatov, a lieutenant general in the Soviet intelligence service. Sudoplatov had been closely involved with the assassination of Stalin's bitter enemy, Leon Trotksy, and other highly secret operations during the Cold War. He had served in the KGB for more than fifty years, and at one time, he claimed, had controlled "more than twenty thousand guerillas, moles, and spies."

In *Special Tasks*, Sudoplatov argued that the Soviets tried to recruit Wallenberg as an agent, "to operate either with his family or with the Swedish government.[23] His interrogators may have bullied him with charges that he was a Gestapo informer or an American agent, but that was not the intention from the top. The goal was to recruit him."[24] But, by July 1947, they had made no progress. "Wallenberg had refused to cooperate and he was eliminated at the same time the leadership continued to tell the Swedes that they knew nothing of his fate."

Sudoplatov speculated that "Wallenberg was [probably] taken to a super-secret cell in the commandant's section of the ministry, a location monitored personally by [Grigori] Maironovsky as chief of the toxicological laboratory. My best estimate is that Wallenberg was killed by Maironovsky, who was ordered to inject him with poison under the guise of medical treatment. According to witnesses who told me the story, Wallenberg was kept in the second block of the jail, where medical checkups and injections were routine for prisoners."[25]

One of the reasons why Sudoplatov believed that Wallenberg was poisoned was that his body was cremated without an autopsy: "An autopsy would have revealed the exact nature of his death. The regulations were that those executed under special government decisions were cremated without autopsy at the Donskoi cemetery crematorium and their ashes buried in a common grave."[26]

If Sudoplatov's thesis is correct, the remains of one of the twentieth century's greatest humanitarians are buried alongside those of one of its most depraved sociopaths—Lavrentiy Beria, the former head of the NKVD, who carried out Stalin's greatest purges, sending hundreds of thousands to their deaths.[27] Arguably the greatest hero of the Holocaust had become the most famous victim of a Stalinist terror that between 1929 and 1953 claimed well over two million lives.[28]

IN HIS QUEST TO FIND HIS BROTHER, Guy von Dardel would eventually sacrifice all his savings and his health. Although doctors could not work out at first why he became ill, his daughter Louise did: "The illness is Raoul Wallenberg illness."[29]

In 2000, the year their mother had told them would finally be the time to accept that Raoul was dead, Guy von Dardel and Nina Lagergren both decided that they in fact could not do so. They continued, despite old age and dwindling resources, to campaign for more information and to speak out about what they saw as the Swedish government's cold indifference to their brother's fate.

Answers to their questions remained just as elusive. In January 2001, a joint Swedish-Russian group published a report on Wallenberg that concluded: "The Russian announcement of Raoul Wallenberg's death could only be accepted if it were confirmed beyond any reasonable doubt. This has not happened, partly for the want of a credible death certificate, and partly because the testimony about Raoul Wallenberg being alive after 1947 cannot be dismissed. The burden of proof regarding the death of Raoul Wallenberg lies with the Russian Government."[30]

It still does.

According to Susanne Berger, who spent six years as a consultant to the Swedish-Russian investigation: "There is no longer a debate: It is clear that Russia has documentation which could help solve the Wallenberg mystery if researchers were given proper access. Russia itself does not deny this fact but stresses that it will not allow review of documentation it deems to be of an operational intelligence nature . . . Why does Sweden not fight to see this material?"[31]

21

The Last Survivors

FOR DECADES AFTER HER ARRIVAL in America, Vera Herman did not talk much about her survival of the Holocaust in Hungary. "There was so much pain," she said in 2009, her hands shaking, seated on a couch in her home in New Jersey. "We lost so many people. The one person who was dearest to me was my grandmother. She was my role model and my idol. The thought that she died, that she ended up . . ." Her voice trailed off. "And then my grandfather—he was such an honorable, charitable, decent, and proud man . . . I tried to tell people about it all, once I learned enough English." But people's reactions dismayed her. "One was—'you've suffered so much, why not put it all behind you.' It was well-meaning but impossible. The other reaction made me shut up for thirty-seven years—'you must be exaggerating. Human beings don't do things like that to other human beings.' . . . I think a lot of Americans felt vaguely guilty for not having stopped it."[1]

Then the past stormed back and her life would never be the same. It all began with a telephone call in August 1983. Vera was told that Rider University in New Jersey was planning to celebrate the deeds of a Holocaust rescuer.

Had she ever heard of Raoul Wallenberg?

Vera laughed.

"If I didn't know who he was I wouldn't be talking to you today."[2]

Vera agreed to speak about Wallenberg and her rescue. Over several weeks, she prepared her speech, knowing her family would be in the audience. The horror and terror returned, mostly during the night, erupt-ing into vivid flashbacks in her sleep. Fastidious, studious to the last, she kept a pencil and pad by her bed. "I would write down the nightmares and sort out what was and was not reality. I had about six weeks of pretty nasty nightmares. There was delayed PTSD [post-traumatic stress disor-der]. We survivors had not stopped to analyze what the experiences had done to us. We were just so grateful to be alive."[3]

On October 5, 1983, at Rider University, near her home in New Jer-sey, Vera walked to a podium before a packed house and spoke at length for the first time about her experiences during the Holocaust. "All of a sudden," she later recalled, "I came to a sobering realization—a discovery of extraordinary importance: I was among the youngest of the survivors of the Holocaust, western civilization's darkest hour. None of us were getting any younger. It was our sacred duty to speak for those who per-ished and, above all, to try to teach love, acceptance, and tolerance to the young through the lessons of the Holocaust in order to stem the ever-rising tide of hatred everywhere in the world."[4]

Vera has since spent much of her free time doing precisely that. She still urges her audiences to remember that "we are all human beings. Only after this do we belong to educational, ethnic, political, racial, reli-gious, or social groups. If we accept that which unites us, our common humanity, the reasons that divide us should not matter."

On a warm spring day in 2009, as sunlight floods through windows in her New Jersey home, Vera tells the story of how her father Emil tried to get his family to safety in America in 1939. Sadly, the Nazis arrived be-fore the Hermans could get away. But Emil did manage to get permission to send two containers of family heirlooms across the Atlantic, where they sat for seven long years in a New York warehouse. Remarkably, when Emil opened the containers in 1947, he discovered that nothing had been touched. He also found Vera's most precious belonging—a Shirley Temple doll—which he proudly returned to her. To this day, Vera treasures it as her only memento of her idyllic childhood before the Holocaust.

"If anyone deserved to at least see the fruits of his labor, it was Raoul Wallenberg," says Vera. "The Russians robbed people of their souls. They would convince their prisoners that no one cared about them. It is just horrendous to think that they did that to him."

Vera doesn't hold out much hope that Vladimir Putin will be any more helpful than Gorbachev was in solving the mystery of Wallenberg's fate: "I don't think Putin is much different from Stalin."[5] As with others who were rescued by Wallenberg, she struggles with the notion that the man who saved her is, in all likelihood, dead. "I don't think we can ever accept his probable death," she says.[6]

If by some miracle Wallenberg were still alive, adds Vera, she would show him her family. They are his greatest legacy.

It is a familiar and deeply affecting refrain repeated around the globe by those rescued—the one hundred thousand lives some credit him with saving have now become, perhaps, a million or more. The living testament to his humanity continues to multiply, growing as the years pass, a perpetual reminder of how one man really can make a difference.

MARIANNE LOWY, like Vera Herman, escaped communism in 1947 and moved to the United States with her husband, Pista Reiss. She had two children, a girl and a boy, both of whom dote on her today. In 1974, she remarried. Today, eighty-six and widowed from her second husband, she still has the high cheekbones and striking looks of the dark-haired teenager who wore an exquisite Wallenstein gown to her first ball in 1942, practiced pirouettes on the polished parquet floors of her parents' Budapest home, and dreamed as a young girl, thanks to her family's friendship with the successful movie producer Adolph Zukor, of being sent to Hollywood to become a child star. "I missed my boat," she smiles, seated in an Upper East Side studio in New York, where she spends each fall before returning to her home in Palm Beach. "I could have been another Shirley Temple."[7]

Like Vera Herman, Marianne sees it as her life's last mission to remind the world about the man who saved her, her family, and so many others. She speaks as often as she can in high schools, telling students to live their lives to the fullest, as Wallenberg did. "Life is very precious," she says. "You have to make the best of every moment that you live. Do not listen to demagogues. Try not to have hatred and prejudice. Try to help others. Never lose hope."

Her memories are still vivid; her gratitude to Wallenberg undiminished. She smiles as she recalls that gold and cans of sardines were the most sought-after items on the black market in Budapest during the Holocaust. Gold could buy life. Sardines sustained it. Although she does not like sardines, she still keeps two cans of them in her home, "just in case."[8]

THERE ARE MANY DATES that eighty-six-year-old Erwin Koranyi cannot forget. One of the most poignant was the day in 1990 when he received a letter from his first wife, Alice Breuer, in Stockholm. Erwin opened it, excited to read Alice's news. The letter included a clipping from the Stockholm newspaper *Expressen*. On January 13, 1990, it had published Wallenberg's 1944 diary, page by page. Alice had sent Erwin photocopies of some of the pages.

Erwin was astonished to read that on August 5, 1944, according to the diary, Raoul Wallenberg had a meeting at 4 p.m. with a certain "Koranyi." Then on another page of the diary, on August 7, was a note in Wallenberg's neat handwriting: "5 fanger"—five prisoners, including a "Mrs. Koran"—Alice.

August 7 had been another unforgettable date—the day Erwin had been reunited with Alice, thanks to Wallenberg.

Erwin read the clipping carefully.

"My eyes filled with tears," he recalled, "as I remembered Wallenberg by this silent reminder from his grave."[9]

Erwin was now married to a fellow Hungarian Holocaust survivor, Edie, some of whose family had died on the death marches in November 1944. Their marriage would last fifty years until Edie died in 2009. They did not have children partly because Erwin was still haunted by Alice's tragic miscarriage in 1945.

Erwin today lives alone in a spacious apartment, full of midcentury European art, overlooking central Ottawa. A large oil painting of Edie dominates the hallway. In his office, he pulls out a photograph of Alice, his first wife. He has never forgotten her mother's last wishes—that he should protect and save Alice. He still feels responsible for her.

Erwin's wise and still handsome face creases with emotion as he casts his mind back to the years before the Nazis stormed into Hungary. He can still smell the three thousand rose bushes his father planted in a vast flower garden surrounding the family home in Budapest. Yet he has no desire to revisit his youth—he is one of many Jewish émigrés who has never been tempted to return, unlike Alice, Vera Herman, and Marianne Lowy. Erwin cites the murder in recent years of Gypsies and the desecration in June 2009 of the Wallenberg memorial on the banks of the Danube, where so many Jews were stripped of their clothing and shoes before being shot to death by the Arrow Cross. Pig's trotters were stuffed into the metal shoes that compose the memorial, just one of many anti-Semitic acts in the country in recent years.[10] "They [also] shat on the shoes," he says bitterly. "And you ask why I have not gone back!"

The increase in anti-Semitism and the rise of the far right in Hungary does not surprise him. Like Austria—the birthplace of Heydrich and Hitler and other mass murderers such as Kaltenbrunner—Hungary is a country that has never properly atoned, in his eyes, for the Holocaust. Erwin implies that perhaps these countries should finally begin to acknowledge the magnitude of their citizens' crimes, as Germany has done, before the last survivors pass on.

"I am very deeply Jewish, in a nationalistic sense," Erwin explains carefully. "I am probably an atheist, but I am definitely, through and through, a Jew. One thing I know; I don't want to live a minute in this world without a state of Israel." During the wars in 1967 and 1973, he volunteered to seve as a doctor in Israel. He didn't get there in 1967 because the war was over so quickly. But the decision to go, magically it seemed, marked an end to his PTSD. During the next war, in 1973, he worked as a field physician on the northern front, treating the severe burns of young Israeli tank crews.[11]

Erwin Koranyi long ago achieved his boyhood ambition of becoming a doctor. And he found great and lasting love with his second wife, Edie. "A happy ending?" he has written at the end of a lyrical memoir. "Perhaps. But everything has a price, and the survivor must pay. He must redeem his existence with the pain of remembrance, with the sorrowful memories of lost loved ones."[12]

OUTSIDE, IT IS A SULTRY AUGUST DAY in Stockholm. The clean, prosperous city's sidewalk cafes are full of Scandinavian tourists, the harbor is busy with pleasure boats and cruise ships. Jewish tourists stand near Stockholm's central synagogue and look slightly mystified by a Raoul Wallenberg memorial, one of several that now grace capital cities around the globe.

Although most well-informed people have heard of Wallenberg today, many, including Jews, know less about him than about Oscar Schindler, who saved far fewer people and in any case profited from their forced labor. And sadly, Wallenberg's extraordinary courage, especially after the Arrow Cross took power, has been overshadowed by speculation about his fate. The voices of those he saved are rarely heard.

The testimony of these last survivors is immensely valuable, more so than any diplomatic cable from Budapest to Stockholm. Their courage and resilience were in many cases just as inspirational as that of their "lost hero." Indeed, they deserve to be remembered too. They were not passive. They fought to stay alive. They did not have diplomatic status. All of them believe they are here today because a young man could not stand by while Adolf Eichmann tried to kill every last one of them.

Eighty-three-year-old Alice Breuer still remembers Wallenberg's heroism only too well. In her apartment in the center of the city, she points to a photograph taken in Hungary in 1944, before Wallenberg saved her life for the first time by issuing her a Schutzpass. The photograph shows her wearing a coat with a yellow star sewn onto it.

Sixty-five years later, Alice is soon on the verge of tears as she recalls the summer of 1944, the most destructive chapter in the Holocaust when more than four hundred thousand of her fellow Hungarians, including almost all her relatives, were sent to their deaths by Adolf Eich-mann. "I never thought it would be so emotional, thinking back," she says. "I don't know why I survived it all. I really don't. It was fated, preor-dained." Nor will she ever forget the cold morning in January 1945 when Raoul Wallenberg saved her for a second time, shouting through a mega-phone, demanding that his Jews—Alice and dozens of others—be re-turned to him rather than shot and dumped into the Danube.

Alice arrived in Wallenberg's homeland in 1952 with nothing but a seemingly fatal disease—tuberculosis—to remind her of all she had lost. "I was very ill when I got here," she says. "A doctor said I was going to die. I didn't want to live, but everyone made a fuss about me. They gave me all they could. Clinically, I was depressed. I had lost all my family."

Alice slowly recovered from tuberculosis, having finally decided she wanted to live. But life for many years was a daily struggle. It wasn't long before her marriage with Laci Revesz began to unravel. "My private life was not good," she says. "I had miscarriages. I couldn't have children. I had treatment. But then, when I was able to get pregnant, we got di-vorced."[13]

She eventually began to work as a doctor in Sweden. She also started therapy, as was required of all those dealing with psychiatric patients. "Analysis was very important to me," she explains. "I was able to think things over. It allowed me to recover."[14] She is today regarded as one of Sweden's most distinguished psychotherapists.

Alice and her first husband, Erwin, whom she married to stay alive, still meet occasionally and correspond regularly. They clearly still care about each other a great deal.[15]

The last time they saw each other for a joyful reunion was in spring 2009, when they visited Erwin's sister, Marta. She also owes her life to Raoul Wallenberg, who would now, in 2010, be ninety-eight years old.

EIGHTY-NINE-YEAR-OLD NINA LAGERGREN, Raoul's half-sister, also lives alone in Stockholm. She has fought her entire adult life to try to find her brother, but she no longer has the energy she once had. In Au-gust 2009, her brother, Guy, died, making her the only living member of

Raoul's immediate family. One senses in speaking to her that the burden of carrying on the fight alone is now too much to bear.

"My family has been fighting, breaking our hearts, for a very long time," says Nina. "Another generation needs to carry on now and do whatever it can to solve the [mystery] and keep his name alive."

Nina still treasures the wooden box she received in Moscow in 1989, containing his passport and diary. In her home hangs an oil painting of Raoul, which her parents adored, and a bust of him is in a hallway. He is also ever-present in her study. "There's not one day I don't spend with him," she says. "He is with me in the books, papers, photographs, and so on that fill this room. He is with me all the time."[16]

Appendix

Losses of Hungarian Jews During World War II

	Budapest	Provinces	Annexed Areas	Total
Number of Jews[a] in 1941	246,803	243,818	334,386	825,007
Losses of Hungarian Jews during the war				
Losses prior to German Occupation[b]	15,350	14,500	33,150	63,000
Losses during the Occupation				
Fled abroad	2,000	1,000	2,000	5,000
Deported, killed, or died	105,453	222,318	290,236	618,007
Total	122,803	237,818	325,386	686,007
Number of Hungarian Jews after the War				
Returned from deportation	20,000	40,000	56,500	116,500
Liberated	124,000	6,000	9.000	139,000
Total	144,000	46,000	65,500	255,500

[a]Includes converts and Christians of Jewish origin.
[b]Begins March 19, 1944.

Source: Adapted from *The Politics of Genocide, The Holocaust in Hungary,* condensed edition, by Randolph L. Braham (Wayne State University Press, Detroit, 2000), p. 252, and based on data found in *Hungarian Jewry before and after the Persecution* (Budapest: Statistical Department of the Hungarian Section of the World Jewish Congress, n.d.), 2.

Notes

CHAPTER ONE. WANNSEE

1. Mark Roseman, *The Wannsee Conference and The Final Solution*, Picador, New York, 2002, p. 94.

2. Mario Dederichs, *Heydrich: The Face of Evil*, Casemate, 2009, pp. 20–30.

3. Ibid.

4. Danny Smith, *Lost Hero*, Harper Collins, London, 2001, p. 21.

5. Mark Roseman, *The Wannsee Conference and The Final Solution*, p. 101.

6. "We [had] decided to employ it for the mass extermination operation," the Auschwitz commandant Rudolph Hoess recalled. "Now we had the gas, and we had established a procedure." The manufacturer later claimed at Nuremberg that it had been developed only as a disinfectant. Danny Smith, *Lost Hero*, p. 21.

7. Auschwitz doctor Miklos Nysizli, a Hungarian, recalled: "For every convoy [delivered to the camp] it was the same. Red Cross cars brought the gas from the outside. There was never a stock of it in the crematorium. The precaution was scandalous, but still more scandalous was the fact that the gas was brought in a car bearing the insignia of the International Red Cross." Source: Ibid.

8. David Ceserani, *Becoming Eichmann*, Da Capo Press, Cambridge, 2004, p. 114.

9. Ibid.

10. So-called Sassen interviews, cited at Eichmann trial, session 75, June 20, 1961.

11. Danny Smith, *Lost Hero*, p. 21.

12. David Ceserani, *Becoming Eichmann*, p. 115.

13. Ibid., p. 117.

CHAPTER TWO. ON THE RUN

1. A few days earlier, Vera had seen her only teacher for the last time. She and other Jewish children had been barred from local schools, but the principal of a former Jewish day school, in the local town of Banska Bystrica, had continued to teach Vera and several others in secret and at great risk to himself. "I loved him," Vera remembered. "I loved him dearly. The day before we were to leave, while doing an errand for my parents, I saw him on the top of a hill, and I started running toward him to say good-bye. But then I stopped dead in my tracks because I remembered that my mother had said that our life depended on no one knowing that we were going to leave. So I stood and I watched that wonderful man disappear over the horizon and I never saw him again." Vera Goodkin, interview with the author.

2. Ibid.

3. Ibid.

4. Ibid.

5. Ibid.

6. Vera Goodkin, e-mail to the author, December 2, 2009.

7. Vera Goodkin, interview with the author.

8. In the beginning, especially, her parents had felt guilty about imposing terrible danger on the people who helped them hide. "As we ran from place to place—as things became more dangerous for the rescuer, and as we were asked to move or we realized that common decency would demand that we move—the times became more turbulent, the fear was sharper, and the lack of food, more acute. There was a lot more hunger as time went on." Ibid.

9. Vera Goodkin, *In Sunshine and Shadow,* Comteq Publishing, Margate, New Jersey, 2006, p. 75.

10. Ibid.

11. Vera Goodkin, interview with the author.

12. Ibid.

13. Ibid.

14. Ibid.

15. Ibid.

16. Ibid.

17. Ibid.

18. Ibid.

19. http://www.raoulwallenberg.net/?en/wallenberg/testimonie/interviews/vera-goodkin.

20. Ibid.

21. Ibid.

22. The family would soon be sent to Auschwitz. The mother and two daughters would survive.

23. Vera Goodkin, interview with the author.

24. Vera Goodkin, *In Sunshine and Shadow,* p. 78.

25. Randolph L. Braham and Scott Miller, editors, *The Nazis' Last Victims,* Wayne State University Press, Detroit, 1998, p. 182.

26. Raphael Petai, *The Jews of Hungary,* Wayne State University Press, 1996, p. 546.

27. Vera Goodkin, interview with the author.

28. Ibid.

CHAPTER THREE. MAUTHAUSEN

1. James Waller, *Becoming Evil: How Ordinary People Commit Genocide and Mass Killing.* Oxford University Press, Oxford, 2002, pp. 3–5.

2. As a boy, Eichmann was allegedly taunted by schoolmates for being a kleine Jude—a little Jew— because he looked so Jewish.

3. The deportation of the Hungarian Jews was destined to be seen as perhaps the most controversial act of the Holocaust, given that the Allied powers and Jewish leaders in Hungary knew about Auschwitz and yet did little to prevent it—for example, there was no bombing of the camp.

4. Neal Bascomb, *Hunting Eichmann,* Houghton Mifflin Harcourt, New York, 2009, p. 2.

5. Ibid.

6. Frederick E. Werbell and Thurston Clarke, *Lost Hero,* 1982, p. 9.

7. Ibid.

8. Ibid.

9. Ibid., p.6.

10. Neal Bascomb, *Hunting Eichmann,* p. 1.

11. Source: http://www.holocaustresearchproject.org/holoprelude/eichmen.html. A die-hard Nazi to the bitter end, Dannecker would commit suicide while in American custody in 1945.

12. Comer Clarke, *Eichmann, the Man and His Crimes,* Ballantine Books, New York, 1960, p. 96. According to Clarke, Dannecker would organize "Karl Nights" when Eichmann visited Paris. "On one occasion, Eichmann organized the nude girls in a line to face the 'firing squad.' Then Eichmann and his party loosened corks from their champagne bottles and, roaring with laughter, aimed them at the ducking, giggling girls. Eichmann had few sexual inhibitions and the orgies often went on until six in the morning, a few hours before the next batch of victims were to be consigned to their deaths." Source: Ibid.

13. *Nazi Conspiracy and Aggression.* Volume VIII. USGPO, Washington, 1946, pp. 606–619.

14. Rafi Benshalom, *We Struggled for Life,* Gefen, Jerusalem, 2001, p. 24.

15. Marianne Lowy, interview with the author. See also Benjamin Balshone, *Determined,* Bloch Publishing, New York, 1984, p. 45.

16. Marianne Lowy, interview with the author. "It was a Sunday, when young people went to walk along the Corso. I had a rendezvous with my fiance who lived on the Buda side. We were supposed to meet around 11 a.m. He called me at 10 a.m. . . . He saw it from Buda. That was the beginning of the end."

CHAPTER FOUR. THE LAST REFUGE

1. Almost half were refugees from other countries like the Hermans.

2. Arthur D. Morse, *While Six Million Died,* The Overlook Press, New York, 1998, p. 350.

3. Jochen von Lang, *Eichmann Interrogated,* Da Capo Press, New York, 1999, p. 212.

4. Anna Porter, *Kasztner's Train,* Walker & Company, New York, 2007, p. 88.

5. John Bierman, *Righteous Gentile,* p. 39.

6. Sassen tapes.

7. Randolph L. Braham, *The Politics of Genocide,* Wayne State University Press, Detroit, 2000, p. 57. Horthy would later claim that he did not know they were going to be killed. Source: Ibid.

8. Anna Porter, *Kasztner's Train,* p. 97.

9. Rudolf Hoess, *Commandant of Auschwitz,* Pheonic Press, London, 1985, p. 214.

10. Ibid., p. 215. According to Hoss, Eichmann was "a vivacious, active man in his thirties, and always full of energy. He was constantly hatching new plans and perpetually on the lookout for innovations and improvements. He could

never rest. He was obsessed with the Jewish question and the order which had been given for its final solution." Ibid., p. 213.

11. Simon Wiesenthal, *The Murderers Among Us,* McGraw-Hill, New York, 1967, p. 98.

12. Alan Levy, *Nazi Hunter,* Carroll & Graff, New York, 2002, p. 119.

13. But Samuel Stern recalled that Eichmann was also charming and persuasive.

14. Frederick E. Werbell and Thurston Clarke, *Lost Hero,* 1982, p. 10.

15. Anna Porter, *Kasztner's Train,* pp. 102–103.

16. Yaacov Lozowick, *Hitler's Bureaucrats,* Continuum, London, 2000, p. 256.

17. Marianne Lowy, interview with the author.

18. Arthur D. Morse, *While Six Million Died,* p. 352.

19. Elie Wiesel, *Night,* Hill and Wang, New York, 2006, p. 31.

20. Marianne Lowy, interview with the author.

21. Benjamin Balshone, *Determined,* p. 52.

22. Ibid., p. 53.

23. Marianne Lowy, interview with the author.

24. Source: http://www.annefrank.dk/Heyman.htm.

25. Elie Wiesel, *Night,* p. 31.

26. Ibid., p. 33.

27. Yaacov Lozowick, *Hitler's Bureaucrats,* p. 56.

28. Erwin Koranyi, interview with the author.

29. Ibid.

30. Ibid.

31. Erwin K. Koranyi, *Dreams and Tears,* General Store Publishing House, Ontario, 2006, p. 53.

32. Erwin Koranyi, interview with the author.

33. Ibid.

34. Alice Breuer, interview with the author.

35. Erwin Koranyi, interview with the author. "When she returned to Budapest," Erwin remembered, "she said that she had promised that she would go back to Kormend. She was afraid that her parents would be harmed. I told her that the only way to live in Budapest was if we got married. I was twenty years old and in love with her. I persuaded her to get married."

36. Erwin K. Koranyi, *Dreams and Tears,* p. 56.

37. Alice Breuer, interview with the author.

38. Ibid.

39. Ibid.

CHAPTER FIVE. ESCAPE FROM AUSCHWITZ

1. Rudolf Vrba, *I Escaped from Auschwitz*, Barricade Books, Fort Lee, New Jersey, 2002, p. 248.
2. Ibid.
3. Paul Lungen, *Canadian Jewish News*, January 27, 2005.
4. Rudolf Vrba, *I Escaped from Auschwitz*.
5. Guido Knopp, *Hitler's Hitmen*, Sutton, 2002, England, p. 34.
6. Rudolf Vrba, *I Escaped from Auschwitz*, p. 263.
7. Anna Porter, *Kasztner's Train*, p. 158.

CHAPTER SIX. THE CRUELEST SUMMER

1. Erwin K. Koranyi, *Dreams and Tears*, p. 58.
2. March 19, 1944, affected the Jews of Kormend "like a stroke of lightning from the clear sky. The blows came in torrential manner: wearing of the Yellow Star of David, segregation, closing of businesses, and confiscation of assets. In Kormend, the ghetto was concentrated within the streets surrounding the Jewish temple; it was fenced by wooden planks, all at the expense of the Jews. Humiliating scenes during concentration and later, during entrainment, were the norm. The train station chief's son was defiantly arrogant with Mr. Frimm, an engineer and his former boss, suggesting that he 'preferably use a rope.' Dr. Havas, a physician from Nagycskny, was the benefactor of the township. Still, while being taken into the ghetto, they stoned him. Jews, ridden by fear and at the mercy of their enemies, were crowded first in the ghetto of Szombathely, then taken to the Motor Factory, and finally, thrown into jam-packed cattle cars and deported in the direction of Auschwitz! The last rabbi of the community, Dr. Jakab Krausz, whose noble activities we already mentioned, became a martyr of the Holocaust together with his congregants. The great majority of the community—children, mothers, young people, and the elderly—were together in the hour of doom. In all, of the 389 people deported, about 20 survived. Today, only three or four Jewish families live in Kormend." Source: http://www.jewishgen.org/yizkor/vas_megye/vas047.html.
3. Ibid.
4. Erwin K. Koranyi, *Dreams and Tears*, p. 57.

5. Erwin Koranyi, interview with the author.

6. He would soon be described as "a very solid type: squarely built, broad nosed, peasant-like, a bit slow and heavy, but with a very clear head and firm grasp of facts. He breathes honestly." Source: Arthur D. Morse, *While Six Million Died,* p. 356.

7. Quentin Reynolds, *Minister of Death,* Dell, New York, 1961, p. 172.

8. Ibid., pp. 173–174.

9. http://www.raoulwallenberg.net/?en/wallenberg/testimonie/interviews/vera-goodkin and Vera Goodkin, interview with the author: Vera was woken one morning by the "sounds of heavy boots along a walkway to the apartment. There was a loud knocking on the door. Men were asking for us by name. We went along. Once we were in the street, we realized that we were not alone, that other people were being rounded up. There were armed men hitting people to make sure we were subdued. There was no talking. I felt terrible fear, terrible fear."

10. Vera Goodkin, *In Sunshine and Shadow,* p. 80.

11. Ibid.

12. Vera Goodkin, interview with the author.

13. Vera Goodkin, *In Sunshine and Shadow,* p. 80.

14. Ibid.

15. Alex Weissberg, *Desperate Mission,* Criterion Books, New York, 1958, p. 159.

16. Ibid., p. 164. "Don't you understand what you're doing?" Brand shouted. "This is plain murder! Mass murder! If I don't go back, our best people will be slaughtered! My wife! My mother! My children! They will be the first to go. You've got to let me return. I have come here under a flag of truce, on a special mission. You can agree or not as you will, but you have no right to seize an emissary. The Germans are my enemies just as much as they are the enemies of the Allies, and far more bitter enemies, too. I am here as a delegate of a million people condemned to death. Their lives depend on my return. Who gives you the right to lay hands on me?" Source: Ibid.

17. Aide-memoire delivered by Lord Halifax to State Department, June 5, 1944. Weizmann Archives, Rehovoth, Israel.

18. Ben Hecht, *Perfidy,* Milah Press, 1999, p. 228.

19. Ibid.

20. Alex Weissberg, *Desperate Mission,* p. 223.

21. Raul Hilberg, *The Destruction of the European Jews,* Yale University Press, 2003, p. 1224.

22. Ira Hirschmann letter to John Pehle, July 3, 1944: War Refugee Board Projects and Documents, Box 70.

23. "All I remember is hearing that a million Jews were to be released somewhere in return for ten thousand all-weather trucks and the promise that these would not under any circumstances be used on the Western front," Eichmann told an interrogator in 1960. "That was the basis of the agreement . . ." Source: Jochen von Lang, *Eichmann Interrogated*, p. 207.

24. Rudolf Vrba, *I Escaped from Auschwitz*, p. 265.

CHAPTER SEVEN. THE SWEDISH PIMPERNEL

1. In 1944, David Ben-Gurion wrote angrily: "What have you done to us, you freedom-loving peoples, guardians of justice, defenders of the high principles of democracy and the brotherhood of man? What have you allowed to be prepared against a defenseless people while you stood aside and let it bleed to death, without offering help or succor, without calling on the fiends to stop, in the language of retribution which alone they would understand? Why do you profane our pain and wrath with empty expressions of sympathy which ring like a mockery in the ears of millions of the damned in the torture houses of Nazi Europe? Why have you not even supplied arms to our ghetto rebels, as you have done for the partisans and underground fighters of other nations? . . . If, instead of Jews, thousands of English, American, or Russian women, children, and aged had been tortured every day, burnt to death, asphyxiated in gas chambers—would you have acted in the same way?" Source: Theodore S. Hamerow, *Why We Watched*, Norton, New York, 2008, p. 353.

2. Arthur D. Morse, *While Six Million Died*, p. 383.

3. Frederick E. Werbell and Thurston Clarke, *Lost Hero*, Signet, New York, 1982, p. 15.

4. Alan Levy, *Nazi Hunter*, p. 172.

5. Arthur D. Morse, *While Six Million Died*, pp. 348–349.

6. Kati Marton, *Wallenberg: Missing Hero*, Random House, 1995, p. 39.

7. Jeno Levai, *Raoul Wallenberg*, University of Melbourne, 1989, p. 36.

8. Martin Gilbert, *The Holocaust*, Henry Holt, New York, 1985, p. 71.

9. Nina Lagergren, interview with the author.

10. Stockholm Military History Museum open display.

11. Jeno Levai, *Raoul Wallenberg*, p. 29.

12. Ibid.

13. Raoul Wallenberg to Gustaf Wallenberg, Haifa, June 19, 1936.

14. Jeno Levai, *Raoul Wallenberg*, p. 38.

15. Kati Marton, *Wallenberg: Missing Hero*, p. 41.

16. War Refugee Board, Hyde Park records.

17. See Levai, pp. 30–39 for more on Wallenberg's background.

18. Jeno Levai, *Raoul Wallenberg*, p. 42.

19. Ibid., pp. 42–43.

20. Ibid., p. 45.

21. Ibid., p. 46.

22. Ibid., p. 44.

23. John Bierman, *Righteous Gentile*, p. 38.

24. Braham, *The Politics of Genocide*, p. 163.

25. John Bierman, *Righteous Gentile*, p. 38. Also see Braham for more details.

26. Guido Knopp, *Hitler's Hitmen*, p. 35.

27. Nina Lagergren, interview with the author.

28. Ibid.

29. John Bierman, *Righteous Gentile*, p. 37.

30. Nina Lagergren, interview with the author.

31. Elenore Lester, *Wallenberg: The Man in the Iron Web*, Prentice Hall, London, 1982, p. 66.

32. Danny Smith, *Lost Hero*, p. 47.

33. Nina Lagergren, interview with the author.

34. John Bierman, *Righteous Gentile*, p. 37.

35. Jeno Levai, *Raoul Wallenberg*, p. 45.

36. Frederick E. Werbell and Thurston Clarke, *Lost Hero*, pp. 24–25.

37. John Bierman, *Righteous Gentile*, p. 38

38. Ibid.

CHAPTER EIGHT. THE MAJESTIC HOTEL

1. Monday, July 9, 1944, Wallenberg's appointment's diary, RA, Raoul Wallenberg Arkiv, Signum, 1, Vol. 9, University of Upsala, Sweden. The small diary was returned to Nina Lagergren in 1989 by the Russians.

2. Arthur D. Morse, *While Six Million Died*, p. 363. See also "Rescue from Hungary," War Refugee Board Projects and Documents, Box 33 and Box 35 and

the "White Papers of Royal Ministry for Foreign Affairs," Stockholm, Raoul Wallenberg case, 1957 and 1965. *The Holocaust in Hungary: Forty Years Later,* Randolph L. Braham, and Bela Vago, eds., Columbia University Press, New York, 1985.

3. Per Anger, *With Raoul Wallenberg in Budapest,* pp. 37–39.

4. See Randolph L. Braham and Bela Vago, *The Holocaust in Hungary,* and Lars Berg interview in 1979 in New York.

5. Jeno Levai, *Raoul Wallenberg,* p. 50.

6. Lutz would survive the war and live into old age, recognized finally around the world as one of the most effective of "righteous gentiles" who had saved thousands of lives.

7. Anna Porter, *Kasztner's Train,* p. 99.

8. Guido Knopp, *Hitler's Hitmen,* p. 29.

9. Theo Tschuy, *Dangerous Diplomacy,* Eerdmans Publishing, Cambridge, UK, 2000, pp. 167–170.

10. Elenore Lester, *Wallenberg: The Man in the Iron Web,* pp. 91–92.

11. It took place on August 3, 1944, according to Wallenberg's daybook.

12. Elenore Lester, *Wallenberg: The Man in the Iron Web,* pp. 91–92.

13. According to Wallenberg's diary, he met with Ferenczy on Thursday, July 20, 1944. This may have been the date that Kasser later recalled. Thursday, July 20, 1944, Wallenberg's appointment's diary, RA, Raoul Wallenberg Arkiv, Signum, 1, Vol. 9, University of Upsala, Sweden.

14. Jeno Levai, *Raoul Wallenberg,* p. 68.

15. Elenore Lester, *Wallenberg: The Man in the Iron Web,* pp. 91–92.

16. Marianne Lowy, interview with the author.

17. Ibid.

18. Benjamin Balshone, *Determined,* pp. 72–73.

19. Arthur D. Morse, *While Six Million Died,* p. 364.

20. For an excellent account of Wallenberg's relationship with Lauer, see Paul A. Levine's *Raoul Wallenberg in Budapest: Myth, History and Holocaust,* Valentine Mitchell, Middlesex, UK, 2010, pp. 165–189.

21. Raoul Wallenberg, *Letters and Dispatches,* Arcade Publishing. New York, 1995, p. 273.

22. These sources may have included Allied and Axis agents. Although his employer at the War Refugee Board, Iver Olsen, later swore that Wallenberg did not know that he, Olsen, was working for the American intelligence organization, the OSS, it is hard to believe that Wallenberg was not in some way in-

volved in Allied intelligence operations. Wallenberg had proven links to the British foreign intelligence service, MI6, according to documents in Sweden's national archives. That summer of 1944, these documents reveal, he sent coded messages and spoke on the telephone with Cyril Cheshire, MI6's wartime head of station in Stockholm. Wallenberg's business partner, Kalman Lauer, may also have been involved with Allied intelligence operations. Two weeks after arriving in Budapest, not long after he learned the fate of Lauer's relatives, Wallenberg sent Lauer a telegram, also using coded language, that asked him to get Olsen to intervene with Cheshire to ensure that an end to the deportation of Hungarian Jews would be a key condition of any peace deal.

23. Susanne Berger, "Stuck in Neutral," Arlington, Virginia, 2005, p. 7.

24. War Refugee Board File, Box 111, Franklin D. Roosevelt Memorial Library, Hyde Park, New York.

25. Elenore Lester, *Wallenberg: The Man in the Iron Web*, p. 93.

26. Alan Levy, *Nazi Hunter*, p.184. See also Wallenberg's daybook on display in the Stockholm Military Museum.

27. Tuvia Friedmann, *The Hunter*, p. 164.

28. Eichmann had good reason to be worried. Manus Diamant, a member of a Jewish resistance group, claimed that his organization "wanted to kill Eichmann at the railway station in Debrecen. I had disguised myself," added Diamant, "as a porter and was carrying a suitcase full of explosives. I watched Eichmann walking up and down the platform, supervising the transports. Things couldn't move fast enough for him . . . Our HQ was against [blowing him up] because they anticipated reprisals, as there had been when Heydrich was assassinated. Our people believed that such an act would only accelerate the deportations." Source: Guido Knopp, *Hitler's Hitmen*, pp. 32–33.

29. Anna Porter, *Kasztner's Train*, p. 120.

30. Ibid.

31. Eichmann's colleague, SS intelligence officer Wilhelm Hottl, then operating in Budapest, had run an extensive network of agents for some time in Hungary. He and other intelligence sources would have been able to provide extensive background information on this well-connected and troublesome scion of the most powerful family in Sweden, a still neutral nation.

32. Alan Levy, *Nazi Hunter*, pp. 184–185.

33. As Marcus later would put it: "I used to say that the definition of being neutral—often called bloody neutral—is that you are bawled out by everybody on all sides. We fulfilled that very well. We were bawled out by everyone. I know that the

different camps always thought that we were doing something more favorable to the other camp, but that was not the policy." *Euromoney* magazine, October 1980.

34. Ibid.

35. For further details, see Eric Sjoquist, *Affaren Raoul Wallenberg*, Bonniers, Stockholm, 1974.

36. Alan Levy, *Nazi Hunter*, pp. 184–185.

37. Ibid.

38. Veesenmayer to German Foreign Office, December 20, 1944, T/1244.

39. Guido Knopp, *Hitler's Hitmen*, p. 36.

40. Jeno Levai, *Raoul Wallenberg*, p. 173. See also Pal Szalai's report in Jeno Levai, pp. 170–175.

41. Ibid. Perhaps Wallenberg, the "Jew dog," needed to be put in his place. Certainly, Wallenberg's activities in Budapest eventually placed his life in danger. Pal Szalai, an Arrow Cross official, would later allege that he warned Wallenberg that an SS intelligence official called Gottstein was working with others to "make Wallenberg disappear, but as a Swedish diplomat was involved, this action had to be prepared very carefully."

42. Vera Goodkin, interview with the author.

43. Later, Vera would discover that Kasser was a member of an Austro-Hungarian aristocratic family: "A very bright man who didn't just sit back and lean on the wealth and prestige of his family. He was a very successful and wealthy exporter-importer, and he, with his volunteer function in the Swedish Red Cross, became friendly with Wallenberg." Source: http://www.raoul wallenberg.net/?en/wallenberg/testimonie/interviews/vera-goodkin.

44. Vera Goodkin, interview with the author.

45. Vera Goodkin, *In Sunshine and Shadow*, p. 81.

46. Ibid.

47. Vera Goodkin, interview with the author.

48. Vera Goodkin, *In Sunshine and Shadow*, p. 83.

49. Ibid.

50. Source: http://www.raoulwallenberg.net/?en/wallenberg/testimonie /interviews/vera-goodkin.

51. Vera Goodkin, interview with the author.

52. Alice Breuer, interview with the author.

53. Erwin Koranyi, interview with the author.

54. Alice Breuer, interview with the author.

55. Ibid.

56. Ibid.

57. Erwin Koranyi, interview with the author.

58. Ibid.

59. Erwin K. Koranyi, *Dreams and Tears,* p. 58.

60. Erwin Koranyi, interview with the author.

61. Erwin K. Koranyi, *Dreams and Tears,* p. 58.

62. Saturday, August 5, 1944, Wallenberg's appointment's diary, RA, Raoul Wallenberg Arkiv, Signum, 1, Vol. 9, University of Uppsala, Sweden.

63. Erwin Koranyi, interview with the author.

64. Monday, August 7, 1944, Wallenberg's appointment's diary, RA, Raoul Wallenberg Arkiv, Signum, 1, Vol. 9, University of Uppsala, Sweden.

65. Alice Breuer, interview with the author.

66. Alan Levy, *Nazi Hunter,* pp. 176–177.

67. Erwin Koranyi, interview with the author.

68. Alice Breuer, interview with the author. More than sixty years later, Alice still marvels at her good fortune. "Can you imagine how confused I was?" she says. "I didn't know anything about him. I had no idea about Sweden."

69. Erwin Koranyi, interview with the author.

70. Ibid.

71. John Bierman, *Righteous Gentile,* pp. 68–69.

72. Harvey Rosenfeld, *Angel of Rescue,* New York, 1982, p. 45.

73. Horthy recalled: "In August, Budapest was to be cleaned up. One hundred seventy thousand Jews were registered in the capital and another one hundred ten thousand were in hiding with their Hungarian friends. The Secretaries of State, Baky and Endre, had planned a surprise action to arrest and deport the Budapest Jews. As soon as news of this reached my ears, I ordered the armored division, which was stationed near Esztergom, to be transferred to Budapest, and I instructed the chief of the Budapest gendarmerie to assist in preventing the forceful removal of the Jews . . . I duly informed the government of the Reich that I would do my utmost to prevent the removal of Jews from Budapest. As the Germans were still striving to keep up the pretence of Hungarian sovereignty, they decided to forgo taking further measures." Nicholas Horthy, *Memoirs,* Robert Speller and Sons, New York, 1957, p. 220.

74. Guido Knopp, *Hitler's Hitmen,* p. 37.

75. Ibid.

76. Uki Goni, *The Real Odessa,* Granta, London, 2003, pp. 293–294.

77. Ibid.

78. Ibid.

79. R. Wallenberg to K. Lauer, September 29, 1944, RA, Raoul Wallenberg Arkiv, Signum 1, Vol. 6.

80. John Bierman, *Righteous Gentile,* p. 70.

81. Ibid.

CHAPTER NINE. OPERATION PANZERFAUST

1. Otto Skorzeny, *Skorzeny's Secret Missions,* Dutton, 1950, p. 193.

2. Ibid.

3. Ibid., p. 196.

4. Ibid., pp. 193–205.

5. Alice Breuer, interview with the author.

6. Source: http://www.hungarian-history.hu/lib/montgo/montgo20.htm.

7. Agnes Adachi, *Child of the Winds,* Adams Press, Chicago, 1989, p. 10.

8. Erwin Koranyi, interview with the author.

9. Miklas Horthy, *Memoirs,* p. 293.

10. Erwin K. Koranyi, *Dreams and Tears,* p. 72.

11. See Randolph L. Braham, *The Politics of Genocide: The Holocaust in Hungary,* vol. 2, revised and enlarged edition, Columbia University Press, New York, 1994.

12. Erwin Koranyi, interview with the author.

13. Christian Ungvary, *The Siege of Budapest,* Yale University Press, New Haven, 2005, p. 289.

14. Erwin Koranyi, interview with the author. "He hid us despite the fact that he knew that if they caught us, he and his wife and children would be killed. I tremendously respected that man. He was so much of an exception."

15. Erwin K. Koranyi, *Dreams and Tears,* p. 86.

16. Ibid., p. 73.

17. Alice Breuer, interview with the author.

18. Erwin Koranyi, interview with the author.

19. Ibid. Eventually, the Arrow Cross would raid the orphanage and place Pipez and others in the ghetto, where he would survive the war.

20. Erwin K. Koranyi, *Dreams and Tears,* p. 76.

21. Erwin Koranyi, interview with the author.

22. Miklas Horthy, *Memoirs,* pp. 253–55.

23. Veensenmayer was released in 1951.

24. Randolph Braham, editor, *The Nazis' Last Victims*, p. 37.

25. Frederick E. Werbell and Thurston Clarke, *Lost Hero*, pp. 64–65.

26. Ibid.

27. Jeno Levai, *Raoul Wallenberg*, p. 103. In a report to the Foreign Ministry in Stockholm, Wallenberg described how on the "first night of the putsch . . . between a hundred and two hundred people are believed to have been killed." The Arrow Cross coup had had a "catastrophic effect" on his rescue organization. "The whole of the personnel as well as the motor car disappeared. During the whole of the first day, the undersigned had to ride around the bandit-infested streets on a lady's bicycle trying to gather together the threads." Source: John Bierman, *Righteous Gentile*, p. 74.

CHAPTER TEN. THE ARROW CROSS

1. Vera Goodkin, interview with the author. "The Arrow Cross were for the most part drunken bums," recalled Vera Herman, who was then under Wallenberg's protection. "They were undisciplined. The Germans had some understanding of international law. They needed the Swedes and respected them. After all, who is more Aryan than the Scandinavians?"

2. Lars Berg, *The Book That Disappeared*, Vantage Press, New York, 1990, p. 34. Berg added: "None of us left his house any longer without a gun in his pocket. A diplomatic passport might be a good protection in theory but an automatic speaks in a quicker and more convincing way." Ibid., p. 35.

3. Frederick E. Werbell and Thurston Clarke, *Lost Hero*, pp. 68–70. They had first met in an empty apartment on the sixth floor of a publishing company owned by one of Wallenberg's Section C staff. It had been clear after only a few minutes of conversation that they had the same ideals and came from similar backgrounds. Wallenberg knew that the Austrian-born baroness now regretted her marriage to the amoral and penniless Baron Kemeny, who had squandered a large dowry provided by her two sisters, who were nuns. She wanted to help Wallenberg but she did not want her husband to be placed in danger. "You must believe me," Wallenberg reportedly told her, "this Hungarian government is doomed. The Allies have already promised to hold war crimes trials. Your husband and the other Arrow Cross leaders will be executed." Source: Ibid.

4. Raoul Wallenberg, *Letters and Dispatches*, Arcade Publishing. New York, 1995, p. 276.

5. Marianne Lowy, interview with the author.

6. Alice Breuer, interview with the author.

7. Erwin K. Koranyi, *Dreams and Tears*, p. 77.

8. Erwin Koranyi, interview with the author.

9. Christian Ungvary, *The Siege of Budapest*, p. 8.

CHAPTER ELEVEN. THE ROAD TO HEGYESHALOM

1. Lars Berg, *The Book That Disappeared*, p. 48.

2. Jochen von Lang, *Eichmann Interrogated*, p. 251.

3. Bronia Klibanski, "The Archives of the Swiss Consul General Charles Lutz," Yad Vashem Studies, XV, Jerusalem 1983, pp. 357–65.

4. Elenore Lester, *Wallenberg: The Man in the Iron Web*, pp. 110–111.

5. Ibid.

6. Tschuy, *Dangerous Diplomacy*, p. 197. The experience was harrowing to others who, like him, had to enter as a diplomat. His colleague Charles Lutz, who had worked closely with him, and accompanied him on several rescue missions, recalled how soul-searing these hours in gathering places could be: "Hundreds of Schutzbrief holders had already been brought to the brickyards . . . I shall never forget their fear-ridden faces. Again and again the police had to intervene, because the people almost tore off my clothes as they pleaded with me. This was the last upsurge of a will to live, before resignation set in which usually ended in death. For us it was mental torture to have to sort out these documents. On such occasions we saw human beings being hit with dog whips. They fell to the ground with bleeding faces, and we were ourselves openly threatened with weapons, if we tried to intervene." Source: Ibid.

7. John Bierman, *Righteous Gentile*, pp. 80–81.

8. Alan Levy, *Nazi Hunter*, p. 188.

9. Juettner also later recalled: "In November 1944, I made an official tour of inspection of the Waffen-SS Divisions fighting in the Hungarian area. In preparation for this tour, I had ordered Obersturmbannfuhrer [Kurt] Becher to meet me in Vienna . . . On the evening of my arrival, Becher told me that on his journey from Budapest to Vienna he had met columns of Jews marching to the Reich frontier. The march had made a strong impression on him, since the terrible exhaustion of these people was apparent at first sight. At first I would not believe his description, since these things appeared to me almost impossible. The next morning, I drove to Budapest accompanied by Becher and my adjutant. About halfway to Budapest or a little later, we met the first columns. Further

columns followed at intervals between 25 and 30 kilometers. As far as I can remember, they consisted mainly of women. Unless my memory fails me, all ages up to 60 were represented . . . The first columns, which had been on the march already for several days, made a truly terrifying impression and confirmed Becher's statement of the day before." Source: Randolph Braham, *Politics of Genocide,* pp. 841–842.

10. Kurt Becher also claimed to have done this.

11. Jochen von Lang, *Eichmann Interrogated,* Da Capo Press, New York, 1999, pp. 253–254.

12. Swedish White Papers, 1957, testimony of Erhard Hille. The Germans had seized the Langfelder family's profitable machine factory when they had occupied Budapest that March.

13. Jeno Levai, *Raoul Wallenberg,* pp.133–136.

14. Frederick E. Werbell and Thurston Clarke, *Lost Hero,* p. 93.

15. Ibid., p. 94.

16. Ibid.

17. Per Anger, *With Raoul Wallenberg in Budapest,* p. 59.

18. Jeno Levai, *Raoul Wallenberg,* pp. 136–138.

19. Per Anger, *With Raoul Wallenberg in Budapest,* p. 59.

20. Alan Levy, *Nazi Hunter,* p. 190.

21. Jeno Levai, *Raoul Wallenberg,* pp. 133–136.

22. Ibid.

23. Ibid.

24. Per Anger, *With Raoul Wallenberg in Budapest,* p. 59.

25. Ibid.

26. Ibid.

27. Ibid.

28. So-called Sassen tapes.

29. Swedish White Papers, 1957.

30. Ibid. Again Veesenmayer cabled Berlin: "The chief executive in the deployment of Jewish labor for the lower Danube region, SS Oberturmbannfuhrer Hoess, has declared that he can only use able-bodied men, preferably under the age of forty."

31. Vera Goodkin, interview with the author.

32. Source: http://www.raoulwallenberg.net/?en/wallenberg/testimonie/interviews/vera-goodkin.

33. Ibid.

34. Vera Goodkin, interview with the author.

35. Vera Goodkin, *In Sunshine and Shadow,* p. 83.

36. Ibid.

37. Vera Goodkin, interview with the author.

38. Ibid.

CHAPTER TWELVE. DINNER WITH EICHMANN

1. Source: http://www.HolocaustResearchProject.org.

2. Two historians have disputed Berg's recollection of the alleged meeting. A. Lajos, *Hjalten och Offren: Raoul Wallenberg och judarna in Budapest* (Vaxjo: Svenska Emigratinstitutes skrifserie, no. 15, 2003), p. 150. Also M. Ember, *Wallenberg Budapesten* (Varoshaza, Budapest, 2000) pp. 71–77. See also Paul Levine, *Raoul Wallenberg in Budapest: Myth, History and Holocaust,* pp. 276–280 and p. 288.

3. *Raoul Wallenberg, Letters and Dispatches,* pp. 274–275.

4. John Bierman, *Righteous Gentile,* p. 98.

5. Berg's account has been dismissed by some scholars and questioned in depth by scholar Paul Levine in his recent study: *Raoul Wallenberg in Budapest: Myth, History and Holocaust,* pp. 276–280.

6. Lars Berg, *The Book That Disappeared,* Vantage Press, New York, 1990, p. 15.

7. John Bierman, *Righteous Gentile,* p. 98.

8. Frederick E. Werbell and Thurston Clarke, *Lost Hero,* p. 89.

9. Lars Berg, *The Book That Disappeared,* p. 15.

10. Ibid., p. 16. Eichmann and his aide then left. "Perhaps Raoul did not win very much by his direct attack," Berg recalled, "but it could sometimes be a great pleasure for a Swede to speak his mind to an SS officer. And I am sure that Eichmann left the house very much impressed by Raoul's fearless and strong personality." Source: Ibid.

11. Janos Beer, interview with the author.

12. Thomas Veres, oral history, U.S. National Holocaust Museum collections.

13. Thomas Veres, written account.

14. Thomas Veres, written account, courtesy U.S. Raoul Wallenberg Association.

15. Janos Beer, written account of his activities. Given to the author by Janos Beer, February 10, 2010.

16. Frederick E. Werbell and Thurston Clarke, *Lost Hero,* p. 105.

17. Janos Beer, interview with the author.

18. Kati Marton, *Wallenberg: Missing Hero,* p. 119.

19. Janos Beer, interview with the author at MIT, February 10, 2010.

20. Ibid.

21. Rudolph Philipp, *Raoul Wallenberg, Diplomat, Kampe, Samarit.* Fredborgs Forlag, Stockholm, 1946.

22. For further details on Voros's meetings with Wallenberg, see Marton Voros, *Aven for din Skull,* Askild & Karnekull, Stockholm, 1978.

23. Janos Beer, interview with the author.

24. Muller affidavit, Swedish White Papers, 1957.

25. See Maria Schmidt, "Mentes Vagy Arulas? A Budapesti Zsido Tanacs." *Medvetanc,* numbers 2–3 (1985).

26. Anna Porter, *Kasztner's Train,* p. 265.

27. Source: http://www.nizkor.org/hweb/people/e/eichmann-adolf/transcripts/Testimony-broad/Kurt_Becher-04.html.

CHAPTER THIRTEEN. DECEMBER 1944

1. Thomas Veres, written testimony, U.S. Wallenberg Association web site.

2. Ibid.

3. According to Levai, Wallenberg also sent a letter to Koloman Lauer on December 8, in which he described the terrible conditions in Budapest and asked him to inquire with his uncle Jacob Wallenberg about a job at Huvudsta. Levai, p. 224.

4. Raoul Wallenberg, *Letters and Dispatches,* 1924–1944, p. 277.

5. Danny Smith, *Lost Hero,* p. 87.

6. Per Anger, *With Raoul Wallenberg in Budapest,* p. 64.

7. Christian Ungvary, *The Siege of Budapest,* p. 3.

8. Anna Porter, *Kasztner's Train,* p. 283.

9. Theo Tschuy, *Dangerous Diplomacy,* p. 217.

10. John Bierman, *Righteous Gentile,* pp. 107–108.

11. Ibid.

12. Elenore Lester, *Wallenberg,* p. 117. Only a few hundred of the thousands of Germans left behind to fight the Soviets would survive.

13. Christian Ungvary, *Siege of Budapest,* p. 292.

14. Ibid. p. 300.

15. Jeno Levai, *Raoul Wallenberg*, p. 172.

16. Janos Beer, interview with the author.

17. Erwin Koranyi, interview with the author.

CHAPTER FOURTEEN. THE INFERNO

1. Veres remembered Wallenberg being cautious and taking great care to avoid unnecessary confrontations with the SS and Arrow Cross. He maximized the advantages and protections that came with diplomatic status. Veres recalled how the car Wallenberg used "bore a series of distinguishing signs, from 'courier service' to 'diplomatic corps,' and other inscriptions and insignia. The rear number plate was different from the front one. When it came to showing our documents, we used the one we thought was best. To the Arrow Cross, 'courier service,' to the German Nazis, 'diplomat.'" Added Veres, "Wallenberg remarked, laughing on one occasion, that one ought to devise number plates that could by pushing a button be changed automatically to suit the occasion." Jeno Levai, *Raoul Wallenberg*, p. 175.

2. Sharon Linnea, *Raoul Wallenberg: The Man Who Stopped Death*, The Jewish Publication Society, Philadelphia, 1993, pp. 132–133.

3. Just five soup kitchens provided a watery soup that was all most people lived on. Conditions behind the high, obscenity-daubed wooden fences that surrounded the ghetto were hellish indeed, as one eyewitness described them: "In narrow Kazicnzy Street, enfeebled men, dropping their heads, were pushing a wheelbarrow. On the rattling contraption, naked human bodies as yellow as wax were jolted along, and a stiff arm with black patches was dangling and knocking against the spokes of the wheel. People were squatting or kneeling around a dead horse and hacking the meat off it with knives. The animal's head was lying a few meters away. The yellow and blue intestines, jellylike and with a cold sheen, were bursting out of the opened and mutilated body." Christian Ungvary, *The Siege of Budapest*, p. 299.

4. Thurston Clarke and Frederick E. Werbell, *Lost Hero*, p. 129.

5. Ibid.

6. Christian Ungvary, *The Siege of Budapest*, p. 292.

7. Thurston Clarke and Frederick E. Werbell, *Lost Hero*, p. 130.

8. Ibid., p. 133.

9. Jeno Levai, *Raoul Wallenberg*, p. 231.

10. Christian Ungvary, *The Siege of Budapest*, p. 288.

11. Ibid. p. 278.

12. Christian Ungvary, *The Siege of Budapest*, p. 292–293. Ungvary's book is the best account of the siege and its effect on civilians and soldiers alike.

13. Erwin K. Koranyi, *Dreams and Tears*, p. 86.

14. Erwin Koranyi, interview with the author. One of Erwin Koranyi's aunts and her son had meanwhile died on the death march. "It was two hundred miles in pouring rain," recalled Erwin Koranyi. "People who stayed behind were shot. Wallenberg had tried to pick up as many people as he could. But there was only so many he could save."

15. Erwin K. Koranyi, *Dreams and Tears*, p. 88.

16. Erwin Koranyi, interview with the author.

17. Ibid.

18. Benjamin Balshone, *Determined*, p. 101.

19. Marianne Lowy, interview with the author.

20. Jeno Levai, *Raoul Wallenberg*, pp. 204–205.

21. Erwin K. Koranyi, *Dreams and Tears*, p. 89.

22. Ibid., p. 90.

23. Erwin K. Koranyi, *Dreams and Tears*, p. 90.

24. Erwin Koranyi, interview with the author.

25. Alan Levy, *Nazi Hunter*, p. 194.

26. Erwin K. Koranyi, *Dreams and Tears*, p. 90.

27. Marianne Lowy, interview with the author.

28. According to the Hungarian historian Jeno Levai, who experienced the siege of Budapest and was under Swedish protection that winter: "It [was] of the utmost importance that the Nazis and the Arrow Cross men were not able to ravage unhindered—they were compelled to see that every step they took was being watched and followed by the young Swedish diplomat. From Wallenberg, they could keep no secrets. Wallenberg was the 'world's observing eye,' the one who continually called the criminals to account. That is the great importance of Wallenberg's struggle in Budapest." Source: Per Anger, *With Raoul Wallenberg in Budapest*, p. 84.

29. Vera Goodkin, interview with the author.

30. Jeno Levai, *Raoul Wallenberg*, p. 277.

31. Agnes Adachi, *Child of the Winds*, p. 37.

32. Ibid.

33. Jeno Levai, *Raoul Wallenberg*, p. 178.

34. Ibid.

35. Agnes Adachi, *Child of the Winds,* p. 37.

36. Source: http://www.ushmm.org/wlc/media_oi.php?lang=en&ModuleId=10005211&MediaId=1077.

37. Agnes Adachi, *Child of the Winds,* p. 43–44.

38. Per Anger, *With Raoul Wallenberg in Budapest,* p. 77.

39. Ibid.

40. Jeno Levai, *Raoul Wallenberg,* p. 162.

41. Lars Berg, *The Book That Disappeared,* p. 50.

42. Jeno Levai, *Raoul Wallenberg,* p. 170.

43. Dr. Gyory Wilhelm, who had been involved in rescue activities with Wallenberg, greeted Wallenberg at the house on January 11, 1945. "I'd like to stay here a few days," an exhausted Wallenberg told him. "I don't feel very secure in my other houses and apartments, and I also think that this district will be among the first in central Pest to be liberated by the Russians. I want to make contact with them as soon as possible so I can begin relief activities on behalf of the Jews." Frederick E. Werbell and Thurston Clarke, *Lost Hero,* p. 137.

44. Jeno Levai, *Raoul Wallenberg,* p. 208.

45. Ibid., p. 209.

46. Ibid.

47. Frederick E. Werbell and Thurston Clarke, *Lost Hero,* p. 142.

48. Source: http://info.jpost.com/C001/Supplements/Shoah/hol_Missing.html. The decision had apparently already been taken in the Kremlin to bring Wallenberg to the capital for further interrogation. It has been alleged that a Soviet spy in the Swedish Embassy, Count Michael Tolstoy-Kutusov, had reported to Moscow that Wallenberg supplied the OSS with intelligence while also feeding information to senior Wehrmacht and SS officers. As a result, the Soviets may have suspected that Wallenberg was a double agent playing all sides, working for his OSS handler Iver Olsen and for the Germans. That Wallenberg could have done so to save lives does not appear to have occurred to the NKVD. In their jaundiced eyes, humanitarian action was always a front for other business.

49. Elenore Lester, *Wallenberg: The Man in the Iron Web,* p. 9.

50. Jeno Levai, *Raoul Wallenberg,* p. 213.

51. Ibid., p. 215.

52. Ibid.

53. Frederick E. Werbell and Thurston Clarke, *Lost Hero,* pp. 144–145.

54. Jeno Levai, *Raoul Wallenberg,* p. 215.

55. Ibid.

56. Frederick E. Werbell and Thurston Clarke, *Lost Hero*, p. 147.

57. Jeno Levai, *Raoul Wallenberg*, p. 216.

58. Four out of five Hungarian Jewish children were killed during the Holocaust.

59. Theo Tschuy, *Dangerous Diplomacy*, p. 217.

60. Frederick E. Werbell and Thurston Clarke, *Lost Hero*, p. 141.

61. To this day, according to the *Guinness Book of Records*, Wallenberg holds the record for the number of lives saved from extinction by any one person. According to the Hungarian historian Jeno Levai, who was the first to document Wallenberg's rescue efforts in a 1947 book, "Wallenberg was the only neutral diplomat who never tried to save only the Swedish [protected Jews] but all sufferers equally." Source: Jeno Levai, *Raoul Wallenberg*, p. 150.

CHAPTER FIFTEEN. LIBERATION

1. Vera Goodkin, interview with the author.

2. Jeno Levai, *Raoul Wallenberg*, p. 210.

3. Erwin Koranyi, interview with the author.

4. Erwin K. Koranyi, *Dreams and Tears*, p. 97.

5. Ibid., p. 98.

6. Ibid.

7. Erwin Koranyi, interview with the author.

8. Erwin K. Koranyi, *Dreams and Tears*, p. 103.

9. Ibid., p. 104.

10. Ibid.

11. Christian Ungvary, *The Siege of Budapest*, p. 355.

12. Marianne Lowy, interview with the author.

13. Ibid.

14. Ibid.

15. Benjamin Balshone, *Determined*, p. 109.

16. Marianne Lowy, interview with the author.

17. Vera Goodkin, interview with the author.

18. Ibid.

19. Ibid.

20. Vera Goodkin, *In Sunshine and Shadow*, p. 59.

21. Christian Ungvary, *The Siege of Budapest,* p. 346.

22. Ibid., p. 581. According to Christian Ungvary, by April 12, 1945, 8,200 "fascist and other reactionary elements" would have been arrested. Only 1,608 of them were released. Source: Christian Ungvary, ibid., p. 368.

23. Erwin Koranyi, interview with the author.

24. Anne Applebaum, *Gulag,* p. 432.

25. Christian Ungvary, *The Siege of Budapest,* p. 348.

26. Vera Goodkin, interview with the author.

27. Christian Ungvary, *The Siege of Budapest,* pp. 374–375.

28. Ibid., p. 255.

29. Erwin Koranyi, interview with the author.

30. Alice Breuer, interview with the author. It took a week to get to Szeged. "At one point I was trying to carry Alice on my shoulder, but she would not let me," recalled Erwin. "That was a very difficult [time]. I was really desperate. When we got there, we rented a room, had a little bit of money, went to university, registered."

CHAPTER SIXTEEN. THE FALL

1. Claudia Steur, *Theodor Dannecker: Ein Funktionar der "Endlosung,"* Tubingen: Klartext, 1997, p. 225.

2. Dieter Wisliceny would be hanged in 1948. Veensenmayer, Winkelmann, and Kurt Becher would all avoid the death penalty. Thanks to Rudolph Kasztner, who appealed on his behalf, Becher was not even tried for war crimes. He would enjoy enormous success as a businessman in postwar Germany.

3. Peter Padfield, *Himmler: Reichsfuhrer SS,* Papermac, 1995, p. 145.

4. It is not known how Muller reacted. Nor is it known what happened to Muller after the war—he was one of only a handful of the most powerful Nazis to disappear without a trace as the Third Reich collapsed.

5. Jochen Von Lang, *Eichmann Interrogated,* Da Capo Press, New York, 1999, p. 257.

6. Roger Manvell and Heinrich Fraenkel, *Heinrich Himmler,* Greenhill Books, 2007, p .69.

7. Uki Goni, *The Real Odessa,* p. 296.

8. John Toland, *The Last 100 Days,* Random House, New York, 1965, p. 412.

9. Simon Wiesenthal, *The Murderers Among Us,* p. 99.

10. Jochen Von Lang, *Eichmann Interrogated,* p. 262.

11. Ibid., pp. 258–59.

12. Quentin Reynolds, *Minister of Death,* p. 189.

13. According to Neal Bascomb: "While Eichmann watched [his sons] play, little Dieter slipped and fell into the lake. Eichmann fished the boy out of the water, took him over his knee, and slapped him hard several times. While his son screamed, Eichmann told him never to go near the water again. He might never see his boys again, he reasoned: It was best to leave them with a bit of discipline. To his mind, this was the most a father could do for his children." Neal Bascomb, *Hunting Eichmann,* p. 25.

14. Ibid.

15. This was indeed Kaltenbrunner's fate. As the International News Service would report on October 16, 1946: "This was Ernst Kaltenbrunner. He entered the execution chamber at 1:36 a.m., wearing a sweater beneath his blue double-breasted coat. With his lean, haggard face furrowed by old dueling scars, this terrible successor to Reinhard Heydrich had a frightening look as he glanced around the room. He wet his lips, apparently in nervousness, as he turned to mount the gallows, but he walked steadily. He answered his name in a calm, low voice. When he turned around on the gallows platform, he first faced a United States Army Roman Catholic chaplain wearing a Franciscan habit. When Kaltenbrunner was invited to make a last statement, he said, 'I have loved my German people and my fatherland with a warm heart. I have done my duty by the laws of my people and I am sorry my people were led this time by men who were not soldiers and that crimes were committed of which I had no knowledge.' This was the man, one of whose agents—a man named Rudolf Hoess—confessed at a trial that under Kaltenbrunner's orders he gassed three million human beings at the Auschwitz concentration camp! As the black hood was raised over his head, Kaltenbrunner, still speaking in a low voice, used a German phrase which translated means, 'Germany, good luck.' His trap was sprung at 1:39 a.m. Field Marshal Keitel was pronounced dead at 1:44 a.m., and three minutes later guards had removed his body." Source: http://www.mindfully.org/ Reform/Nazi-Execution-Smith16oct46.htm.

16. John Toland, *The Last 100 Days,* p. 571.

17. "I myself returned from American captivity in November 1947, having been taken [as a] prisoner of war in Alt Aussee on May 14, 1945." Source: http:// www.nizkor.org/ftp.cgi/people/e/eichmann.adolf/ftp.py?people/e/eichmann.adolf //transcripts/Testimony-Abroad/Wilhelm_Hoettl-08.

18. Uki Goni, *The Real Odessa,* p. 296.

19. Jochen Von Lang, *Eichmann Interrogated,* p. 262.

20. Ibid.

21. Adolf Eichmann, *Meine Flucht,* Hessisches Hauptstaatsarchiv, Allierte Prozesse, 6/247, folder 1.

22. Guido Knopp, *Hitler's Hitmen,* p. 39.

CHAPTER SEVENTEEN. LOST HERO

1. Swedish White Papers, 1957.

2. In Budapest, Wallenberg had reportedly told Baroness Kemeny, on the day they last saw each other, that "If anything should happen to you, I have told Kollontai about you and the child." Source: Kati Marton, *Wallenberg: Missing Hero,* p. 107.

3. Frederick E. Werbell and Thurston Clarke, *Lost Hero,* pp. 178–180.

4. Lars Berg, *The Book That Disappeared,* p. 215.

5. Frederick E. Werbell and Thurston Clarke, *Lost Hero,* pp. 179–181.

6. Source: http://info.jpost.com/C001/Supplements/Shoah/hol_Missing.html. Once on Soviet soil, these returnees were more often than not sent into its gulag, as was standard practice with any Soviet who had been tainted by contact with the capitalist West.

7. Ibid.

8. In recent years, it has been suggested that Wallenberg may have been associated with a super-secret intelligence organization, separate from the OSS, code-named Pond, which was run by a man named John Grombach as a private intelligence organization. Speculation that Wallenberg was some kind of operative, either for Pond or the OSS, increased when the CIA acknowledged in the early 1990s that Iver Olsen had worked for the OSS, the CIA's predecessor, when he recruited Wallenberg for the Budapest mission. A 1979 State Department memo puts the question of Wallenberg's links, or lack thereof, to American intelligence in the proper perspective: "Whether or not Wallenberg was involved with espionage during WWII is a moot point at this stage in history. His obvious humanitarian acts certainly outweigh any conceivable 'spy' mission he may have been on." Source: http://info.jpost.com/C001/Supplements/Shoah/hol_Missing.html.

9. Decision to commence investigation into Katyn Massacre, Malgorzata Kuzniar-Plota, Departmental Commission for the Prosecution of Crimes against the Polish Nation, Warsaw, November 30, 2004.

10. Jozsef Gazsi, *The Man They Honored Like Moses: Wallenberg pamphlets II,* Budapest, 1995. It would not be until 1991 that Russian President Boris Yeltsin admitted Soviet responsibility for the massacre, which continues to poison Russian-Polish relations to this day. Had Wallenberg produced powerful evidence of Soviet culpability in 1945, there would have been a fierce media outcry in the West. And Stalin's plans to subjugate all of Soviet-occupied Europe, including devastated Poland, would perhaps have been met with stronger opposition.

11. Per Anger, *With Raoul Wallenberg in Budapest,* p. 147.

12. Elenore Lester, *Wallenberg: The Man in the Iron Web,* p.131.

13. Dr. Vladim J. Birstein, "The Secret of Cell Number Seven," *Nezamisimaya Gazeta,* April 25, 1991, p .4.

14. This allegedly happened on March 2, 1948. Source: Report of Swedish-Russian Working Group, 2000, pp. 111–112.

15. Source: http://info.jpost.com/C001/Supplements/Shoah/hol_Missing. html. In 1947, an official Soviet announcement stated that Wallenberg was not in the Soviet Union. In 1948, the Wallenbergs' family friend, Alexandra Kollontay, was told that Wallenberg had died the previous year of a heart attack in prison. Source: Ibid.

16. Nina Lagergren, interview with the author.

17. Kati Marton, *Wallenberg: Missing Hero,* p. 161.

18. Sweden, like Switzerland, profited handsomely from neutrality. In 1998, a U.S. government inquiry would state that: "It was a generally held view among Allied economic warfare experts early in the war that the German war effort depended on iron ore from Sweden and oil from the Soviet Union, and that without these materials, the war would come to a halt." Sweden had allowed Germans transit rights across its territory, and supplied vital ball bearings and even parts for the lethal V-2 rockets, which killed many innocent Londoners.

19. According to journalist Danny Smith: "One of the most audacious cloaking schemes between the Nazis and the Wallenbergs concerned the 'acquisition' of the American Bosch Corporation (ABC), a U.S. subsidiary of the Nazi German firm Robert Bosch GmbH. The Wallenbergs had allegedly agreed to return ABC to the Nazis after the war had ended with a German victory." Source: Danny Smith, *Lost Hero,* p. 143.

20. The U.S. Treasury Department began to put together a case at Nuremberg. But the brothers once more benefited from their connections, this time to future Secretary of State John Foster Dulles, who allegedly stopped the investigation in the U.S. State Department. Source: Hugh Thomas, *The Strange Death*

of Heinrich Himmler, St. Martin's Press, New York, 2002, p. 88. See also "Red House Report," 1999.

21. According to researcher Susanne Berger, an authority on Wallenberg's fate in the Soviet Union: "Numerous questions about the Wallenberg family's behavior in the Raoul Wallenberg case remain unanswered: What about the unresolved questions about Raoul's background and his rumored professional ties to both Jacob and Marcus Wallenberg? How and why exactly did Jacob in 1954 approach Czech intermediaries about Raoul Wallenberg's fate, and what did he learn? Did Jacob and Marcus see eye to eye in the matter? Why did Marcus Wallenberg tell former Cabinet Secretary Arne Lundberg in 1951 that he firmly believed Raoul Wallenberg to be dead? On what information did he base this conviction?" Source: Susanne Berger, "The Fight of Their Lives." http://www.raoul-wallenberg.eu/articles/the-fight-of-their-lives/.

22 Lars Berg, *The Book That Disappeared,* p. 227.

23 Kati Marton, *Wallenberg,* p. 161.

24. Alan Levy, *Nazi Hunter,* p. 205.

25. Swedish White Papers, 1957.

26. Ibid.

27. Swedish White Papers, 1957.

28. Report of Swedish-Russian Working Group, 2000, pp. 90–91.

29. Alan Levy, *Nazi Hunter,* p. 206.

30. Ibid.

31. John Bierman, *Righteous Gentile,* p. 129.

32. Alan Levy, *Nazi Hunter,* pp. 207–208.

33. Swedish White Papers, 1957.

34. Ibid.

35. Frederick E. Werbell and Thurston Clarke, *Lost Hero,* p. 157.

36. Ibid., p. 158.

CHAPTER EIGHTEEN. BRAVE NEW WORLDS

1. Erwin K. Koranyi, *Dreams and Tears,* p. 114.

2. Ibid., p. 120.

3. Erwin Koranyi, interview with the author.

4. Erwin K. Koranyi, *Dreams and Tears,* pp. 121–122.

5. Ibid., p. 125.

6. Ibid.

7. Ibid., p. 131.

8. Ibid., p. 132.

9. Vera Goodkin, interview with the author.

10. Ibid.

11. Ibid.

12. Vera Goodkin, *In Sunshine and Shadow,* p. 109.

13. Vera Goodkin, interview with the author.

14. Ibid.

15. Erwin K. Koranyi, *Dreams and Tears,* p. 144.

16. Ibid., p. 146.

17. Ibid., p. 149.

18. Ibid., p. 159.

19. Ibid., p. 185.

20. Vera Goodkin, *In Sunshine and Shadow,* p. 99.

21. Ibid., p.104.

22. Ibid., p.124.

23. Ibid.

CHAPTER NINETEEN. GOING AFTER THE MASTER

1. Tuvia Friedman, *The Hunter,* p. 164. See Wisliceny affidavit.

2. Manus Diamant didn't like the idea at first. "That's a terrific idea," he told a Haganah agent. "You want me to become that bitch's lover. Are you crazy? I have feelings, too. You want me to kiss the same mouth that Eichmann kissed? You want me to move right in and live with her? Hah!" Source: Alan Levy, *Nazi Hunter,* p. 131.

3. Tuvia Friedman, *The Hunter,* pp. 170–176.

4. Simon Wiesenthal, *The Murderers Among Us,* pp. 123–124.

5. Ibid., p. 124.

6. Parts of the Sassen interviews were later famously published in two articles in *Life* magazine. They were highly damning. In private, with Sassen, Eichmann had given vent to his true feelings and was far more honest than in the self-pitying autobiography Eichmann wrote later while in prison in Israel. In 1980, the Sassen documents, or Sassen tapes, some six hundred pages of material from the interviews, were given to Eichmann's widow, Veronika. Source: Gerard Groeneveld: *"Kriegsberichter," Nederlandse SS-oorlogsverslaggevers 1941–1945,* Nijmegen, Vantilt, 2004, pp. 356–368.

7. Moshe Pearlman, *The Capture and Trial of Adolf Eichmann,* Simon and Schuster, New York, 1963, pp. 527–528.

8. Source: Wiesenthal, *Murderers Among Us,* p. 97.

9. Ibid.

10. Peter Malkin and Harry Stein, *Eichmann in My Hands,* New York, 1990, pp. 181–187.

11. Eichmann even signed the following statement: "I, Adolf Eichmann, the undersigned, declare of my own free will: Since my identity is now known, I recognize that there is no sense in attempting to evade justice any longer. I declare myself willing to go to Israel and face proceedings there before a competent court. It goes without saying that I shall receive legal defense and I will try to put the facts of my final years in office in Germany into the record without any embellishments, so that posterity will be given a true picture. I am making this declaration of my own free will. No promises were made to me, nor was I threatened in any way. I wish finally to find peace of mind again. Since I cannot recall all of the details and tend to confuse or mix things up, I request that I receive help in my desire to find the truth by having documents and testimony put at my disposal. Buenos Aires, May 1960."

12. Isser Harel, *The House on Garibaldi Street,* Viking, New York, 1975, p. 154.

13. Guido Knopp, *Hitler's Hitmen,* p. 46.

14. Isser Harel, *The House on Garibaldi Street,* p. 190.

15. Guido Knopp, *Hitler's Hitmen,* p. 47.

16. Ibid. When news broke in Argentina of Eichmann's abduction, it provoked a major diplomatic crisis, with Argentina making vehement protests to the UN about Israel's violation of Argentine sovereignty. Fascists in Argentina, meanwhile, took matters into their own hands and killed, tortured, and bombed Jews in reprisal.

17. "All my life I have been accustomed to obedience," Eichmann also told Less, "an obedience which in my years of membership in the SS became blind and unconditional. Though there is no blood on my hands, I shall certainly be convicted of complicity in murder. But be that as it may, I am inwardly prepared to atone for the terrible events. I know the death penalty awaits me. I am not asking for mercy, because I am not entitled to it. In fact, if it seems to be a greater act of atonement, I am prepared, as an example and deterrent to all anti-Semites of the earth, to hang myself in public. But let me first write a book

about these horrible events as a warning and example for the young people of the present and the future, and then let my life on earth end."

18. "Something seemed completely wrong, and I kept thinking about it while the incomprehensible bill of indictment ('the murder of six million men, women, and children') was being read. Suddenly I knew what it was. In my mind, I'd always been SS Obersturmbannfuhrer, supreme arbiter of life and death. But the Eichmann I now saw did not wear the SS uniform of terror and murder. Dressed in a cheap, dark suit, he seemed a cardboard figure, empty and two-dimensional. Fifteen times, after each item of the indictment, Eichmann was asked whether he was guilty. Each time, he said 'Not guilty.' This procedure, too, seemed inadequate to me. I thought that Eichmann should have been asked six million times, and he should have been made to answer six million times." Simon Wiesenthal, *Murderers Among Us*, pp. 98–99.

19. Hannah Arendt, *Eichmann in Jerusalem*, 1963, Epilogue.

20. Dutch journalist Harry Mulisch was just one of seven hundred journalists from around the world who reported on the trial in detail. He concluded that: "In the final analysis, it all boils down to the fact that Eichmann only believed in his own oath. This oath was his God and it lent godliness to the orders he received. It was stronger than the sufferings and the deaths of millions of innocents. The saying, 'one man, one oath,' held true for Eichmann. He had sworn his oath to Himmler personally in 1932, under totally different circumstances, when there was no talk of yet exterminating the Jews; he at least was certainly not aware of such a possibility. And later on, there was no escape from the murder oath sworn long ago." Zvi Aharoni and Wilhelm Dietl, *Operation Eichmann*, Cassell, London, 1997, p. 40.

21. Protocol, C.C. 124/53 in the D.C. Jerusalem, cited in Hecht, *Perfidy*, Milah Press, 1961, p. 229, and footnote 199, p. 280.

22. The Trial of Adolf Eichmann, Record of Proceedings in the District Court of Jerusalem, 9 vols. (Jerusalem, 1992–1995) 5: 2195–2206.

23. Moshe Pearlman, *The Capture and Trial of Adolf Eichmann*, London, 1963, p. 370.

24. Gideon Hausner, *Justice in Jerusalem*, London, 1967, pp. 436–437.

25. Guido Knopp, *Hitler's Hitmen*, p. 51.

26. Gideon Hausner, *Justice in Jerusalem*, pp. 431.

27. William Hull, *The Struggle for a Soul*, Doubleday, New York, 1963, p. 83.

28. Rachel Ginsberg, *Hamishpacha* magazine, May 1, 2005.

29. Vera Goodkin, interview with the author.

30. Erwin Koranyi, interview with the author.

CHAPTER TWENTY. THE WALLENBERG MYSTERY

1. "A very remarkable conversation took place on December 26, 1945, between Staffan Soderblom and Abramov, a head of department at the Soviet Foreign Ministry, MID. According to the Soviet Foreign Ministry's notes, Soderblom gave an account of what he knew about Raoul Wallenberg's last days in Budapest, but added: 'I would genuinely like to give you my personal opinion on this matter. I know of course that my opinion cannot be of a personal nature, but in this case I would like you to consider it as personal. I take it that Wallenberg is not alive. It is possible that he died in a German air raid or in an attack by some Hungarian or German military unit operating behind the Soviet troops. The Red Army began an extensive attack shortly after Wallenberg was taken to Debrecen. As a result, staff and archives were being moved out and at that point it appeared to be impossible to obtain any information on Wallenberg's fate. It would be splendid if the mission were to be given a reply in this spirit, that is to say, that Wallenberg is dead. It is necessary first and foremost because of Wallenberg's mother, who is still hoping her son is alive. She is wasting her strength and health on a fruitless search. I have consulted Mme Kollontay about this in the past few days. She agrees with me and recommended that I spoke to you openly about it, which is what I am doing. I stress once again that my request for a reply from the Soviet government, and the contents of this reply, is a personal request and my personal opinion.'" Source: 2000 Swedish-Russian Working Group report, p. 88.

2. *Wall Street Journal,* February 28, 2009.

3. Frederick E. Werbell and Thurston Clarke, *Lost Hero,* p. 199.

4. Tim Tzouliakis, *The Forsaken,* Penguin, New York, 2008, p. 300. Hammarskjold would die in a controversial plane crash in 1961. He was the only person to be awarded a Nobel peace prize posthumously; attempts were made in 1948 to have Wallenberg awarded the prize.

5. Susanne Berger, "The Fight of Their Lives," http://www.raoul-wallenberg.eu/articles/the-fight-of-their-lives/.

6. *Wall Street Journal,* February 28, 2009.

7. Kati Marton, *Wallenberg: Missing Hero,* p. 12.

8. Frederick E. Werbell and Thurston Clarke, *Lost Hero,* p. 214.

9. Ibid., p. 216.

10. Report of the Swedish-Russian Working Group, 2000.

11. Alan Levy, *Nazi Hunter*, p. 213.

12. Susanne Berger, "The Fight of Their Lives." http://www.raoul-wallenberg.eu/articles/the-fight-of-their-lives/.

13. *Wall Street Journal*, February 28, 2009.

14. Ibid.

15. Kati Marton, *Raoul Wallenberg, Missing Hero*, p. 3.

16. Ibid.

17. Speech on October 5, 1981. The president spoke at 2:35 p.m. at the signing ceremony in the Rose Garden at the White House. Participants in the ceremony included the Swedish ambassador and Mrs. Wilhelm Wachtmeister, members of the Senate and House of Representatives, representatives of the Jewish community, and Mr. Wallenberg's sister and brother, Nina Lagergren and Guy von Dardel, who came from Sweden for the ceremony. Also in attendance were Representative Tom Lantos of California, the principal sponsor of the resolution in the House of Representatives, and his wife. While a sixteen-year-old youth working for the Hungarian Underground, Representative Lantos was saved in Budapest by Mr. Wallenberg. As enacted, S.J. Res. 65 is Public Law 9754, approved October 5. Source: http://www.presidency.ucsb.edu/ws/index.php?pid=44341.

18. "In 1989 the wooden shelves in the archival repository of the KGB, housed in the same building as the Lubianka prison, were replaced by metal ones. After an investigation of the KGB files, the staff went through a storage-room containing rubbish, office material, and so on, all in a mess. From the top shelf, a parcel fell down. If it had not been for a cigarette case which dropped to the floor, nobody would have paid any attention to it. The parcel had been sealed with glue. When the contents were examined, the archivist found Raoul Wallenberg's diplomatic passport, his car registration certificate, his prison file card, his golden cigarette case, some foreign currency, and his pocket agenda. This is how, according to the Russians, the remaining belongings of Raoul Wallenberg turned up." Source: http://www.osaarchivum.org/guide/rip/1/a.html.

19. Source: http://www.telegraph.co.uk/news/worldnews/europe/hungary/1376789/What-happened-to-Wallenberg.html.

20. Alan Levy, *Nazi Hunter*, p. 228.

21. Vera Goodkin, interview with the author.

22. *Wall Street Journal*, February 28, 2009.

23. Pavel A. Sudoplatov, *Special Tasks*, Backbay Books, New York, 1995, p. 265.

24. Ibid., p. 270.

25. Per Anger, who would campaign throughout his life for information on Wallenberg's fate, strongly refuted Sudoplatov's thesis: "I strongly disagree with the conclusion that the Wallenberg mystery is solved and that he was killed in 1947. That conclusion is based on circumstantial evidence with no firsthand confirmation. Central to the argument that he died in 1947 is a memorandum, dated May 14, 1947, which outlines unsuccessful Soviet efforts to recruit Wallenberg as a double agent, and directs a top Soviet security officer to submit 'suggestions for liquidation.' Former KGB officer Sudoplatov admits that the key phrase in Russian can mean either Wallenberg's murder or the 'liquidation' (resolution) of his case. Those, like Sudoplatov, who accept Wallenberg's death in 1947 accept the view that this meant the elimination of the man. Sudoplatov, however, admits that he never met Wallenberg, had no firsthand knowledge of his fate, and does not know anyone who had direct knowledge of his death." Source: Per Anger, *With Raoul Wallenberg in Budapest*, pp. xv–xvi.

26. Ibid.

27. Ironically, there have been suggestions that Beria may have had something to do with Wallenberg's death.

28. Exact numbers of those killed in the gulag under Stalin are impossible to ascertain, but the historian Otto Pohl cites the figure of 2,749,163 in his book *The Stalinist Penal System*, Jefferson, NC, 1997, p. 131. For an excellent discussion on the numbers who passed through the Soviet gulag and how many were killed, see Anne Applebaum's *Gulag, A History*, Anchor Books, New York, 2004, pp. 578–586.

29. *Wall Street Journal*, February 28, 2009.

30. Report of the Swedish-Russian Working Group, 2000. In April 2010, there was a further development. According to the Associated Press: "The archives of the Russian Security Services say a man identified only as Prisoner No. 7, who was interrogated six days after the diplomat's reported death, was 'with great likelihood' Wallenberg. The security services reported the find last November to Susanne Berger and Vadim Birstein, two members of a research team that conducted a ten-year investigation into Wallenberg's disappearance in the 1990s. The researchers informed Wallenberg's relatives in a letter released for publication Thursday. The findings also were reported in the Swedish magazine *Fokus*. The information still has to undergo in-depth verification, Berger

wrote in the letter, 'but if indeed confirmed, the news is the most interesting to come out of Russian archives in over fifty years.'" Source: Arthur Max and Karl Ritter. "New evidence on WWII mystery of Raoul Wallenberg." Ove Bring, professor in international law at the National Defense College in Stockholm, said the report by the Russian security services warranted reopening Wallenberg's case. "Everything we believed earlier [about Wallenberg's death] is turned upside down by this," he told The Associated Press. "This has to be investigated again. If he was still alive six days later, then maybe he was alive for a longer period of time," Bring said. "Did he live another week, or a year or 10 years? Suddenly that's an open question." Source: Arthur Max and Karl Ritter (AP), "New evidence on WWII mystery of Raoul Wallenberg."

31. Susanne Berger, "The Fight of Their Lives," http://www.raoul-wallenberg.eu/articles/the-fight-of-their-lives/.

CHAPTER TWENTY-ONE. THE LAST SURVIVORS

1. The emotional floodgates opened much later, after the birth of a grandson, William, who was diagnosed as severely autistic. The news punctured something in Vera. It seemed so terribly unfair after all her family had lost during the Holocaust. "It was as if the walls crumbled—it brought back everything." Vera Goodkin, interview with the author.

2. Vera Goodkin, interview with the author.

3. Ibid.

4. Vera Goodkin, *In Sunshine and Shadow,* pp. 145–146.

5. Vera Goodkin, interview with the author.

6. Ibid.

7. Marianne Lowy, interview with the author.

8. Ibid.

9. Erwin K. Koranyi, *Dreams and Tears,* p. 196.

10. *The Economist,* June 20, 2009.

11. Erwin Koranyi, interview with the author.

12. Erwin K. Koranyi, *Dreams and Tears,* p. 209.

13. Ibid.

14. Ibid.

15. Erwin Koranyi, interview with the author.

16. Nina Lagergren, interview with the author.

Bibliography

Aalders, Gerard, and Cees Wiebes. *The Art of Cloaking Ownership*. Amsterdam: Amsterdam University Press, 1996.

Adachi, Agnes. *Child of the Winds: My Mission with Raoul Wallenberg*, Chicago: Adams Press, 1989.

Afonso, Rui. *One Good Man*. "Nosso Mundo," n. 61. Lisboa: Editorial Caminho.

Aharoni, Zvi, and Wilhelm Dietl. *Operation Eichmann*. London: Cassell, 1997.

Alexander, Lynn. *Safe Houses*. New York: Atheneum, 1985.

Amick, George. "Hell's Angel: Raoul Wallenberg." *Judaica Philatelic Journal*. (Fall 1983).

Anger, Per. *With Raoul Wallenberg in Budapest, Memories of the War Years in Hungary*. New York: Holocaust Library, 1981, paperback 1985, and Washington, DC: Holocaust Library, The United States Holocaust Memorial Museum, 1995 and 1996.

Applebaum, Anne. *Gulag: A History*. New York: Anchor Books, 2004.

Arendt, Hannah. *Eichmann in Jerusalem,* 1963.

Balshone, Benjamin. *Determined*. New York: Bloch Publishing, 1984.

Bartal, David. *Imperiet; hur Wallenbergarna byggde Europas mäktigaste familjedynasti*. Stockholm: Dagens Industri, 1996.

Bascomb, Neal. *Hunting Eichmann*. New York: Houghton Mifflin Harcourt, 2009.

Bejski, Moshe. "The 'Righteous Among the Nations' and Their Part in the Rescue of Jews." *Rescue Attempts During the Holocaust*. Jerusalem: Yad Vashem, 1977, pp. 637–638.

Benshalom, Rafi. *We Struggled for Life*. Jerusalem: Gefen, 2001.

Berg, Lars G:son. *Boken som forsvann, Vad hände i Budapest*. Arboga. Textab Förlag, 1983.

Berg, Lars G. *The Book That Disappeared: What Happened in Budapest*. New York: Vintage Press, 1990.

Berger, Susanne. "The Fight of Their Lives."

Berger, Susanne. "Stuck in Neutral," Arlington, VA, 2005.

Bierman, John. *Righteous Gentile, The Story of Raoul Wallenberg, Missing Hero of the Holocaust.* Harmondsworth: Penguin Books, 1981 and 1995, paperback 1982.

Bondor, Vilmos. *A Mikó-rejtély. Mikó Zoltán és Raoul Wallenberg kapcsolata a magyar ellenállásban 1944–1945 (The Mikó enigma. The contact between Zoltán Mikó and Raoul Wallenberg in the Hungarian resistance 1944–1945)* Püski, Budapest, 1995.

Braham, Randolph L. *The Politics of Genocide: The Holocaust in Hungary.* 2v. Revised and Enlarged Edition. New York: Columbia University Press, 1994.

Braham, Randolph L., and Scott Miller, eds., *The Nazis' Last Victims.* Detroit: Wayne State University Press, 1998.

Braham, Randolph L. and Bela Vago, eds., *The Holocaust in Hungary: Forty Years Later.* New York: Columbia University Press, 1985.

Brown, Gordon. *Courage. Eight Portraits.* London: Bloomsbury, 2007.

Carlbäck-Isotalo, Helene. "Glasnost and the Opening up of Soviet Archives, Time to Conclude the Raoul Wallenberg Case?" *Scandinavian Journal of History,* 17 (1992): 3, pp. 175–207.

Ceserani, David. *Becoming Eichmann.* Cambridge: Da Capo Press, 2004.

Cherry, Robert. "Raoul Wallenberg: Savior of Hungarian Jewry." *Midstream* (April 1995): 17–21.

Clarke, Comer. *Eichmann, the Man and His Crimes.* New York: Ballantine Books, 1960.

Cooper, Abraham. "Wallenberg Held Hostage: Day 14,000." *Jewish Chicago.* (July 1982): 34–38.

Daniel, Jamie, Michael Nicolson, and David Winner. *Raoul Wallenberg: One Man Against Nazi Terror.* Milwaukee: Gareth Stevens Children's Books, 1992.

Dardel, Fredrik von. *Raoul Wallenberg. Fakta kring ett öde.* Stockholm: Propius, 1970.

Dardel, Maj von. *Raoul.* Stockholm: Rabén & Sjögren, 1984.

Dederichs, Mario. *Heydrich: The Face of Evil.* Casemate, 2009.

Derogy, Jacques. *Le Cas Wallenberg.* Paris: Édition Ramsay, 1980.

Ehrenstråhle, Britt och Hans. *Sju dagar i oktober 1947.* Uppsala: Brombergs, 1980.

Eichmann, Adolf. *Meine Flucht.* Hessisches Hauptstaatsarchiv, Allierte Prozesse, 6/247, folder 1.

Ember, Mária. *A lengyel menekültek és Wallenberg (The Polish refugees and Wallenberg.)* Barátság nr 2 1999, Budapest.

Ember, Mária. *Wallenberg Budapesten (Wallenberg in Budapest).* Budapest: Varoshaza, 2000.

Fant, Kenne. *Nära bilder.* Stockholm: Norstedts, 1997.

Fant, Kenne. *"R"—Dokumentärroman.* Stockholm: Norstedts, 1988.

Fralon, Jose-Alain. *Le Juste de Bordeaux.* Bordeaux: Mollat, 1998.

Forbes, Malcolm, Jr. "Raoul Wallenberg." *They Went That-a-Way.* New York: Simon and Schuster, 1988.

Freed, G. B. "Humanitarianism vs. Totalitarianism: The Strange Case of Wallenberg." *Papers of the Michigan Academy of Sciences, Arts and Letters,* 46 (1961): 503 28.

Friedman, Philip. *Their Brothers' Keepers.* New York: Crown Publishers, 1957. pp. 159–167.

Friedman, Tuvia. *The Hunter.* London: Anthony Gibbs & Phillips, 1961.

Gann, Christoph. *So viele Menschen retten wie möglich.* München: Verlag C.H. Beck, 1999.

Gazsi, József. *Akit Mózesként titeltek. Feltevések egy politikai krimi hátteréhez, avagy töprengés Raoul Wallenberg balsorsaról. (He who was worshipped like Moses. Assumptions about the background of a political thriller, or thoughts on Raoul Wallenberg's fate).* Budapest: Wallenberg-füzetek (Wallenberg booklets), Raoul Wallenberg-Alapítvány (foundation) 1995.

Gilbert, Martin. *The Holocaust.* New York: Henry Holt, 1985.

Ginzburg, Eugenia. *Journey into the Whirlwind.* New York: Harcourt, Brace, 1967.

Goni, Uki. *The Real Odessa.* London: Granta, 2003.

Goodkin, Vera. *In Sunshine and Shadow.* Margate, NJ: Comteq Publishing, 2006.

Hamerow, Theodore S. *Why We Watched.* New York: Norton, 2008.

Handler, Andrew. *A Man for all Connections: Raoul Wallenberg and the Hungarian State Apparatus, 1944–1945.* Westport, CT: Praeger, 1996.

Harel, Isser. *The House on Garibaldi Street.* New York: Viking, 1975.

Harmincad utca 6, A Twentieth Century Story of Budapest, Nigel Thorpe and Petra Matyisin, eds. Budapest: British Embassy, 1999.

Haspel, Rachel Oestereicher. *Raoul Wallenberg: A Hero for Our Time.* New York: Raoul Wallenberg Committee of the United States, 1981, revised 1985.

Hausner, Gideon. *Justice in Jerusalem.* London, 1967.

Hecht, Ben. *Perfidy.* Milah Press, 1999.

Heimerson, Staffan. *Sarajevo och tusen platser till.* Stockholm:Wahlström & Widstrand, 1995.

Hellman, Peter. *Avenue of the Righteous.* New York: Atheneum, 1980.

Hernod, Torsten. *Raoul Wallenberg—hans liv, gärning och fångenskap/*en bibliografi sammanställd av Torsten Hèrnod. Borås: Högskolan i Borås, Institutionen Bibliotekshögskolan, 1997.

Hilberg, Raul. *The Destruction of the European Jews.* New Haven: Yale University Press, 2003.

Hinshaw, David. "Sweden's Neutral Policy in Two Wars." *Sweden: Champion of Peace.* New York: G. P. Putnam's Sons, 1949.

Hoess, Rudolf. *Commandant of Auschwitz.* London: Pheonic Press, 1985.

Horthy, Nicholas. *Memoirs.* New York: Robert Speller and Sons, 1957.

Hull, William. *The Struggle for a Soul.* New York: Doubleday, 1963.

Isakson, Börje. *Omöjligt uppdrag, Raoul Wallenbergs kamp i Budapest.* Stockholm: Lindblad, 1975.

Jarring, Gunnar. *Utan glasnost och perestrojka.* Stockholm: Bonniers, 1989.

Joseph, Gilbert. *Mission sans Retour; l'affaire Wallenberg.* Paris: Albin Michel, 1982.

Karelin, Victor. *Damals in Budapest, Das Buch von Raoul Wallenberg.* Freiburg: Herder, 1982.

Karlbom, Rolf. *Raoul Wallenbergs fångenskap i Sovjet.* Gothenburg: Författaren, 1987.

Knopp, Guido. *Hitler's Hitmen.* England: Sutton, 2002.

Koblik, Steven. *The Stones Cry Out; Sweden's Persecution of the Jews 1933–1945.* New York: Holocaust Library, 1988.

Koranyi, Erwin K. *Dreams and Tears.* Ontario: General Store Publishing House, 2006.

Korey, William. *The Wallenberg Mystery, Fifty-five Years Later.* New York: The American Jewish Committee, 2000, 199.

Kovach, Kim. "In Search of the 'Hero of Budapest': The Disappearance of Raoul Wallenberg." *Israel Horizons,* 28: 3–4 (March/April 1980): pp. 11–28.

Kung, Andres. *Raoul Wallenberg, Igår, idag.* Stockholm: Timbro, 1985.

Lajos, A. *Hjalten och Offren: Raoul Wallenberg och judarna in Budapest.* Vaxjo: Svenska Emigratinstitutes skrifserie, no. 15, 2003.

Lambert, Gilles. *Operation Hasalah.* Indianapolis: Bobbs-Merrill, 1974.

Lang, Jochen von. *Eichmann Interrogated.* New York: Da Capo Press, 1999.

Langlet, Nina. *Kaos i Budapest.* Vällingby: Harriers Bokförlag, 1982.

Langlet, Valdemar. *Verk och dagar i Budapest.* Stockholm: Wahlström & Widstrand, 1946.

Larsson, Jan. *Raoul Wallenberg (Swedish Portraits).* Stockholm: The Swedish Institute, 1995.

LeBor, Adam. *Hitler's Secret Bankers, The Myth of Swiss Neutrality During the Holocaust.* Secaucus, NJ: Birch Lane Press, Carol Publishing Group, 1997.

Lester, Elenore. "Raoul Wallenberg: The Righteous Gentile from Sweden." *The Holocaust in Hungary: Forty Years Later.* Randolph L. Braham and Bela Vago, eds. New York: Columbia University Press, 1985.

Lester, Elenore. *Wallenberg, The Man in the Iron Web.* New York: Prentice-Hall, cop., 1982, paperback.

Lester, Elenore, and Werbell, Frederick E. "Wallenberg." *New York Times Magazine.* (March 30, 1980).

Levai, Jeno. *Black Book on the Martyrdom of Hungarian Jewry.* Zurich: Central European Times, 1948.

Levai, Jeno. *Raoul Wallenberg, His Remarkable Life, Heroic Battles and the Secret of His Mysterious Disappearance.* West Melbourne: WhiteAnt Occasional Publishing, 1989.

Levine, Paul A. *From Indifference to Activism, Swedish Diplomacy and the Holocaust, 1938–1944.* Uppsala: Acta Universitatis Upsaliencis, 1996.

Levine Paul A. *Raoul Wallenberg in Budapest: Myth, History and Holocaust.* Middlesex, UK: Valentine Mitchell, 2010.

Levy, Alan. *Nazi Hunter.* New York: Carroll & Graff, 2002.

Levy, Alan. *The Wiesenthal File.* London: Constable, 1993.

Lichtenstein, Heiner. *Raoul Wallenberg, Retter von Hunderttausend Juden, ein Opfer Himmlers und Stalins.* Köln: Bund Verlag, 1982.

Lindqvist, Herman. *Historien om Sverige, Drömmar och verklighet.* Stockholm: Norstedts, 2000.

Lindström, Ulla. *I regeringen: Ur min politiska dagbok 1954–1959.* Stockholm: Bonniers, 1969.

Linnea, Sharon. *The Man Who Stopped Death.* Philadelphia: The Jewish Publication Society, 1993.

The Lost Hero of the Holocaust, Raoul Wallenberg, Report and Analysis (International Hearings in Stockholm, January 1981). Los Angeles: Simon Wiesenthal Center, 1981.

Lozowick, Yaacov. *Hitler's Bureaucrats.* London: Continuum, 2000.

Lungen, Paul. *Canadian Jewish News,* January 27, 2005.

Malkin, Peter, and Harry Stein. *Eichmann in My Hands.* New York, 1990.

Mandel, Connie L. *Raoul Wallenberg: A Chronicle of Courage.* Los Angeles: Simon Wiesenthal Center, 1981.

Manvell, Roger, and Heinrich Fraenkel. *Heinrich Himmler.* Greenhill Books, 2007.

Marton, Kati. *Wallenberg.* New York: Random House, 1982; reprinted, Arcade Publishing, New York, 1995.

Marton, Kati. "The Wallenberg Mystery." *Atlantic Monthly* (Nov. 1980): pp. 33–40.

Milton, Sybil. "The Righteous Who Helped Jews." *Genocide: Critical Issues of the Holocaust.* Ed. Alex Grobman and Daniel Landes. Los Angeles: Simon Wiesenthal Center; Chappaqua, NY: Rossel Books, 1983, pp. 280–287.

"Missing: Raoul Wallenberg, the Hero of the Holocaust." *Christian Science Monitor* (July 23, 1980).

Morse, Arthur D. *While Six Million Died.* New York: The Overlook Press, 1998.

Moshinsky, Efim. *Raoul Wallenberg Is Alive.* Jerusalem: Rescue Publishing Company, 1987.

Nazi Conspiracy and Aggression. Vol. VIII. Washington, DC: USGPO, 1946.

Nicholson, Michael, and David Winner. *Raoul Wallenberg, the Swedish Diplomat Who Saved 100,000 Jews from the Nazi Holocaust.* Watford: Exley, 1989.

Nicholson, Mike, *Raoul Wallenberg.* Baarn: Tirion/Davidsfonds, 1995.

Olsson, Ulf. *Att förvalta sitt pund: Marcus Wallenberg 1899–1982.* Stockholm: Ekerlids, 2000.

Padfield, Peter. *Himmler: Reichsführer SS.* Papermac, 1995.

Paldiel, Mordecai. *Diplomat Heroes of the Holocaust.* New Jersey: KTAV Publishing House, Inc., 2007.

Pearlman, Moshe. *The Capture and Trial of Adolf Eichmann.* New York: Simon and Schuster, 1963.

Persson, Carl. I samarbete med Sundelin, Anders. *Utan omsvep, Ett liv i maktens centrum.* Stockholm: Norstedts, 1990.

Petai, Raphael. *The Jews of Hungary.* Detroit: Wayne State University Press, 1996.

Petri, Lennart. *Sverige i stora världen, Minnen och reflexioner från 40 års diplomattjänst.* Stockholm: Atlantis, 1996.

Philipp, Rudolph. *Raoul Wallenberg, Diplomat, kämpe, samarit.* Stockholm: Fredborgs Förlag, 1946.

Philipp, Rudolph. *Raoul Wallenberg, Diplomat, kämpe, samarit-och martyr.* Höganäs: Förlags AB Wiken, 1981.

Philipp, Rudolf. *Raoul Wallenberg: Fighter for Humanity.* Stockholm: Fredborgs Förlag, 1946, revised edition, 1980.

Pierrejean, Claudine et Daniel. *Les secrets de l'Affaire Raoul Wallenberg.* Paris: L'Harmattan, 1998.

Pohl, Otto. *The Stalinist Penal System.* Jefferson, NC, 1997.

Porter, Anna. *Kasztner's Train.* New York: Walker & Company, 2007.

Proceedings, the Stockholm International Forum on the Holocaust, a Conference on Education, Remembrance and Research. Stockholm: Regeringskansliet, 2000.

Raoul Wallenberg. Stockholm: The Swedish Institute, 1988.

Raoul Wallenberg. Stockholm: Ministry for Foreign Affairs, 1987 (UD informerar).

Raoul Wallenberg Committee of the United States. *Raoul Wallenberg's Children.* New York: Raoul Wallenberg Committee for the United States. 1981 (December).

Reynolds, Quentin. *Minister of Death.* New York: Dell, 1961.

Roseman, Mark. *The Wannsee Conference and The Final Solution.* New York: Picador, 2002.

Rosenfeld, Harvey. *Raoul Wallenberg—Angel of Rescue.* Buffalo, NY: Prometheus Books, 1982.

Rosenfeld, Harvey. *Raoul Wallenberg.* New York: Holmes & Meyer, 1985.

Runberg, Björn. *Valdemar Langlet, Räddare i faran.* Bromma: Megilla-Förlaget, 2000.

Samuelson, Maurice. "How Wallenberg Fooled the Nazis." *Jewish Chronicle* (January 11, 1985).

Schiller, Bernt. *Varför ryssarna tog Raoul Wallenberg.* Stockholm: Natur och Kultur, 1991.

Skorzeny, Otto. *Skorzeny's Secret Missions.* Dutton, 1950.

Shifrin, Avraham. *The First Guidebook to Prisons and Concentration Camps.* Berne: Stephanus Edition Verlags AG, 1980.

Sjoquist, Eric. *Affären Raoul Wallenberg.* Stockholm: Bonniers, 1974.

Sjoquist, Eric. *Raoul Wallenberg: diplomaten som försvann.* Stockholm: Askild & Kärnekull, 1981.

Sjoquist, Eric. *Raoul Wallenberg,* Normans förlag, Stockholm 1985 och Den Kristna. Stockholm: Bokringen, 1985.

Skoglund, Elizabeth R. *A Quiet Courage, Per Anger, Wallenberg's Co-Liberator of Hungarian Jews.* Grand Rapids, MI: Baker Books, Baker Book House Company, 1997.

Smith, Danny. *Wallenberg, Lost Hero.* Basingstoke: Marshall Pickering, 1986.

Ströbinger, R. *Das Rätsel Wallenberg.* Stuttgart: Burg Verlag, 1982.

Sudoplatov, Pavel, and Anatoli Sudoplatov. *Special Tasks, The Memoirs of an Unwanted Witness—A Soviet Spymaster.* London: Little, Brown and Company (UK) Limited, 1994.

Swedish Institute. *Raoul Wallenberg.* Stockholm: Swedish Institute, 1988.

Szekeres, József. *A Pesti gettók 1945 januári megmentése* (The saving of Pest ghettos in January 1945). Budapest: Várostörténeti tanulmányok (City historical studies) Budapest F város Levéltára (City archives of Budpest), 1997.

Szel, Elisabeth. *Operacion Noche y Niebla.* Madrid: Escelicer, 1961.

Terelya, Josyp. *Witness.* Milford, OH: Faith Publishing Company, 1991.

Thomas, Hugh. *The Strange Death of Heinrich Himmler.* New York: St. Martin's Press, 2002.

Toland, John. *The Last 100 Days.* New York: Random House, 1965.

Trepper. Leopold. *The Great Game: Memoirs of the Spy Hitler Couldn't Silence.* New York: McGraw-Hill, 1977.

The Trial of Eichmann, Record of Proceedings in the District Court of Jerusalem (Vol. 1–6), Jerusalem 1992–1994; *Statement made by Adolf Eichmann to the Israel Police prior to his Trial in Jerusalem* (Vol. 7–8), Jerusalem 1995, and *Microfiches Copies of the Exhibits Submitted by the Prosecution and Defence* (Vol. 9), Jerusalem 1995.

Tschuy, Theo. *Dangerous Diplomacy.* Grand Rapids, MI: Wm. B. Eerdmans Publishing Company, 2000.

Tzouliakis, Tim. *The Forsaken.* New York: Penguin, 2008.

Ungvary, Christian. *The Siege of Budapest.* New Haven: Yale University Press, 2005.

Vaksberg, Arkadij. *Aleksandra Kollontaj.* Stockholm: Norstedts, 1997.

Villius, Elsa och Hans. *Fallet Raoul Wallenberg.* Stockholm: Almqvist & Wiksell/ Gebers, 1966.

Vrba, Rudolf. *I Escaped from Auschwitz.* Fort Lee, NJ: Barricade Books, 2002.

Voros, Marton. *Aven for din Skull.* Stockholm: Askild & Karnekull, 1978.

Wallenberg, Gustaf. *Älskade farfar, brevväxling mellan Gustaf & Raoul Wallenberg 1924–1936.* Stockholm: Bonniers, 1987.

Wallenberg, Raoul, Dokumentsamling jämte kommentarer rörande hans fången-skap i Sovjetunionen. Utrikesdepartementet, Stockholm, 1957 (Atkstycken utgivna av Kungl. utrikesdepartementet, N.S. II. 9).

Wallenberg, Raoul, Handlingar i Utrikesdepartementets arkiv om Raoul Wallen-berg, Vol. 1–7 (1944–49), offentliggjorda 1980, Vol. 8–49 (1950–69), offent-liggjorda 1982 (Copies).

Wallenberg, Raoul. *Letters and Dispatches 1924–1944.* New York: Arcade Pub-lishing, 1995.

Waller, James. *Becoming Evil: How Ordinary People Commit Genocide and Mass Killing.* Oxford: Oxford University Press, 2002.

Weissberg, Alex. *Desperate Mission.* New York: Criterion Books, 1958.

Werbell, Frederick E., and Thurston B. Clarke. *Lost Hero: The Mystery of Raoul Wallenberg.* New York: McGraw-Hill, 1982.

Werbell, Frederick E., and Thurston B. Clarke. *Raoul Wallenberg, En försvun-nen hjälte.* Stockholm: B. Wahlström, 1985, paperback.

Wiesel, Elie. *Night.* New York: Hill and Wang, 2006.

Wiesenthal, Simon. *The Murderers Among Us.* New York: McGraw-Hill, 1967.

Wiesenthal, Simon. *Recht nicht Rache, Erinnerungen.* Frankfurt am Main: Ull-stein, 1988.

Wulf, Joseph. *Raoul Wallenberg.* Berlin: Colloquium Verlag, 1958.

Wulf, Joseph. *Il fut leur espérance.* Tournai: Casterman, 1968.

Wynn, Greville. *Contact on Gorky Street.* New York: Atheneum, 1968.

Yahil, Leni. "Raoul Wallenberg—His Mission and His Activities in Hungary." *Yad Vashem Studies.* XV: pp. 7–53. 1.

Index